The Private Sector and Water Pricing in Efficient Urban Water Management

T0300188

This book focuses on participation of the public and private sectors in urban water management and on the role of water pricing. It discusses in-depth topics such as public choices of urban water service management; dynamics of privatization and regulation of water services; adoption of water demand instruments; impacts of price and non-price policies on residential water demand; quality of water services; lessons from not-for-profit public–private partnerships; and critical examinations of models and projections of demands in water utility resource planning in England and Wales. Appropriateness of water prices and tariffs in achieving socially desirable outcomes is also analyzed and a global survey of urban water tariffs is approached with a focus on sustainability, efficiency and fairness.

This book was originally published as a special issue of the *International Journal of Water Resources Development*.

Cecilia Tortajada is the President of the Third World Centre for Water Management, Mexico.

Francisco González-Gómez is Professor in the Department of Applied Economics, Faculty of Economics and Business, and Researcher at the Institute of Water Research, University of Granada, Spain.

Asit K. Biswas is a Distinguished Visiting Professor at the Lee Kuan Yew School of Public Policy, Singapore.

Miguel A. García-Rubio is Associate Professor in the Department of Applied Economics, Faculty of Economics and Business, and Researcher at the Institute of Water Research, University of Granada, Spain.

Routledge Special Issues on Water Policy and Governance

Edited by:

Cecilia Tortajada (IJWRD) – Third World Centre for Water Management, Mexico
James Nickum (WI) – International Water Resources Association, France

Most of the world's water problems, and their solutions, are directly related to policies and governance, both specific to water and in general. Two of the world's leading journals in this area, the *International Journal of Water Resources Development* and *Water International* (the official journal of the International Water Resources Association), contribute to this special issues series, aimed at disseminating new knowledge on the policy and governance of water resources to a very broad and diverse readership all over the world. The series should be of direct interest to all policy makers, professionals and lay readers concerned with obtaining the latest perspectives on addressing the world's many water issues.

Water Pricing and Public-Private Partnership
Edited by Asit K. Biswas and
  Cecilia Tortajada

Water and Disasters
Edited by Chennat Gopalakrishnan and
  Norio Okada

Water as a Human Right for the Middle East and North Africa
Edited by Asit K. Biswas, Eglal Rached
  and Cecilia Tortajada

Integrated Water Resources Management in Latin America
Edited by Asit K. Biswas,
  Benedito P. F. Braga,
  Cecilia Tortajada and
  Marco Palermo

Water Resources Management in the People's Republic of China
Edited by Xuetao Sun, Robert Speed and
  Dajun Shen

Improving Water Policy and Governance
Edited by Cecilia Tortajada and
  Asit K. Biswas

Water Quality Management
Present Situations, Challenges and
  Future Perspectives
Edited by Asit K. Biswas,
  Cecilia Tortajada and Rafael Izquerdo

Water, Food and Poverty in River Basins
Defining the Limits
Edited by Myles J. Fisher and
  Simon E. Cook

Asian Perspectives on Water Policy
Edited by Cecilia Tortajada and
  Asit K. Biswas

Managing Transboundary Waters of Latin America
Edited by Asit K. Biswas

The Private Sector and Water Pricing in Efficient Urban Water Management

Edited by
Cecilia Tortajada, Francisco González-Gómez,
Asit K. Biswas and Miguel A. García-Rubio

Routledge
Taylor & Francis Group

LONDON AND NEW YORK

First published 2015
by Routledge

2 Park Square, Milton Park, Abingdon, Oxon OX14 4RN
711 Third Avenue, New York, NY 10017, USA

Routledge is an imprint of the Taylor & Francis Group, an informa business

First issued in paperback 2016

British Library Cataloguing in Publication Data
A catalogue record for this book is available from the British Library

ISBN 13: 978-1-138-77998-3 (hbk)
ISBN 13: 978-1-138-69301-2 (pbk)

Typeset in Times New Roman
by Taylor & Francis Books

Publisher's Note
The publisher accepts responsibility for any inconsistencies that may have arisen during the conversion of this book from journal articles to book chapters, namely the possible inclusion of journal terminology.

Disclaimer
Every effort has been made to contact copyright holders for their permission to reprint material in this book. The publishers would be grateful to hear from any copyright holder who is not here acknowledged and will undertake to rectify any errors or omissions in future editions of this book.

Contents

CONTENTS

Citation Information

The chapters in this book were originally published in the *International Journal of Water Resources Development*, volume 29, issue 3 (September 2013). When citing this material, please use the original page numbering for each article, as follows:

Chapter 13
State-of-the-art review: designing urban water tariffs to recover costs and promote wise use
Sonia Ferdous Hoque and Dennis Wichelns
International Journal of Water Resources Development, volume 29, issue 3
(September 2013) pp. 472–491

Please direct any queries you may have about the citations to
clsuk.permissions@cengage.com

Foreword

Esteban de las Heras Balbás

AguaGranada Foundation, Granada, Spain

Water resources all over the world are expected to come under greater pressure in the future unless water resource management practices can be significantly improved. Consequently, many countries, organizations and institutions are attempting to improve management practices, including through legislation and regulation, so that efficient, rational and sustainable use of this resource is possible in the coming years. Such improvements must occur for all different use sectors, including domestic, agriculture, industry, energy, tourism and recreation.

Within this overall framework of increasing needs and therefore growing pressure on available water resources, there are many ongoing debates on how best to improve urban water management. Some of these issues include: achieving universal access to safer water in developing countries; sustainable management of water resources; infrastructure development; maintaining quality; improving management efficiency; better regulation and control of industry; efficient and equitable tariff systems; and broadening supply using non-conventional water sources.

To address the complex issues associated with the provisioning of urban water and wastewater management services, the Third World Centre for Water Management in Mexico and the University of Granada, with the support of the AguaGranada Foundation, organized the *Workshop on Water Pricing and Roles of Public and Private Sectors in Efficient Urban Water Management*, which was held in Granada, 9–11 May 2011. The International Water Resources Association and Global Water Intelligence also collaborated in organizing the event. In addition, the Euro-Arab Foundation for Higher Studies, the Caja Rural de Granada, the Spanish Ministry of Science and Innovation and the Andalusia Regional Ministry of Economy, Innovation and Science also provided support. It was attended by some 30 leading international experts from academia and the public and private sectors, and from institutions in many parts of the world. They were selected for their expertise and specially invited to participate in the meeting.

Following the workshop, the authors modified their papers based on the discussions at Granada and additional peer review. This special issue contains the papers that were discussed, as well as additional ones which the editors believed to complement them.

Michael Rouse and David Lloyd Owen address the complex issue of regulation in the industry. Dennis Wichelns covers how to enhance the performance of water prices and tariff structures to achieve socially desirable outcomes. David Zetland and Christopher

Gasson provide a comprehensive assessment of global water tariffs with a view toward making the systems sustainable, efficient and fair.

Gareth Walker provides a critique of the models available for predicting water demand within the context of England and Wales. Arnaud Reynaud assesses the impact of price and non-price policies on residential water demand in Wisconsin. Germà Bel, Francisco González-Gómez and Andrés J. Picazo-Tadeo consider a the dynamics of privatization and regulation of water services by comparing experiences from two Spanish regions. Alberto Ruiz-Villaverde, Francisco González-Gómez and Andrés J. Picazo-Tadeo consider multi-criteria approach to analyzing public choice in urban water service management.

Roberto Martínez-Espiñeira and Maria A. García-Valiñas discuss "adopting versus adapting" in terms of adoption of water-saving technology versus water-conservation habits in Spain. María A. García-Valiñas and Josepa Miquel-Florensa discuss access and management of water service quality in Tanzania. Eduardo Araral and Yahua Wang discuss the water demand management situation in South-East Asia. Finally, Sonia Ferdous Hoque and Dennis Wichelns present a state-of-the-art review on urban water tariff structures to meet local challenges.

I am confident that the papers in this special issue will be of considerable interest to water professionals from different parts of the world and will contribute to the current ongoing global debates on these complex and evolving issues. The AguaGranada Foundation would like to thank all the authors and the co-sponsors of this stimulating event, as well as the editors of this publication.

The private sector and water pricing in efficient urban water management

Cecilia Tortajada* and Miguel A. García-Rubio**

* *Third World Centre for Water Management, Mexico*
** *Department of Applied Economics and Water Research Institute, University of Granada, Spain*

Abstract. Traditional approaches to water management have led to unsustainable use of the water resources in much of the world. With population growth and economic development, promoting more efficient water management has become a priority. In institutional frameworks characterized by the existence of competitive markets, price mechanisms guarantee economic efficiency. By contrast, in markets where there is limited competition, demand and supply may be partially independent of costs, and political and social factors may play an important role in determining the price. This paper critically examines the limited scope that the privatization of urban water management has in promoting competition in the industry. In addition, it discusses the limitations of using urban water rates as a single instrument to address often-conflicting objectives and the role public participation should play in the management of water services in urban areas.

Introduction

There have been considerable debates in recent decades among water professionals and decision-makers as to how best water available can be allocated efficiency, equitably and cost-effectively, promoting at the same time water conservation. For the domestic sector, a series of institutional arrangements and policy interventions have been developed in order to mitigate cost-effectively quantity and quality dimensions of water scarcity under specific economic social, environmental and political conditions, and also try to increase the efficiency of water delivery and use (Dinar & Saleth, 2005).

Institutional arrangements include public and private utilities that operate either on their own or under agreements of different types. With time, the real and perceived failure of the public sector to provide water and wastewater-related services efficiently and reliably has encouraged the participation of the private sector in the provision of such services. The importance of the private sector is its potential to finance investment costs and contribute directly to the efficiency of the water sector by reducing costs and improving creditworthiness and ability to attract additional financing (Akhmouch & Kauffman, 2013). Nevertheless, private sector performance has fallen short of expectations in many parts in the world. In addition, neither public nor private ownership alone have guaranteed a more efficient access to the service or its more efficient management.

Water pricing and tariffs structures are some of the most important components of public policies for the delivery of water and wastewater services in urban areas efficiently, equitably and sustainably. Their financial and economic roles are expected to lead to increased capital investments and reduced demands. That is, recovering the investment on operation and maintenance costs of the water systems and also signalling the scarcity value and opportunity cost of water for allocation decisions (Wichelns, 2014).

There is an extensive body of literature that argues that the performance of private sector in many urban areas has not always been satisfactorily or sustained over time. Questions related to the cost-effectiveness of the private sector utilities, as well as to what extent they are willing to provide good services to the poor and their interest in promoting water conservation, have become increasingly contentious (Cotta, 2012). Concerning urban water pricing, it has also been argued that, for this to be sustainable, full-cost pricing with equity should promote conservation and also attract the very large investments that are necessary. This should be done by considering resource-use efficiency, full cost recovery (supply and opportunity costs and economic externalities) and economic viability of the water utilities (Worthington & Hoffmann, 2006). While the conceptual arguments behind these ideas are easy to understand, the process to implement them has proved to be very difficult in both developed and developing countries mostly because of social and political reasons.

Given the importance of the private sector and water pricing in efficient urban water management, this paper critically examines the limited scope that the privatization of urban water management has in promoting competition in the water industry. In addition, it discusses the limitations of using urban water rates as a single instrument to address often-conflicting objectives and the role the public should play in the management of water services in urban areas.

The public-private debate in urban water management

The participation of the private sector in the urban water sector is not a new phenomenon. From the late 19th to the early 20thcentury, private companies financed, constructed and managed the modern system of water supply in many cities of America and Europe (Pérard, 2009). The limited investment and neglected service quality that resulted from the primordial role played by private managers led to the nationalization of these services in almost all cases.

However, in the 70s, the role of the public sector in the economy was profoundly questioned as a result of the inefficiencies arising from failures in government interventions associated with the bureaucracy and political competition. From this, a new philosophy on the management of public services emerged and found a strong theoretical foundation in the theory of public choice (Downs, 1967) and agency theory

(Alchian & Demsetz, 1972). The theory of public choice highlights the difficulties the administrative bureaucracy faces to promote the efficiency of the public sector. Meanwhile, the agency theory shows that the achievements of the principal's objectives depend on the actions performed by the agent, in which the first has delegated. At the same time, these actions can be far from the interests of the principal, especially in the case of asymmetric information. In the case of public administration, there could be two types of agency relationship: delegation of responsibility of citizens-voters to the politicians, and the delegation of the latter to policy makers.

Thus, in the following decade a 'conservative revolution' began advocating market deregulation and the privatization of hither to public monopolies. This wave of privatization also extended to local public services and, in some countries, allowed private participation in the management of urban water services.

In this context, organizations like the World Bank and the International Monetary Fund sustain that private entities can invest capital to improve infrastructure and its efficiency, reduce water tariffs and be more responsive to the needs of consumers. Especially since the 90s, these agencies support the privatization of urban water services, including it as one of the conditions many emerging and developing countries have had to comply with to receive international aid (Goldman, 2005). In 2012, it was estimated that private companies were supplying water to 962 million people worldwide (Pinsent Masons, 2012). Currently, the austerity measures imposed on southern European countries are resulting in a new wave of privatization in urban water services. This is the case of Spain, which is currently undergoing local government reforms.

Some scholars (Barlow & Clarke, 2002; Lobina & Hall, 2008; Shiva, 2008; Araral, 2009) are present arguments against the private management of urban water services. On one hand, it is argued that the participation of the private sector could detonate a permanent ongoing conflict between public and private interests and the for-profit motive of the private sector could marginalize the poor. Even the World Bank has recognized that concession contracts have not generated a significant number of new water connections (World Bank, 2005). In addition, the difficulty of promoting effective competition in the sector could result into the private sector becoming a dominant actor as the private sector seeks to consolidate its market share. Finally, many criticize what is interpreted as the commodification of water, access to which should be treated as a human right.

Some of the privatization processes of the past decades are being reversed and the public sector has recovered the management of previously privatized water services. The reversal (or remunicipalization) has occurred in cities in developed countries such as Paris, Hannover, Berlin (Beveridge et al., 2014) and Budapest, and also developing ones, like Jakarta, and most notably in Latin America (Lobina & Hall, 2007) such as in Cochabamba (Pigeon et al., 2012). However, the public ownership alone does no guarantee the increased access to the service or its more efficient management. Most of the water utilities that have gone back under public control in less developed countries continue to face the same problems of underinvestment and are unable to expand the water distribution networks as it was the case before (Spronk et al., 2012).

Privatization, competition and efficiency

Economic theory provides important arguments to show that, under certain conditions, market competition maximizes economic efficiency and social welfare. More specifically, competitive forces ensure that economic agents produce their outputs at the lowest cost-production efficiency and that consumers have access to these outputs at prices that accurately reflect these minimum costs-allocative efficiency. Efficient management of urban water utilities result in users not having to deal with excessive service cost. Further promoting efficiency can help achieve improvements in the quality of services without simultaneous increases in tariffs. Nevertheless, these results correspond to the theoretical ideal of perfect competition.

One of the most important characteristics of the urban water industry, and one often ignored in certain discourses, is the existence of significant economies of scale. Being a very capital-intensive industry and facing high fixed costs, it is inefficient to duplicate supply and sanitation networks. Total costs are thus lower when the service is in the hands of a single provider. Furthermore, the presence of high sunk costs poses barriers to entry and exit of different firms, making the market not contestable (Baumol et al., 1982). Similarly to other network industries, the case of urban water industry exhibits the conditions of a classic natural monopoly.

Ownership changes in urban water service providers are part of the 'economic solutions' to the management of problems affecting the sector. This is not the case in the presence of a natural monopoly, where the free market cannot produce an economically efficient outcome since there will be no competition regulating how the monopoly behaves. In other words, in the management of urban water, privatization assumes no sector liberalization; quite the opposite, it involves the mere transfer of a public to a private monopoly, where the consolidation of market power can lead to abuses. Despite this, one of the primary reasons justifying the privatization role of the urban water industry has been promotion of efficiency.

In this sense, there is a large volume of applied research that has attempted to compare public and private management in the urban water sector from the point of view of efficiency. A literature review suggests that there is no conclusive empirical evidence to imply that one form of management is more efficient than the other (Abbott & Cohen, 2009; González-Gómez & García-Rubio, 2008; Rouse, 2013). It should be pointed out that these studies rarely consider variables such as the level of satisfaction of service users, water quality or the prevention of network leakages (Worthington, 2014). In addition, some studies conclude that public initiative tends to operate in scenarios with diseconomies of scale and scope (Carvalho et al., 2012), which might explain why in some cases private companies have higher performance than public ones. In fact, private participation in the sector can be geographically segmented, sometimes not being a real management choice; for instance, the private sector could avoid serving low-income areas that could compromise the returns on investment (Jiménez & Pérez-Foguet, 2009), or areas where environmental factors make service management more complex and the expected returns lower (González-Gómez et al., 2011).

In any case, empirical evidence challenges the argument that promotion of efficiency has to be the priority element to decide whether urban water services are privatized or not. It is difficult to establish an unequivocal set of factors determining service privatization since research shows mixed results. The objectives of privatization are often political and ideological in nature (Bel & Fageda, 2007), and in some other cases, decisions are determined by the financial difficulties faced by local governments (Ruiz-Villaverde et al., 2014). Beyond the public-private controversy, mere privatization cannot respond to important sector challenges (Rouse, 2014) where the decision is made taking into consideration factors that have nothing to do with service promotion and improvement.

The importance of institutional factors

Similarly to other economic activities, private sector involvement in the management of urban water systems demands the existence of clear and reliable rules of the game and, consequently, the development of appropriate institutions. Rules of the game would be the very much needed political stability, an appropriate definition of property rights and legal certainty. Moreover, given the characteristics of the sector, privatization of urban water services cannot lead to the complete withdrawal of the public sector, but rather a change in the way the government is involved in this industry. Since the public sector retains responsibility for the provision of water services, even when the operators are private companies, the establishment of an appropriate regulatory framework should become crucial. Bel et al. (2014) observed that, in Spain, differences in regulatory models result in different privatization models. Yet, at the operational level, it has not been resolved how best to regulate privatized urban water services. In practice, problems on how best to regulate private sector management, lack of human and financial resources and staff with appropriate training, and information asymmetry between large private operators and public service managers, are not uncommon.

Furthermore, although the role of efficiency in regulating the sector is important, in practice, it is rare that this is one of objectives of regulation. Thus, the possible merits of public and private management cannot be clearly established and it is necessary that they be evaluated within the particular institutional and policy context (Walter et al., 2009). Moreover, the identification of good practices in water management, whether in the public or private sector, cannot be seen as a widely generalized panacea and instead should take into account the specific institutional and regulatory framework in which these take place. For example, in Tanzania, the results of García-Valiñas & Miquel-Florensa (2014) suggest that community management is the best alternative for water delivery. This model has been widely used in rural areas in sub-Saharan Africa, but faces significant challenges and requires appropriate institutions (Kamruzzaman et al., 2013). In this region, the community management model was driven by the donors themselves. However, there is no guarantee that the model in the region will remain because it requires the support of national and local governments in strengthening and promoting community management institutions. By contrast, government bureaucracies in these countries are not the most suitable for the successful implementation of this approach. This could be as a consequence of the so-called Western individualistic influence that weakens the spirit of community values and undermines traditional values. Lack of incentives for community members, lack of adequate replacement policy of water committee members and their lack of legal status, questionable transparency in accountability issues, lack of support of the local government institutions and financial difficulties to replace capital assets are some of the main challenges facing this management model. In the context of developed countries, Owen (2014) shows how the model used in Wales has been effective in reducing prices, improving the service and promoting environmental sustainability; the key to success residing in a proper regulatory and political support.

In any case, the governance deficit the sector faces worldwide (Tortajada, 2010) cannot be solved through a simple change of management. Equally, the debate surrounding the relative merits of public and private management has instead deflected attention from the more pressing problem that is the need of governance reforms. Probably, this situation is further complicated as water management is still largely referred to as a strictly technical problem, with little consideration of its political and social dimensions (Transparency International, 2008). Walker (2014) shows how a seemingly technical matter, such as demand modelling, has been handled in England and Wales with an obvious lack of transparency. The current institutional structure creates conflicting incentives between national resource planners and financial planners firms, as a result of which predicting demand becomes a highly strategic issue. Consequently, transparency in modelling demand weakens, future uncertainties become unclear, and objectives that conflict with each other become vague. This reflects the need to implement more participatory policies in the management of water resources.

In this sense, the European Water Framework Directive provides for three levels of citizen participation in water planning: public information, public consultation and active participation (European Commission, 2003). In several specific situations, citizen participation has influenced management outcomes. In countries such as Bolivia, Uruguay, Argentina, South Africa and Tanzania, strong citizen protest movements against the privatization of the service that have been key to the cancellation of concessions.

Corrupt practices, although with unequal frequency and intensity, affect most of the world and should be discussed separately. Corruption is one of the most important manifestations of the existing crisis in water governance, and affects not only the public sector but also non-governmental organizations and private companies. Therefore, among the solutions is increasing transparency by encouraging the participation of civil society in setting priorities according to the specific situations and monitoring activities (González de Asis et al., 2009). All stakeholders should have the right to access to information, public consultation and active participation in the management of urban water services.

In urban water management, the choice of a public or private manager is a question with a low scientific consensus. In these circumstances, the democratic and participatory ways of conflict resolution should take a greater role to ensure social control management. This would improve the transparency and also the development of engaged stakeholders in the management of basic services. In the field of urban water, regardless of the type of property management, public agencies should encourage and ensure the active participation of different stakeholders: elected politicians, interest groups, institutions and associations involved with consumer and environmental protection, media, various spheres of government involved, scientific community and the general public. This, in turn, requires institutional reforms that include different paths for citizen participation in organizations responsible for urban water management. For example, local politicians should not unilaterally impose the privatization of the management of services when there is an important public opposition. However, this is, unfortunately, quite common in many countries. Under these circumstances, it is essential to develop mechanisms for public information and consultation. In conclusion, the involvement of the society can result in more just and sustainable results (Susskind, 2013).

Water pricing and participation of the public in water services management

Pricing of water and wastewater services are designed primarily to achieve cost recovery and also to raise sufficient revenue to cover operations, maintenance and investments. Properly structured, they can play important roles in promoting behavioural changes and improving affordability and access for the poor. However, pricing of water, subsidies and any type of support, need to be targeted and appropriately adjusted according to the conditions of populations who live in poverty (Hoque & Wichelns, 2014). As argued by the Human Rights Council (UNGA, 2013:17-18), "Scarcity pricing, penalties or higher pricing structures for non-essential use, well-designed increasing-block tariffs, subsidies for those in need, institutional and distributive taxes, are all examples of approaches used to raise revenue and recover costs. These should be implemented in a fair manner that promotes sustainability and access for all to water and sanitation services."

In a survey of 308 cities in 102 countries that examines the relations between tariffs and sustainability, efficiency and equity, Zetland & Gasson (2014) found that the relations among water prices, efficiency and fairness vary largely around the world and that water prices are the result of a complex interrelation between economic, political and social factors and have evolved over time. In another study, Hoque & Wichelns (2014) assessed domestic and non-domestic water and wastewater tariffs in 60 cities and 43 countries. The findings also confirmed the relation between local water scarcity and political considerations for water tariffs in urban areas.

The ability to pay of low-income sectors of the population all over the world has been discussed by numerous authors. There has been the erroneous idea for decades that poor members of the society are unable to pay for water services when in reality they are already overpaying for the quality of service they get. As mentioned by Rouse (2013), what low-income population is unable to do is to save, pay a lump sum or monthly or quarterly bills, making these the constraints that need to be addressed. The many times mentioned subsidies to provide assistance to the poor should be on access charges as well as on either low tariff pre-payment meters or means that test direct support on water bill payments.

In all the above cases, the gradual involvement of members of the public through consultative, deliberative and engagement processes has the potential to result in positive additions to the complex task of efficient provision and management of water services in urban areas, including their pricing. In order to be effective, participation strategies should not be limited to encouraging participation of the public but to actually develop participation modalities and setting broader involvement framework by introducing governance aspects.

Governance aspects, when incorporated in public processes in spite of their complexity, provide the possibility to engage participants to play a more active and comprehensive role. Members of the public have thus the possibility to engage as advisors, co-decision makers or cooperating partners depending on their expertise as well as on the degree to which they are willing to collaborate in the processes established and, in consequence, also take responsibility of their decisions and actions. The obvious gains of more meaningful degrees of interaction and participation would be the better understanding of the goals that are commonly discussed. This, in turn, is likely to lead (although not necessarily) to the joint decision of compromises and trade-offs between competing values and priorities and achieve outcomes that have the potential to be more transparent and accountable (Tortajada & Joshi, 2013). Communication, collaboration and cooperation among those involved also open the door for broader public acceptance and support for different initiatives (Lenihan, 2009). After all, it is the engagement of the different parties that determines the degree of success of implementing long-term strategies.

Politics at the national level and the rule systems administered by state agencies do play a specific role, but the essence of governance is that individuals and organizations may also engage as actors in politics and policy making. It is governance aspects that point in the direction of understanding, engaging and become part of policy making as well as social and institutional change processes, that have the potential to consider multiple categories of actors and heterogeneity within each identified actor category; multiple relationships and networks between actors; multiple institutional arrangements with connected rule systems; multiple levels in administrative or territorial terms from the local to the global; and multiple scientific, ideological and other perspectives (Söderbaum & Tortajada, 2011).

It is important to note that ideological perspective or 'ideology' is about means–ends relationships: where the parties are at present, where they want to go in future, and what strategy they can develop to get there. While ideology is often a word with negative connotations, it is also a fact that actors, individually and collectively are guided by their ideological orientations. In consequence, ideology plays an important role in the world of policy-making both from the point of view of the public sector but also many times the actors involved (Söderbaum, 2013).

Processes that involve dialogue, interaction and debate between members of the public and formal and information organizations, are enormously intricate; and so are the means by which stakeholders can have a say in decision-making as this is through the interest groups to which they belong. When only specific groups are involved in decision-making, it is a reality that the views that are discussed may not always represent those of all the individuals making the group as a whole. This is because groups of stakeholders neither include all of the citizenry nor represent all of its needs and concerns. Additionally, stakeholders who are affected by a particular decision or problem may not necessarily be represented in the groups that are prepared to take part in decision-making on the specific issues, including members of local institutions, groups of users, or members of the public (Tortajada, 2006).

Even when participation can help in understanding the reasons that support any given decision, it provides no final assurance that any agreement can be reached among the parties involved. It is commonly assumed that participation is an essential element to build consensus and prevent conflicts and that dialogue provides an opportunity for stakeholders to discuss and have a better understanding of the different viewpoints. However, although participation processes represent an opportunity for stakeholders to share objectives, experiences, responsibilities, and be more agreeable to the solutions that will be reached, this is clearly not always the case. In many cases, interests and ideologies prevail and make no allowance for interaction and exchange of ideas, blocking any initiative towards a common objective. Participation is not, therefore, some lofty ideal: stakeholders and members of the society interested in an issue may join a process of participation for specific motives that, far from implying the quest for a common goal, represent an effort to impose specific interests. The challenge is thus not that people and organizations, both formal and informal, take part per se in processes of participation. The challenge is that they do so be fully aware of the facts and the accompanying sense of responsibility that commits them to making constructive contributions to the common cause, and stand by group decisions even when the results do not coincide with their very own interests (Söderbaum & Tortajada, 2011).

Therefore, participation must not be understood as an end in itself with the organization of participative processes as the final objective. Participation has to be a means of achieving joint responsibility of the different economic and social sectors in the decisions-making of which they form part of the problems as well as of the solutions. The role of governments is to promote processes and establish spaces for communication, information and participation where proposals are discussed, decisions are taken, and mechanisms are established that link government actors and members of the public. The role of the actors or stakeholders is to engage into decision-making fully aware of the responsibility of the decisions they take.

Conclusions

Within a framework of efficient urban water management, the main challenges the sector faces for the solutions of the complex problems that affect it, is to avoid generic answers that are based on theoretical premises. Rather, such responses should be based on practical experiences that have stood the test of time, and also take into account the institutional framework within which these experiences have succeeded.

The debate on the relative merits of public and private provision has diverted attention from the urgent problem of governance reform. A main priority is to resolve the problems associated with the regulation and management in the water service industry to address the governance gap in the management of urban water services.

The fundamental importance of governance is that it embraces not only regulations and institutions but also value-related issues such as responsibility, accountability, transparency, equity and fairness of multiple actors and institutions. Its importance is that it also points in the direction of understanding policy-making as well as social and institutional change. In this respect, the involvement of all stakeholders in urban water management, including different paths for public participation, can produce more just and sustainable results.

Ideally, members of the public should not be predominantly passive and be limited to compliance with voting, but instead have a dynamic attitude to be able to place limits on the actions of governments. Equally, governments are responsible for promoting processes and create opportunities for communication, information and participation through which proposals are discussed, decisions are made, and binding mechanisms for government and society to enable the different parties are established. Public participation in the management of water and water services in urban areas would remain as a simple statement of good intentions if more comprehensive and dynamic mechanisms to ensure more inclusive involvement in decision-making are not articulated.

Acknowledgements

Miguel A. García-Rubio gratefully acknowledges the financial support from the following Spanish institutions: the *Consejería de Economía, Innovación, Ciencia y Empleo* from the Government of Andalusia (P11-SEJ-7039) and the Spanish Ministry of Economics and Competitiveness of Spain (Project ECO2012-32189).

References

Abbott, M. & Cohen, R. (2009). Productivity and efficiency in the water industry. *Utilities Policy* 17(3-4), 233–244.

Akhmouch, A., & Kauffmann, C. (2013). Private-sector participation in water service provision: Revealing governance gaps. *Water International*, 38(3), 340–352.

Alchian, A. & Demsetz, H. (1972). Production, information cost and economic organization. *American Economic Review*, 62(5), 777–795.

Araral, E. (2009). The failure of water utilities privatization: Synthesis of evidence, analysis and implications. *Policy and Society*, 27(3), 221–228.

Barlow, M., & Clarke, T. (2002). *Blue gold: The battle against corporate theft of the world's water.* New York: The New Press.

Baumol, W.J. (1982). Contestable markets: An uprising in the theory of industry structure. *American Economic Review*, 72(1), 1–15.

Bel, G. & Fageda, X. (2007). Why do local governments privatize public services? A survey of empirical studies. *Local Government Studies*, 33 (4), 517–534.

Bel, G, González-Gómez, F. & Picazo-Tadeo, A.J. (2014). The dynamics of privatization and regulation of water services: A comparative study of two Spanish regions. In Tortajada, C., González-Gómez, F., Biswas, A.K. & García-Rubio, M.A. (Eds.), *The private sector and water pricing in efficient urban water management*. London: Routledge.

Beveridge, R., Hüesker, F. & Naumann, M. (2014). From post-politics to a politics of possibility? Unravelling the privatization of the Berlin Water Company. *Geoforum*, 51, 66–74.

Carvalho, P., Marques, R.C. & Berg, S. (2012). A meta-regression analysis of benchmarking studies on water utilities market structure. *Utilities Policy*, 21, 40–49.

Cotta, S. A. (2012). Privatization and water service provision in the United States: A recommendation for expanded oversight and the development and adoption of best practices. *Water International*, 37(7), 818–830.

Dinar, A. & Saleth, R.M. (2005). Issues in water pricing reforms: from getting correct prices to setting appropriate institutions. In Folmer, H. & Tietenberg, T.H. (eds.). *The International Yearbook of Environmental and Resource Economics 2005/2006. A survey of current issues.* Gheltemham and Northampton: Edward Elgar Publishing.

Downs, A. (1967). *Inside bureaucracy.* Boston: Little Brown.

European Commission (2003). Public Participation in relation to the Water Framework Directive. Common Implementation Strategy for the Water Framework Directive [2000/60/EC] Guidance Document n. 8. Luxemburg: Office for Official Publications of the European Communities.

García-Valiñas, M.A. & Miquel-Florensa, J. (2014). Water service quality in Tanzania: Access and management. In Tortajada, C., González-Gómez, F., Biswas, A.K. & García-Rubio, M.A. (Eds.), *The private sector and water pricing in efficient urban water management*. London: Routledge.

Goldman, M. (2005). *Imperial Nature: The World Bank and struggles for social justice in the age of globalization.* New Haven, CT: Yale University Press.

González de Asís, M., O'Leary, D., Ljung, P. & Butterworth, J. (2009). *Improving transparency, integrity, and accountability in water supply and sanitation*. Washington DC: The World Bank.

González-Gómez, F. & García-Rubio, M.A. (2008). Efficiency in the management of urban water services. What have we learned after four decades of research? *Hacienda Pública Española. Revista de Economía Pública*, 185(2), 39–67.

González-Gómez, F., Picazo-Tadeo, A.J. & Guardiola, J. (2011). Why do local governments privatise the provision of water services? Empirical evidence from Spain. *Public Administration*, 89(2), 471–492.

Hoque, S.F., & D. Wichelns. (2014). State-of-the-art review: designing urban water tariffs to recover costs and promote wise use. In Tortajada, C., González-Gómez, F., Biswas, A.K. & García-Rubio, M.A. (Eds.), *The private sector and water pricing in efficient urban water management*. London: Routledge.

Jiménez, A., & Pérez-Foguet, A. (2009). International investments in the water sector. *International Journal of Water Resources Development*, 25(1), 1–14.

Kamruzzaman, A.K.M., Said, I. & Osman, O. (2013). Overview on management patterns in community, private and hybrid management in rural water supply. *Journal of Sustainable Development*, 6(5). DOI: 10.5539/jsd.v6n5p26.

Lenihan, D. (2009). Rethinking the public policy process. A public engagement framework. Public Policy Forum, Ottawa. Retrieved from http://www.ppforum.ca/publications/rethinking-public-policy-process-public-engagementframework

Lobina, E., & Hall, D. (2007). *Water privatisation and restructuring in Latin America, 2007*. London, England: Public Services International Research Unit.

Lobina, E., & Hall, D. (2008). The comparative advantage of the public sector in the development of urban water supply. *Progress in Development Studies*, 8(1), 85–101.

Owen, D.L. (2014). Glas Cymru: Lessons from nine years as a not-for-profit public-private partnership. In Tortajada, C., González-Gómez, F., Biswas, A.K. & García-Rubio, M.A. (Eds.), *The private sector and water pricing in efficient urban water management*. London: Routledge.

Pérard, E. (2009). Water supply: public or private? An approach based on cost on funds, transaction costs, efficiency and political costs. *Policy and Society*, 27(3), 193–219.

Pigeon, M., McDonald, D.A., Hoedeman, O. & Kishimoto, S. (2012). *Remunicipalisation: Putting Water Back in Public Hands*. Amsterdam: Transnational Institute.

Pinsent Masons (2012). *Pinsent Masons Water Yearbook 2012–2013*. London: Pinsent Masons.

Rouse, M. (2013). *Institutional governance and regulation of water services. The essential elements* (2nd edition). London: IWA.

Rouse, M. (2014). Policy brief: The urban water challenge. In Tortajada, C., González-Gómez, F., Biswas, A.K. & García-Rubio, M.A. (Eds.), *The private sector and water pricing in efficient urban water management*. London: Routledge.

Ruiz-Villaverde, A., González-Gómez, F. & Picazo-Tadeo, A.J. (2014). Public choice of urban water service management: A multi-criteria approach. In Tortajada, C., González-Gómez, F., Biswas, A.K. & García-Rubio, M.A. (Eds.), *The private sector and water pricing in efficient urban water management*. London: Routledge.

Shiva, V. (2008). From water crisis to water culture. *Cultural Studies*, 22(3–4), 498–509.

Söderbaum, P. (2013). Ecological economics in relation to democracy, ideology and politics. *Ecological Economics*, 95, 221–225.

Söderbaum, P., & C. Tortajada (2011). Perspectives for water management within the context of sustainable development. *Water International*, 36(7), 812–827

Spronk, S., Crespo, C., & Olivera, M. (2012). Struggles for water justice in Latin America: Public and "social-public" alternatives. In McDonald, D.A. & Ruiters, G. (Eds.), *Alternatives to privatization: Public options for essential services in the global South*. New York: Routledge, pp. 421–452.

Susskind, L. (2013). Water and democracy: new roles for civil society in water governance. *International Journal of Water Resources Development*, 29(4), 666–677.

Tortajada, C. (2006). *Instruments for public participation in water management (Instrumentos de participación pública en la gestión del agua)*. Zaragoza: University of Zaragoza.

Tortajada, C. (2010). Water governance: Some critical issues. *International Journal of Water Resources Development*, 26(2), 297–307.

Tortajada, C., and Y. K. Joshi (2013). Water demand management in Singapore: Involving the public. *Water Resources Management*, 27(8), 2729–2746.

Transparency International (2008). *Global corruption report 2008. Corruption in the water sector.* New York: Cambridge University Press.

UNGA (United Nations General Assembly) (2013). Report of the Special Rapporteur on the human right to safe drinking water and sanitation, Catarina de Albuquerque. A/HRC/24/44. New York: United Nations.

Walker, G. (2014). A critical examination of models and projections of demand in water utility resource planning in England and Wales. In Tortajada, C., González-Gómez, F., Biswas, A.K. & García-Rubio, M.A. (Eds.), *The private sector and water pricing in efficient urban water management*. London: Routledge.

Walter, M., Cullmann, A., von Hirschhausen, C., Wand, R. & Zschille, M. (2009) Quo vadis efficiency analysis of water distribution? A comparative literature review. *Utilities Policy*, 17(3–4), 225–232.

Wichelns, D., (2014). Enhancing the performance of water prices and tariff structures in achieving socially desirable outcomes. In Tortajada, C., González-Gómez, F., Biswas, A.K. & García-Rubio, M.A. (Eds.), *The private sector and water pricing in efficient urban water management*. London: Routledge.

World Bank (2005). *Infrastructure development: The roles of the public and private sectors. World Bank group's approach to supporting investments in infrastructure*. Washington, DC: World Bank.

Worthington, A.C. (2014). A review of frontier approaches to efficiency and productivity measurement in urban water utilities. *Urban Water Journal*, 11(1), 55–73.

Worthington, A.C. & Hoffmann, M. (2006). A state of the art review of residential water demand modelling. University of Wollongong, School of Accounting and Finance. Working Paper Series No. 06/27, 2006.

Zetland, D. & Gasson, C. (2014). A global survey of urban water tariffs: are they sustainable, efficient and fair? In Tortajada, C., González-Gómez, F., Biswas, A.K. & García-Rubio, M.A. (Eds.), *The private sector and water pricing in efficient urban water management*. London: Routledge.

POLICY BRIEF

The urban water challenge

Michael Rouse

Oxford University Centre for the Environment, University of Oxford, Oxford, UK

There are major challenges associated with the provision of urban water services which meet acceptable standards of service for present and future generations. Unless there is significant investment in the underground networks there will be an increasing loss of access to acceptable service. There has been a mistaken belief that water resource difficulties can be solved through "hours of day" water rationing. Successful case studies help to point the way forward. In the developed world there are wake-up calls for major investment. In many parts of the developing world the most fundamental change required is the adoption of a policy of continuous ("24/7") supply. There should be sustainable cost recovery from water charges, with subsidies being targeted to make provision for low-income groups. With rapid urbanization, water service planning has to be integrated with city planning.

Introduction

There are many challenges to be faced in providing sustainable urban water services. The two most commonly discussed are the impact of climate change on water sources and financing the associated infrastructure. It is almost a prerequisite that every paper make reference to climate change. Having fulfilled that requirement, this article can now address the extensive challenges which have to be faced to achieve universal water and sanitation services to meet the aspirations of the UN Human Rights Declaration on water and sanitation (UNHRC, 2010).

Of course water resources are important, and the design criteria and environmental implications of climate change have to be understood, but there are other, potentially more difficult, challenges. Rapid population growth (UN, 2012) is predicted, and this will require large-scale investment in new infrastructure; but equally large-scale investment (Doshi, Schulman, & Gabaldon, 2007) is required to refurbish existing infrastructure. Without addressing the latter, it will not be possible to extend the infrastructure to serve the "new" population in the expanded cities. Both developed and developing countries have major investment, source of funding, cost recovery and sustainability issues to address.

The existing infrastructure

In many parts of the developed world there has been neglect of infrastructure, particularly water mains and sewers. These systems cannot easily be inspected, and their deterioration does not become evident until there are major service failures. These systems have long lives, and generally provision has not been made in accounting systems for their replacement. As a consequence, water charges have been too low to accumulate reserves to fund the large sums of money necessary for their replacement. Although the managers responsible for the operation of the systems have recognized the need for system refurbishment and have put forward programmes for refurbishment, the impact on government subsidies or charges has been politically too difficult. In England and Wales (Rouse, 2007), it required privatization and pressure from the market to reduce uncertainty on future costs before there was political recognition of the large investment to be faced. Once tariff setting became an objective regulatory process based on levels of service, rather than a political one, the process began of addressing 30–40 years of infrastructure neglect. The same was true of Scotland, although still public-sector managed when independent regulation was introduced. Northern Ireland will have to face up to major investment in the old infrastructure. The logistics of dealing with years of neglect are not generally recognized. It is a salutary thought that if all the water mains in England and Wales were put end to end they would go round the world six times.

Imagine the scale of the problem facing the United States, where the alarm bells are now ringing loudly. The American Water Works Association (AWWA, 2011), in a well-documented study called *Buried No Longer*, estimated the investment requirements for water mains at USD1 trillion over the next 25 years and USD1.7 trillion up to 2050, of which 54% is required to replace existing systems. As the report points out, the good news is that the investment is not all needed immediately; the bad news is that delays in starting will increase the likely costs due to ongoing deterioration. The impact on cost recovery and the implication for water charges are discussed below.

There is a similar backlog of investment in existing systems in developing countries. Many of the systems were constructed in colonial times. Although the cities have grown since that time, water supply systems have not been able to keep pace with urban development. The results of decades of little or no pipe replacement or refurbishment are low pressure and high leakage. Low pressure is a symptom of systems not being able to cope with expansion. Leakage alone is estimated to have an equivalent cost of USD1 billion per year in selected African cities (Banerjee & Morella, 2011). Refurbishment will have to be funded first to make possible the extension of water services to match rapid urban growth. Although in theory there is a source of increased revenue with expanding cities to pay for new water service infrastructure, there is no such new revenue associated with refurbishment of existing systems. This means that costs per capita (for the same level of operational efficiency) will increase and result in a required increase in per capita cost recovery, which, will be argued later, can only come from water charges.

Faced with low pressure, and in the belief that water rationing could be achieved by limiting supplies to any particular area, intermittent supplies are now common. I have always been sceptical (Rouse, 2007) of this means of demand control because I have observed how much water is stored in household containers; how taps are left on to avoid missing the time of delivery; and how much water is thrown away when fresh supplies are flowing. In addition to the risk of ingress of contaminated water when there is no water pressure, I have been concerned about the impact of depressurizing and repressurizing on water-main structures. Monitoring of the impact of intermittent supplies in Cyprus (Waterloss, 2011) during a severe-drought period confirmed that concern. In Nicosia, non-revenue water measured in the years before and after the 2008–09 period of intermittent supplies showed an increase from $7,300 \, \text{m}^3$ to $13,700 \, \text{m}^3$ per day, an increase of 87%. There was also an increase in pipe bursts.

Rapid growth

It is estimated (UN, 2011) that the world's population will increase from 7 billion to 9.3 billion by 2050. Given increasing urbanization (UN, 2012), most of the additional 2 billion plus will impact urban areas in developing countries. This has major implications for water resources and for integrated city and water and sanitation planning. Over recent decades water development has tended to be focussed on integrated river basin management. Concern over the equitable and effective use of river basins will increase, but there should be integration of water and sanitation provision planning with city infrastructure planning. Currently water networks often do not keep pace with growth in cities. An Oxford student in 2012 studied 29 rapidly growing cities in India and developed a conceptual model (yet to be published) that describes water network coverage, urban spatial characteristics, and urban growth patterns. Estimating population growth is difficult enough; determining the shape of that growth and what it means for water network design is more difficult. Much more research in this area is required. There has been progress on considering how water reuse can be integrated into water resource management. A "model" city approach is being adopted in Quingdao in China (Novotny, 2011). There is research work on "smart" network thinking (Vairavamoorthy, 2012) to enhance existing networks. It would be good to see much more research on water network "spines" within which the more local network thinking could be incorporated.

Why the situation is serious

The UN's (2000) Millennium Development Goals for water and sanitation sought to halve the number of people without safe water or basic sanitation by 2015. The WHO/UNICEF (2012) Joint Monitoring Programme Report gives progress in meeting those goals, with reported success in water but not sanitation. Although since 1990 an estimated additional 2 billion people have access to "improved" water sources, official estimates refer to 1 billion people still without access to safe drinking water. Given that in the monitoring programme "safe" is not defined, it is likely that the figure for safe drinking water (Onda, LoBuglio, & Bartram, 2012) is much larger, possibly 2–3 billion people. The equivalent figures for sanitation are an estimated additional 1.8 billion people having access since 1990 but 2.4 billion still without access to basic sanitation (accessible hygienic toilets), and certainly more without satisfactory collection and treatment of their wastewater. The poor tend to live either in run-down city centres or on the extremity of cities, including in informal settlements. It is the urban poor who most miss out on water and sanitation provision. What are the key elements which are preventing universal and sustainable access to safe drinking water and basic sanitation?

What we can learn from success stories?

European Union directives, though focused on drinking water-quality and environmental water quality, have driven investment in infrastructure improvements. For example, some of the aesthetic problems with drinking water arising from corrosion of old cast-iron water mains could not be corrected without attention to the refurbishment or replacement of those systems. In the UK, this has required increases in water tariffs to pay for the investment. Without regulatory pressures to improve efficiency, the tariff increases would have been greater. The impact on charges has been greatest in Scotland, which in 2012 had the highest domestic charges in the world. This is an example of having to face up to the reality of water service sustainability. There are similar situations in most of northern

Europe where sustainable water services have been achieved – where there are efficient operations, but where water charges are high compared with those parts of the developed world which have yet to face up to the problems.

Any section on success stories must include Phnom Penh. It is very important because it is a demonstration of what can be achieved in a poor country, given sound policies and excellent management. The remarkable manager, Ek Sonn Chan, focused on some key fundamentals, including developing staff, removing corruption, controlling leakage and collecting revenue. Vital to this was consulting and informing the consumers, and making service provision affordable to the poor. Efficient operations contributed to effective cost recovery, to the point where Phnom Penh is now financially self-sufficient and able to self-finance system enhancements. There have been a number of articles describing the Phnom Penh achievements (Biswas & Tortajada, 2010; Chan, 2009; Vermersch, Chan, & Vaughan, 2012). Some of the key performance improvements are shown in Table 1. But the full story has yet to be told. Hopefully, Ek Sonn Chan will find the time to give a full personal account of how it was, from the dark days of Khmer Rouge right through to the exemplary water service of today. He has shown that water service for all is achievable, affordable and financially sustainable.

There was also a successful turnaround (Muhairwe, 2009) in the National Water and Sanitation Corporation (NWSC) of Uganda. The problems faced by the NWSC were identified as poor customer service, poor organizational culture, large debt, low cost recovery, high non-revenue water and corruption amongst the staff. The improved performance, over a similar period of time to that of Phnom Penh (13 years), is shown in Table 2. The manager responsible, William Muhairwe, was dealing with a different inheritance from Phnom Penh and a more diverse geographical operation. Although income now exceeds operational and maintenance costs, it has not yet been possible to become self-financing, because it is considered politically necessary to raise tariffs slowly. Muhairwe refers to the need for donor support: "We know we can't do everything on our own without a helping hand from development partners." There is some way to go to achieve 100% service coverage. Without cost recovery at the Phnom Penh level, donor support will be required for capital works to extend coverage. This difference between Phnom Penh and the NWSC raises the question as to whether donor support to finance new developments can result in long-term sustainability or whether it can only be achieved through self-financing.

The downward spiral was mentioned earlier that arises from intermittent supplies due to the destructive impact of the cycle of depressurization and repressurization on distribution systems. Continuous supplies (24 hours a day) are now commonly referred to as 24/7. Three 24/7 pilot projects were completed in 2010 in the State of Karnataka, India,

Table 1. Urban water performance indicators in Phnom Penh, 1993–2006.

	1993	2006
Coverage area (%)	25	90
Number of connections (thousands)	27	147
Supply duration (hours per day)	10	24
Revenue collection (%)	48	99.9
Non-revenue water (%)	72	8
Staff per 100,000 connections	22	4
Financial situation	Subsidy	Full cost recovery

Source: Ek Sonn Chan (2007).

Table 2. Urban water performance indicators in Uganda, 1998–2011.

	1998	2011
Service coverage (% of population served)	48	75
Total piped connections	50,826	272,406
New connections per year	3,317	25,000
Household metered connections	37,217	271,734
Staff per 1000 connections	36	6
Collection efficiency	60%	98%
Non-revenue water	60%	33%
Metered accounts	65%	99%
Annual turnover (USD millions)	8	51
Profit (USD millions)	− 3 (loss)	12 (surplus)

Source: Muhairwe (2009).

which demonstrated the importance of 24/7 in managing water resources and in providing continuous sustainable water services for all. A full account of these projects is given in a World Bank Water and Sanitation Programme Field Note (WSP, 2010). The projects yielded some important findings. They showed that refurbishing or replacing the distribution systems lowered the overall water resource requirement, achieving 24/7 service without additional water resources, even though the service was extended to the whole population. Importantly, the low-income consumers, whose service had changed from intermittent unreliable supplies to reliable 24/7 delivery, were willing to pay for that service. Apparently, the only complaints were from some higher-income consumers who were suddenly expected to pay an economic price for the service being provided. As a result of these trials, 24/7 is now becoming policy across India. The myth of intermittent supplies to reduce water resource requirements has been shattered.

"The Singapore Water Story" has now been documented in detail in a book (Tortajada, Joshi, & Biswas, 2013) published 22 March 2013. It provides a comprehensive account of the development of water and sanitation services integrated into city planning right from Singapore's independence in 1965 to the present day. In 1965 the city-state was facing the same problems of intermittent supplies and industrial pollution, whilst being relatively poor, that many other countries are facing today. There can be a tendency to think an investment like Singapore's in water and sanitation infrastructure is only possible in a wealthy country. However economic success was achieved because water and environmental developments were an essential part of Singapore's sustainable development. There was continuous and sustainable political commitment, with long-term planning. Singapore took a holistic approach. There was integration with city planning; both the supply and the demand sides of water resources were pursued equally; water and wastewater management were combined; and private-sector suppliers were incorporated into solutions. Pricing of water services was based on sustainable cost recovery but also used part of managing water demand.

It can take some incident or crisis to stimulate reform. Two examples from the United States (Rouse, 2007) are Seattle and Atlanta. In 1995, the city of Seattle was cited by the Environment Protection Agency for failures in wastewater handling. The city reorganized in 1997 with a new management team to integrate water, wastewater, drainage and solid waste. At that time there was significant cost recovery shortfall, deteriorated infrastructure and unwillingness to increase charges to address the problems. The cost of refurbishing the infrastructure was estimated to be USD1 billion. The management team, with political support from city councillors, took a comprehensive approach to reform covering water sources, water demand management, customer consultation and the introduction of a programme of increased tariffs. Tariffs rose by 10% a year for 10 years, and there are ongoing increases today. Special provision was made for low-income customers. The service in Seattle was transformed, and steps were taken to achieve sustainability for future generations.

In Atlanta, a crisis arose in 2002 from the failure of an attempt by the city to deal with its problems merely by placing a contract with a private operator. The problems were much more fundamental and required to be addressed as in Seattle. Once there was recognition of the need for major investment in the water and sewerage infrastructure, it was necessary to embark on a programme of increasing tariffs. Through significant increases in water charges, state loans and a short-term special sales tax, Atlanta is now well on its way to dealing with the backlog of investment towards sustainability.

Efficiency for affordability

In the success stories outlined above, operational efficiency was essential as part of providing a good water supply service and in controlling costs so that sustainable cost recovery was affordable. In contrast, in many cases where there is poor service there are no incentives for management to improve efficiency. There can be overstaffing, because it is politically unacceptable to reduce staff numbers, or even a policy of requiring water service providers to recruit extra staff to reduce unemployment numbers. There are different views on the desirability of such social objectives, but achieving good, efficient water service must be beneficial to all. The alternative is a downward spiral of decline (see Figure 1). Why should people pay for poor service? In practice, they don't – with the consequence that there is less revenue for operations and maintenance, more reliance on subsidies (which encourages political interference in day-to-day operations), lower motivation of management and staff, and a further decline in the level of service.

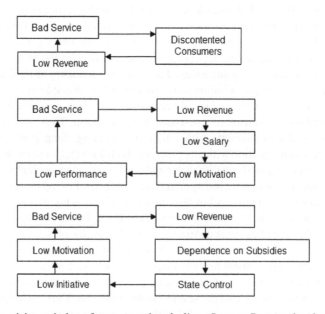

Figure 1. The vicious circles of water service decline. *Source:* Presentation by Eero Kontula (2004).

Sustainable cost recovery

A commonly used definition of sustainable cost recovery, issued by the International Water Association, is "costs that are recovered so that a water services undertaking can achieve and maintain a specified standard of service, both for the present and future generations". It is important to note that this relates to a specified standard of service, which is critical to willingness to pay. The inclusion of future generations relates to the need for ongoing maintenance and system refurbishment, as required to achieve sustainability of service. The failure to carry out that ongoing maintenance and refurbishment is one of the main reasons why so many systems are failing to provide acceptable service today. Unless this is addressed, the situation can only get worse.

There are a number of reasons why water charges are set too low to achieve sustainable cost recovery. One already mentioned is inefficiency, but most common is the political fear of raising tariffs. In many countries the life of governments is quite short compared with water and sanitation planning horizons. Therefore, it is easy to sidestep the painful process of increasing tariffs and leave it to the next government. Making the necessary changes becomes more difficult over time, because the differential between existing and necessary tariffs increases each year. This is the situation facing many cities in the United States. In the two cases outlined above, Seattle and Atlanta found it necessary to increase tariffs by around 10% a year for 10 years or more.

Another issue, particularly important in developing countries, is provision for low-income groups. Well-meaning pressure groups resist attempts to move towards sustainable cost recovery in the belief that those on low incomes will suffer. The reality is that they suffer far more without reliable, continuous water supply; and, as in the 24/7 developments in India, they are prepared to pay for good service. What is important is the method of payment. Those with low incomes have difficulty saving and cannot pay in large amounts, whether for an access charge or a water bill. The best way to assist them is through targeted subsidies for access and easy ways of paying for the water they consume. One approach now becoming common in Africa is payment through mobile-phone accounts (Hope, Foster, Rouse, & Money, 2012). The consumers benefit through low transaction costs, and there is improved cash flow and revenue collection for water service providers.

General subsidies benefit the wealthy more than those on low incomes, because the wealthy consume more water. The use of general subsidies is associated with low cost recovery, so there is a lack of sustainability. A change to targeted subsidies can direct government assistance toward improving provision for the low-income groups. In Chile, (Rouse, 2007) water service providers achieve sustainable cost recovery through water charges but those on a means-tested register obtain assistance through local authorities for payment of bills. Also, capital subsidies are targeted at extending distribution systems to reach unserved areas where many of the low-income people live. In Phnom Penh there are low tariff provisions for low income consumers.

Transparency and public participation

There are a number of levels of public participation, from receiving information to directly managing a water service. In the context of this paper, the critical area is public consultation on problems faced with deteriorating infrastructure and the need for increases in charges to provide for effective maintenance and refurbishment. Particular attention has to be given to low-income groups. In a deteriorated service there has to be recognition that addressing the backlog of investment takes time. As in the Indian 24/7 cases, pilot improvement projects to demonstrate what can be achieved are a good way forward. Such pilots give confidence in the actions being taken; they can also encourage external sources of money for the infrastructure improvements. Such investment is more likely if donors see the commitment of the public to paying for sustainable service. Equally, once the public "sign up" to their part, water service providers have to meet the public's expectations.

Conclusions

Water services are in crisis or approaching crisis conditions due to the neglect of infrastructure, particularly underground water mains and sewers, largely because of political unwillingness to allow charges to be set high enough to achieve sustainable cost recovery. This is true in developed and developing countries. In developed countries the solutions are relatively affordable; what is needed is the political commitment to take action. In developing countries the situation is more serious due to a combination of neglect and rapidly growing urban populations. The sanitation challenges in developing countries are different, due to the current low level of access and lack of sewage-handling facilities. Therefore, the conclusions given here are limited to water supply issues. In water supply the problems have intensified because of the mistaken belief that rationing through intermittent supplies is an effective policy in sharing out limited water resources. In practice, it makes the situation even worse, both through detrimental impact on the physical condition of water mains and by reducing willingness to pay. So, how to get out of this downward spiral? The first and most important point is that it can be done, as demonstrated in Phnom Penh, in Uganda, and in the 24/7 projects taking place in India. In all those cases, donors have assisted (initially only in Phnom Penh) through the supply of funds for the capital works necessary for both system expansion and system refurbishment. There has been a tendency for donors to be willing to provide funding only for new resource and treatment works. Unless the first step is refurbishment of existing systems, there will be no capability to deliver that additional water. *The first conclusion is that new-facility funding has to be preceded by refurbishment of existing systems.* Indeed, the Indian 24/7 experience suggests that additional water resources may not be necessary.

The capital funds could be grants, in which case cost recovery needs to cover only operations and maintenance and provision for future refurbishment. In the case of loans there is the additional financial burden of debt repayment. The requirement for long-term low-interest loans is a big issue in itself not addressed in this paper. The important question here is how to achieve sustainable cost recovery so that future generations won't be faced with repetition of the challenges of today. General subsidies are common but are generally inadequate and unreliable, especially in difficult economic times. They are associated with political unwillingness to face up to the need for tariffs to be set high enough to achieve sustainable cost recovery. The result is inadequate monies for effective maintenance and refurbishment, and a spiral of decline in service. *The second conclusion is that there is no known alternative to sustainable cost recovery from water charges.* Such statements are frightening, but nothing else has been shown to work. Policies of sustainable cost recovery from charges have to be accompanied by provisions for the low-income groups, and are not affordable unless the water service operations are efficient. The former requires sound policies which abolish general subsidies and direct them to the poor. Easy payments methods are vital. The latter requires good management personnel who are not stymied by political interference and conflicting social responsibilities but are able to concentrate on the effectiveness and efficiency of operations. Social concerns, as in Chile, should be the responsibility of a separate part of local government.

Water service provision thinking has to be based on long-term horizons. Infrastructure development takes time, beyond the life of most governments. Singapore's success has been based on continuous political commitment and rigorous long-term planning. In those countries without such political continuity there is a need for all political factions to agree on goals, policies and plans. It is unlikely that water can ever be separated from politics, but city political consensus must be attempted. *Water and sanitation planning has to be an integral part of city planning.* This is critical in an era of rapid urbanization.

It might be noticed that privatization has not been mentioned here, other than in passing in the case of Atlanta. The reason is very simple: I don't see the public/private debate as achieving anything but hot air. Both public and private operations can work, given necessary governance provisions, but nothing will be achieved without attention to the policy and management basics, especially cost recovery. *Please let us concentrate our efforts on what will successfully implement the UN declaration of water and sanitation as a human right* (UNHRC, 2010).

This paper began with a flippant reference to the need to mention climate change. Of course it is important, and it affects the design criteria for water service systems. *However, we must give more attention to the fundamentals of water service delivery, including the achievement of sustainable cost recovery.*

References

AWWA. (2011). Buried no longer: Confronting America's water infrastructure challenge. American water works association. Retrieved from at www.climateneeds.umd.edu/reports/American-Water-Works.pdf [accessed 23 March 2013].

Bannerjee, S. G., & Morella, E. (2011). *Africa's water and sanitation infrastructure: Access, affordability, and alternatives.* Washington, DC: World Bank.

Biswas, A. K., & Tortajada, Cecilia (2010). Water supply of Phnom Penh: An example of good governance. *International Journal of Water Resources Development, 26*(2), 157–172.

Chan, E. S. (2009). Bringing safe water to Phnom Penh's city. *International Journal of Water Resources Development, 25*(4), 597–609.

Chan, Ek Sonn (2007). Presentation, Stockholm WWW.

Doshi, V., Schulman, G., & Gabaldon, D. (2007). *'Lights! Water! Motion! in global perspective. Strategy+business issue.* Washington DC: Booz, Allen, Hamilton.

Hope, R., Foster, T., Rouse, M., & Rouse, A. (2012). Harnessing mobile communications innovations for water security. *Global Policy, 3*(4), 433–442, http://dx.doi.org/10.1111/j.1758-5899.2011.00164

Kontula, Eero (August 2004). Finnida at World Bank/WaterAid Workshop. London.

Muhairwe, W. T. (2009). *Making public enterprises work* From despair to promise: A turn around account. London: IWA.

Novotny, V. (2011). Holistic approach for distributed water and energy management in the cities of the future. IWA International Conference. Cities of the Future Xi'an Technologies for Integrated Urban Water Management. September 15–19, Xi'an, China.

Onda, K., LoBuglio, J., & Bartram, J. (2012). Global access to safe water: Accounting for water quality and the resulting impact on MDG progress. *International Journal of Environmental Research and Public Health, 9*(12), 880–894.

Money, M. J. (2007). *Institutional governance and regulation of water services: The essential elements.* London: IWA Publishing.

Tortajada, C., Joshi, Y., & Biswas, A. K. (2013). *The Singapore water story: Sustainable development in an urban city state.* London: Routledge.

United Nations. (2000). *Millennium Declaration 55/2,* 8 September 2000, http://www.un.org/millennium/declaration/ares552e.htm

UN (United Nations). (2011). *World population prospects: The 2010 revision.* New York: United Nations.

UN (United Nations). (2012). *World urbanisation prospects: The 2011 revision*. New York: United Nations.

UNHRC (United Nations Human Rights Council). (2010). *Resolution adopted by the UN General Assembly 64/292. The human right to water and sanitation*. 3 August 2010.

UNICEF and World Health Organisation. (2012). *Progress on Drinking Water and Sanitation, 2012 Update*, http://www.unicef.org/media/files/JMPreport2012.pdf

Vairavamoorthy, K. (2012). *Networks of the future (smart, multipurpose and flexible by design)*. Paper presented at the World Water Congress and Exhibition. Busan, Korea, September.

Vermersch, M., Chan, E. S., & Vaughan, P. (2012). Are we going to win the war against NRW? *Water 21, 14*(4), 57–59.

Waterloss. (2011). Management of water losses in a drinking water supply system. *Waterloss Newsletter*, No. 2.

World Bank. (2010). *The Karnataka urban water sector improvement project: 24×7 water supply is achievable*. Water and Sanitation Programme. New Delhi: World Bank.

Enhancing the performance of water prices and tariff structures in achieving socially desirable outcomes

Dennis Wichelns

Institute of Water Policy, Lee Kuan Yew School of Public Policy, National University of Singapore

Water prices can convey critical information regarding scarcity, availability, and opportunity costs. Carefully crafted water tariffs enable public officials to achieve socially desirable objectives, such as providing subsidies to poor households and discouraging inefficient water use by higher-income households and commercial customers. Yet water tariffs have not been fully successful in generating desired outcomes, particularly in urban areas of developing countries. Some of the shortcomings of water tariffs in light of the desired goals of equity, efficiency and sustainability are reviewed. Experience with increasing block-rate tariffs is highlighted, and the potential usefulness of a volume-differentiated tariff in conveying subsidies to poor households in developing countries is demonstrated.

The goals we assign to water prices and tariff structures

The goals most often cited in discussions of water pricing and tariff structures include efficiency, equity and sustainability (Kanakoudis, Gonelas, & Tolikas, 2011; Nleya, 2008; Rogers, de Silva, & Bhatia, 2002). Efficiency is achieved when the incremental values obtained through the use of water are equal to the incremental costs. Both the direct costs of securing and delivering water, and the opportunity costs of water in alternative uses, must be considered. Water prices, when set correctly, can communicate the pertinent costs and scarcity conditions in a manner that encourages consumers to choose water volumes that reflect an efficient allocation of water between competing uses and over time.

The equity criterion pertains to the notion of ensuring that all members of a community have access to an affordable supply of water for domestic uses and to support livelihood activities. Equity is particularly prevalent in discussions of water tariff structures, given that water is essential and that in many settings, a purely market-based allocation of water between competing users would deprive poor residents of their access to a safe and reliable supply. Positive externalities accrue to the larger community when all residents have affordable access to safe water. Thus, the larger community has an economic rationale for subsidizing water deliveries to poor households.

Sustainability is achieved when the revenues received from water sales are sufficient to offset the annual operation and maintenance costs and the fixed costs of a water delivery system, including the depreciation and replacement of buildings, pipelines, wells and equipment. Sustainability requires also that the sources of water supply are managed in a manner that ensures the continuation of service deliveries over time. For example, surface water supplies must be managed and allocated in accordance with expected rainfall, streamflow and surface runoff. Groundwater supplies must be managed to ensure that annual withdrawals are consistent with a community's long-term goals regarding groundwater availability and pumping depths. The goals and management strategy should reflect a good understanding of groundwater volumes, aquifer recharge, and the effects of annual withdrawals on groundwater levels.

Water prices and tariff structures are the critical components of public policies designed to achieve the goals of efficiency, equity and sustainability. Yet, they are not the only policy tools needed to ensure success. The policy objectives regarding water service include several dimensions. The primary goal is to provide affordable access for all citizens, while encouraging wise use of water and raising sufficient revenue to operate, maintain and invest in the water delivery system. Corollary objectives include minimizing water losses, maintaining water quality, motivating customers to pay their bills in a timely fashion, and engendering political support for the water delivery operation. This is quite a bit to ask of a single policy tool, such as water pricing. Success will require complementary policies and interventions, some of which will involve careful targeting of programme components and strategic adjustments in policy parameters over time.

Increasing block-rate tariffs

The dual objectives of efficiency and equity motivate adoption of pricing structures that provide some amount of water to poor residents at very low prices, while requiring wealthier residents to pay higher prices. Increasing block-rate tariffs have been implemented in many countries, as they enable water agencies to establish a very low (or zero) price for the volume of water required for subsistence, while charging much higher prices for water deliveries in excess of minimal requirements (Brocklehurst, Pandurangi, & Ramanathan, 2002; Whittington, Boland, & Foster, 2002). The price in the first consumption block is generally set below the cost of water production and delivery, while prices in higher blocks can be set equal to − or higher than − the incremental costs of production (Figure 1).

In theory, increasing block-rate tariffs provide a subsidy to low-income households by enabling them to purchase water at a price below the cost of production and delivery (Foster, Pattanayak, & Prokopy, 2002). Revenue to pay those costs can be recovered from wealthier residents who purchase water in the higher consumption blocks, in which the per-unit price of water is greater than the incremental cost. Water prices that exceed

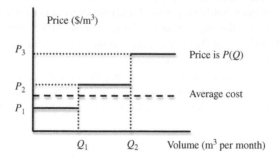

Figure 1. A typical increasing block-rate tariff, with three prices and consumption blocks. $P(Q)$ denotes that the unit price of water increases with the volume delivered each month.

the incremental cost of production and delivery also can motivate consumers to use water wisely, as they are encouraged to avoid purchasing large volumes in the higher consumption blocks. Water agency officials can modify the sizes of the blocks, and the prices assigned to each block, over time, with changes in production costs and water-scarcity conditions. Adjustments in parameter values will also be needed as consumers respond to changes in prices and alter the volumes of water they purchase.

Examples of increasing block-rate tariffs for water service in developing countries include those in Côte d'Ivoire (Diakité, Semenov, & Thomas, 2009), India (Gessler, Brighu, & Franceys, 2008; Mckenzie & Ray, 2009), Kenya (Gerlach, 2008), Malawi (Kalulu & Hoko, 2010), Mauritius (Madhoo, 2011), Nicaragua (Angel-Urdinola & Wodon, 2012), and Zimbabwe (Mkandla, Van der Zaag, & Sibanda, 2005). One goal of implementing block-rate tariffs in these countries is to provide affordable water to poor households. Yet, the programmes generally have not been successful in conveying the intended subsidies to the poor. Many poor households remain unconnected to public water systems and thus are unable to receive the benefits of a safe and reliable water supply. At the same time, many wealthier households purchase some of their water at low prices in the first price block, thus gaining a portion of the subsidy intended for poorer households.

In some cities, the prices of water in higher consumption blocks are set below the average cost of production, thus providing a direct subsidy to wealthier households. Several of the six cities in South Asia surveyed by Brocklehurst et al., (2002) price water substantially below the average cost of production in the first two consumption blocks (Table 1). In two of the cities (Dhaka and Hyderabad), the prices are the same in both blocks, while in Colombo, the prices in both blocks are quite low. In Bangalore, Chennai and Kathmandu, the price of water becomes higher than the average cost of production in the third consumption block. Yet, much of the water sold to customers is billed in the first two blocks. For example, in Bangalore in 2001, 66% of water deliveries were billed in the first block and 28% in the second block (Brocklehurst et al., 2002). Thus, only 6% of deliveries were billed at a price above the average cost of production. Given this distribution, the very low prices of water in the first two consumption blocks essentially prevent the collection of sufficient revenue to pay for the costs of operation and maintenance, or to invest in new equipment and facilities.

These examples suggest that in many settings, the increasing block-rate tariff is not successful in achieving the three desired goals of a water pricing system: efficiency, equity and sustainability. In most cases, the tariffs have presumably been established with good

Table 1. Costs of production and water prices, by consumption block, in selected cities in South Asia, in US dollars per cubic metre, 2001.

City	Estimated production cost	Price of water, by consumption block			
		First	Second	Third	Highest
Bangalore	0.34	0.07	0.14	0.40	0.70
Chennai	0.27	0.05	0.21	0.31	0.53
Colombo	n.a.	0.01	0.02	0.09	0.27
Dhaka	0.08	0.07	0.07	0.07	0.07
Hyderabad	0.26	0.07	0.07	0.12	0.29
Kathmandu	0.17	0.05	0.12	0.28	0.32

Source: Brocklehurst et al. (2002).
Notes: The water pricing structure in Dhaka is uniform, rather than increasing in block rates. We include the data for Dhaka for completeness, and to enable comparison with data for the five other South Asian cities. For Colombo, n.a. denotes not available.

intent and the parameter values are based on a reasonable understanding of water supply and demand conditions. Yet the subsidies intended for poor households might not be targeted with sufficient care, and the incremental prices of water might be too low to motivate wise use on the part of wealthier consumers. As a result, cost-recovery efforts might fall short of expectations, while the notion of sustainability remains unfulfilled.

The goals of this paper are to describe the inherent difficulties in attempting to achieve desired objectives through the use of increasing block-rate tariffs, and to propose an alternative pricing structure that might enhance the likelihood of achieving those outcomes. In a review of recent evidence regarding the use of increasing block-rate tariffs, issues are highlighted, including the numbers of households sharing meters in many cities and the challenge of ensuring that poor households receive the water consumption subsidies intended for them. A volume-differentiated tariff structure is then presented, in which the subsidy component is targeted more carefully toward poor households and the prices of water in higher blocks are selected to achieve cost-recovery and investment objectives.

Conceptually appealing, but empirically challenged

Water agencies in many countries in Asia, Africa and Latin America have implemented increasing block-rate tariffs for household water service delivery (Banerjee, Foster, Ying, Skilling, & Wodon, 2010; le Blanc, 2008). The sizes of consumption blocks and the per-unit prices of water vary across settings and with differences in production costs and household income levels, but the goals are often similar. Water utilities are encouraged to provide subsidized service to poor residents, while collecting sufficient revenue to pay for operation and maintenance. In some cases, utilities are expected also to expand their service delivery to include new areas of rapidly growing cities, often with the explicit goal of enhancing the service provided to poor households (Gerlach, 2008; Nleya, 2008; Venkatachalam, 2006). Increasing block-rate tariffs are conceptually well suited for water utilities in developing countries because they enable purveyors to differentiate prices between wealthy and poor households. However, not all households are connected to public water supply systems; cost recovery is incomplete; and many poor households do not receive the subsidies intended for them in the design of increasing block-rate tariffs.

Too few households connected

One reason that increasing block-rate tariffs are not successful in achieving equitable water distribution is the small proportion of poor households connected to public supply systems in many cities of developing countries. The subsidy inherent in the low price of water provided in the initial consumption block is not received by residents who do not have access to the system or cannot afford the fixed cost of a connection. In most cases, such households must purchase water from vendors, kiosks, or household resellers, often at much higher prices than they would pay to a public water agency (Gerlach & Franceys, 2009; Keener et al., 2010). The connection issue is particularly challenging because many water purveyors prefer to extend service to middle- and high-income neighbourhoods, where the prospects for timely payment of bills and full cost recovery are much brighter (Berg & Mugisha, 2010; Chitonge, 2011; Hadipuro, 2010).

The low price of water in the first consumption block contributes to the disincentive to extend water supply coverage to poor households. Thus, the very design of an increasing block-rate system can complicate efforts to ensure that poor households receive the intended subsidy. Angel-Urdinola & Wodon (2012) suggest that tariffs should be raised in some settings to provide revenue for expanding delivery service. Using water tariff and consumption data for Managua, Nicaragua, the authors show that providing greater water delivery access to the poor improves the targeting performance of a water consumption subsidy programme. They recommend investing greater resources in providing access and ensuring that poor households connect to water delivery systems.

Many poor residents of developing countries lack both the income and the risk tolerance to invest in a water service connection. Kagaya & Franceys (2007) note that the median connection cost of $197 in Uganda is excessive for households earning less than $2 per day (all monetary units are in US dollars). In addition, the households are not prepared to accommodate the uncertainty of some cost components, such as the expenses for additional digging or road cutting that can arise as a connection project moves forward or the "speed money" that might be needed to encourage timely approval of applications and permits.

India provides a partial subsidy of service connection costs by maintaining official charges for connecting to municipal water services at rates that are less than the typical costs of expanding service to new communities. The official connection charge in many cities is about $20, while the typical cost of expanding the service area is $150 per connection (Raghupati & Foster, 2002). Yet, even with such a substantial subsidy, many poor households are unable to afford a water service connection.

Household connection rates are particularly low in many countries of Sub-Saharan Africa. In a survey of 24 countries, Keener et al. (2010) report connection rates ranging from 28% in western Africa to 65% in southern Africa, while the average rate of connection is 38% (Table 2). The connection rates in some of the urban areas included in the study are less than 20%. Standpipes are the primary source of water for unconnected households in most of the cities, providing up to 53% of the water supply for those households (Keener et al., 2010). Other important sources include water tankers, household resellers, small piped networks, and other water vendors. Household resellers are particularly important: they provide up to half the water for households in some African cities, and up to 80% of water for the urban poor (Keener et al., 2010).

The prices paid to alternative water sources can have a substantial impact on household welfare. The average prices of water at standpipes in a sample of 23 cities in Sub-Saharan Africa range from $0.48 to $9.44/m^3, while the average prices at household connections range from just $0.04 to $2.66/m^3 (Table 3). Prices are also substantially higher when

Table 2. Proportions of urban households connected and unconnected to piped water systems, by region of sub-Saharan Africa, 2007.

Status	West	Central	East	South	All
Connected	0.28	0.34	0.37	0.65	0.38
Not connected	0.72	0.66	0.63	0.35	0.62
Sources of water for those households not connected					
Standpipes	0.21	0.32	0.31	0.22	0.25
Wells and boreholes	0.37	0.14	0.20	0.09	0.24
Surface	0.06	0.16	0.08	0.03	0.07
Vendor	0.07	0.01	0.01	0.00	0.04
Others	0.00	0.03	0.03	0.00	0.02

Source: Keener, Luengo, and Banerjee (2010).
Notes: The proportions of water sources for those households not connected pertain to the full set of households. Thus, those proportions sum to the proportions of households not connected to a piped water system.

Table 3.   Water prices in selected cities of sub-Saharan Africa, by type of service provider, in US dollars per cubic metre, 2007.

Country	Largest city	Household connection	Stand-pipe	Household reseller	Water tanker	Water vendor
Cote d'Ivoire	Abidjan	0.04	0.93	1.82	.	3.35
South Africa	Johannesburg	0.05	.	.	.	.
DR Congo	Kinshasa	0.05	1.02	1.01	.	.
Madagascar	Antananarivo	0.11	1.24	.	.	2.33
Malawi	Blantyre	0.12	1.16	3.38	.	.
Nigeria	Kaduna	0.17	.	.	3.43	5.71
Kenya	Nairobi	0.18	1.73	.	3.74	3.47
Ethiopia	Addis Ababa	0.19	0.87	1.44	3.85	.
Chad	N'Djamena	0.22	.	.	.	.
Uganda	Kampala	0.25	1.40	1.40	.	4.50
Senegal	Dakar	0.37	1.53	.	.	2.29
Sudan	Khartoum	0.37	1.15	.	4.32	3.00
Tanzania	Dar es Salaam	0.39	0.87	0.98	2.40	2.56
Lesotho	Maseru	0.40	2.58	.	.	.
Benin	Cotonou	0.41	1.91	1.91	.	.
Rwanda	Kigali	0.44	1.79	1.79	4.48	.
Niger	Niamey	0.52	0.48	.	.	1.79
Ghana	Accra	0.52	5.51	1.53	5.46	6.89
Zambia	Lusaka	0.56	1.67	.	.	3.00
Burkina Faso	Ouagadougou	0.90	0.48	.	.	1.67
Mozambique	Maputo	0.96	0.98	0.98	.	.
Namibia	Windhoek	1.45	.	.	.	.
Cape Verde	Praia	2.67	9.44	.	9.67	11.38
Mean		0.49	1.93	1.63	4.67	4.00
Median		0.37	1.24	1.49	4.08	3.00
Minimum		0.04	0.48	0.98	2.40	1.67
Maximum		2.67	9.44	3.38	9.67	11.38

Source: Keener et al. (2010).
Notes: Empty cells in the table denote missing or unavailable information. The prices given for household connections represent consumption levels of 4 cubic metres of water per month.

purchasing water from households reselling water from a private tap or when acquiring water from a tanker or vendor (Keener et al., 2010). Such high prices cause poor households to expend much of their income on water, while causing them also to minimize the volume of water they consume each month.

Standpipes, kiosks and household resellers of water serve an important role in providing water to unconnected households in many cities, yet the cost of the service is substantial. Operators of informal standpipes and kiosks charge prices that are much higher than prices at formal water delivery points, while household resellers apply a non-trivial mark-up when reselling water from private taps. The ratio of informal to formal prices at standpipes and kiosks ranges from 1.5 to 4.7 in a sample of data from nine cities in Sub-Saharan Africa (Table 4). In those same cities, the ratios of average sale prices to the average costs of water for household resellers range from 1.6 to 6.6. Such ratios enable households with private taps to generate revenue to pay for their own consumption, in addition to the water they sell, while also generating additional household income (Keener et al., 2010).

Households not connected to the municipal water system in Jakarta, Indonesia, face a similar situation regarding high water costs. The price of water from vendors in Jakarta is from 10 to 32 times the price of water delivered by the public supply network, yet many

Table 4. Prices charged at formal and informal standpipes and kiosks, and by household resellers in selected cities in sub-Saharan Africa, in US dollars per cubic metre, 2007.

City	Standpipes and kiosks (average prices)			Household resellers		
	Formal	Informal	Ratio	Average cost	Average sale price	Ratio
Addis Ababa	0.19	0.87	4.6	0.36	1.44	4.0
Blantyre	0.29	1.16	4.0	0.51	3.38	6.6
Maputo	0.31	0.98	3.2	0.62	0.98	1.6
Kampala	0.39	1.40	3.6	0.67	1.40	2.1
Cotonou	0.41	1.91	4.7	0.79	1.91	2.4
Kigali	0.44	1.79	4.1	0.63	1.79	2.8
Abidjan	0.45	0.93	2.1	0.53	1.82	3.4
Dar es Salaam	0.58	0.87	1.5	0.50	0.98	2.0
Accra	3.64	5.51	1.5	0.63	1.53	2.4

Source: Keener et al. (2010).
Notes: The household reseller cost is based on the domestic tariff rate pertaining to consumption of 40 cubic metres per month.

poor households choose not to connect (Bakker, 2007). Their decisions are based partly on the initial cost of obtaining a connection and partly on other monthly charges that must be paid by connected households. For example, households must pay a meter fee and an annual charge for maintaining the connection. For a household consuming 6 m^3 per month, the fixed monthly charges would be 5 to 10 times as high as the volumetric water charge (Bakker, 2007). Households are dissuaded also by the perception that network water is of lower quality than water available from other sources, including groundwater. Household perceptions in Jakarta might be similar to those in other cities across Indonesia, as just 36% of the urban population is connected to a municipal water supply. Among the poorest urban households (those earning about $80 per month), only 16% are connected (Bakker, Kooy, Shofiani, & Martijn, 2008).

Water purveyors in some cities find the competition with household resellers to be undesirable, while others appreciate the role such resellers play in extending the service area (Keener et al., 2010). Given either perspective, the high prices paid for water by the poor might motivate public officials to expand formal delivery service at subsidized prices, while recovering costs by utilizing an appropriately crafted increasing block-rate tariff. Alternatively, public officials might consider recovering the operation and maintenance costs of water delivery from all consumers, while using general revenues to subsidize household connections.

A progressive structure, with non-progressive outcomes

One goal of an increasing block-rate tariff is to enable poor households to spend less for water than wealthier households. If poor households purchase water only within the first consumption block, their marginal and average prices will be much lower than the prices pertaining to higher rates of water use. The total expenditure by a small household also will be less than that of a wealthier household, because both the price and the volume of water consumed will be smaller. Yet the proportion of household income expended for water might still be larger in poor households.

The difference in price responsiveness in poor and non-poor households is also an important policy consideration. Empirical estimates of price elasticity in block-rate pricing environments suggest that poor households are less elastic than higher-income households (Jansen & Schulz, 2006). Thus, the same proportional increase in water price (e.g. 10%) will act largely as a tax on poor households, while encouraging wealthier households to reduce non-essential water consumption. For this reason, the equity implications of a change in water price can be substantial.

Public officials must also consider the demographics of a municipal population when designing an increasing block-rate tariff. In areas with many poor households and few non-poor households, the goal of cross-subsidizing water deliveries to the poor might not be achievable. The very high prices required in upper consumption blocks might be politically unacceptable. High prices might also discourage much of the non-essential water use in wealthier households, such that the revenue collected would not increase substantially with increases in water prices. In areas with challenging demographics, it might be helpful to design block-rate tariffs that include more than two blocks, and to consider combinations of fixed and variable components of water pricing structures.

The water company serving the metropolitan region of São Paulo, Brazil, applies a combined regressive-progressive block-rate tariff, in which the price for the initial consumption block (up to 10 m^3 per month) is highest (Ruijs, Zimmermann, & van den Berg, 2008). The prices for subsequent blocks increase stepwise, yet all of those prices are lower than the initial price. The goal of this partially inverted increasing block-rate tariff is to ensure that the utility collects the revenue needed to cover its costs of operation and maintenance. Yet, poor residents who purchase water primarily in the first consumption block pay the highest average and marginal prices. Ruijs et al., (2008) suggest that the poorest consumers spend about 4.5% of their monthly income for water, while the wealthiest consumers spend about 0.45%.

The increasing block-rate tariff for water in urban areas of Rajasthan has not been modified since 1998 (Gessler et al., 2008). Thus, the value of revenue collected from consumers has not kept pace with inflation, and the revenue is not sufficient to support operation, maintenance and investment. While an estimated 92% of customers receive metered supply, 50% of the meters are not functional (Gessler et al., 2008). The initial consumption block in the Rajasthan tariff extends to 15 m^3 per month. As a result, 31% of domestic consumption falls within the first block and is purchased at the lowest price. Thus, many non-poor families likely benefit from consuming water in the lowest price block, while revenues fall short of the amount required to sustain and improve the delivery system.

So many households per connection

The size of the initial consumption block in most increasing block-rate tariffs is determined by the volume of water required each month to satisfy a household's basic requirements for drinking, bathing and cooking. Typical sizes of the first block fall within the range of 6 to 20 m^3 of water per month (Diakité et al., 2009; Madhoo, 2011; Nleya, 2008; Smith, 2004). The goal is to ensure that each poor household can obtain sufficient water to meet basic requirements at an affordable cost. The design is sensible and effective in settings where each household is home to one family.

In settings where more than one family shares a household or a water meter, the group can quickly exceed the volume of water allowed for a single household within the first consumption block, thus requiring each family to pay a much higher incremental price for water. In such settings, the families do not receive the subsidy intended for them when implementing the increasing block-rate tariff. To ensure that all poor households receive the subsidy, water agencies would need to adjust the size of the initial consumption block to reflect the number of residents in each household (Dahan & Nisan, 2007).

Residents of Kumasi, the second-largest city in Ghana, are charged a flat rate of about $3.00 per month for water consumption up to 7 m^3 (Donkor, 2010). Consumption of 8 through 20 m^3 per month is billed at the rate of $0.40/m^3, while the price of water beyond 20 m^3 per month is $0.55/m^3. Almost 60% of household connections examined in a survey conducted in 2003 provide water for more than one household (Donkor, 2010). Taken together, the 73 connections serve 348 households, or about 4.8 households per connection. Household size in the sample ranged from 2.3 to 18.7 persons, with a median value of 5.8 persons. Due to the large numbers of individuals served by each connection, 93% of the households purchase water in all three consumption blocks. Thus, nearly all of the households pay the highest price per unit for some of the water they consume (Donkor, 2010). Slightly less than half (49%) of the water consumed is delivered within the first consumption block, and a similar proportion (48%) is delivered within the second block. Many households likely pay substantially more for water than they would pay if they were served by individual connections.

Almost all urban residents in Jordan have access to a household water connection, yet many connections serve more than one household. Gerlach & Franceys (2009) report that 60% of the households they interviewed in 2005 had access to their own water connection. Nearly 20% of the households shared a connection with three or more households. Potter & Darmame (2010) report that 56% of the low-income households they interviewed in Greater Amman share a water meter, while just 12% of high-income households report sharing a meter. This issue is particularly pertinent in Jordan, given that residents are charged for water according to the incremental price at which their consumption takes place (Gerlach & Franceys, 2010). For example, a household consuming water in the third consumption block of an increasing block-rate tariff is charged for all water at that price. Given this unusual structure and the prevalence of multiple households per connection, many of the poorest households probably do not benefit from the water consumption subsidy intended for low-income consumers.

Madhoo (2011) shows that the increasing block-rate tariff for water service in Mauritius is progressive, largely because the average size of poor households is smaller than the average sizes of middle- and high-income households. In addition, most of the poor households purchase water primarily within the lowest consumption block (up to 15 m^3 per month). The author notes that 85% to 90% of the homes in Mauritius are owner occupied, and there is very little sharing of houses and apartments by several families. In that setting, it appears the increasing block-rate tariff provides the intended cross-subsidy of water costs from wealthier to poorer households.

So much water not accounted for

Many water purveyors in developing countries report that large volumes of water are lost at some point along the delivery system to physical or commercial losses. Physical losses include leakage from pipes and canals, while commercial losses involve illegal connections, unmetered public uses, and meter reading or performance errors (González-Gómez, García-Rubio, & Guardiola, 2011; Wyatt, 2010). The problem of unaccounted-for water imposes direct costs on water utilities and indirect costs on consumers. Utilities are unable to recover the costs of production, treatment and delivery for water that does not flow through a meter at the point of consumption. As the proportion of unaccounted-for water increases, so too does that average cost of production and delivery, when assessed against only the volume of water delivered to consumers. The shortfall in net revenue to the water agency diminishes the funds it could invest in repairing and extending the delivery system. All else being equal, a water agency's efforts to serve poor households will be slowed by the reduction in net revenue caused by water losses in the system.

In Zambia, the proportions of unaccounted-for water range from 30% to 50% of water produced by the primary purveyors in Kitwe and Lusaka, respectively (Ntengwe, 2004). The simple mean of estimates of unaccounted-for water reported by commercial utilities serving 11 cities and regions in Zambia is 45% (Chitonge, 2011). Regional water boards in Malawi report unaccounted-for-water losses ranging from 20% to 50% of the total volume supplied (Kalulu & Hoko, 2010; Mulwafu et al., 2003). The Nairobi City Water and Sewerage Company reports unaccounted-for water at about 50%, with much of the lost volume pertaining to commercial rather than physical losses (Gerlach, 2008).

Differentiating the blocks for poor and non-poor residents

When an increasing block-rate tariff is applied uniformly across households, both the poor and non-poor may purchase water in the first consumption block. When that occurs, the non-poor also receive some portion of their monthly water consumption at a price well below the average production cost. That unintended subsidy to the non-poor can complicate efforts of municipal purveyors to collect revenue sufficient to operate, maintain and improve the delivery system. In areas where it is feasible to differentiate between poor and non-poor residents, water purveyors may wish to disallow non-poor residents from purchasing water at the subsidized price intended for the poor. In a sense, the utilities would be applying a volume-differentiated tariff (le Blanc, 2008; Komives, Halpern, Foster, Wodon, & Abdullah, 2006) rather than implementing a single form of an increasing block-rate tariff across all consumers.

Volume-differentiated tariffs are generally more effective in targeting the intended subsidies of a pricing programme, and they provide opportunities for generating revenue to support investments in the delivery system. Here, the subsidies and revenue streams pertaining to differentiated tariffs are simulated using a small model of utility water pricing. The goal is to demonstrate the possibility of crafting a tariff structure in which the prices are selected to achieve specific revenue targets and the programme is implemented in a manner that does not allow non-poor households to purchase water in the first consumption block. Thus, the likelihoods of providing consumption subsidies to poor households and of expanding the service area are notably increased.

To begin, a three-price, volume-differentiated tariff is described in which the purveyor establishes the size and price of the lowest consumption block in accordance with the social objective of ensuring affordable water to the poor. The purveyor also establishes the size of the second consumption block according to the expected volume of water desired by non-poor households to support their livelihood activities. After selecting those three parameter values, the utility then determines the prices of the second and third consumption blocks by considering two objectives. The first is to generate sufficient revenue to pay for the subsidy granted to poor residents who purchase water in the first consumption block. The second is to generate the revenue needed to expand and improve the delivery system.

The volume-differentiated tariff is embedded in the utility's total revenue equation as follows:

$$\text{Total Revenue} = P_1V_1 + P_2V_2 + P_3V_3$$

where V_1 is the volume of water purchased by poor residents in Block 1; V_2 is the volume of water purchased by non-poor residents in Block 2; V_3 is the volume of water purchased by non-poor residents in Block 3; and P_1, P_2 and P_3 are the prices of water in each block.

The characteristic that distinguishes this model from a typical increasing block-rate tariff is the prohibition of purchases by non-poor residents of water in Block 1. All of the water purchased by non-poor residents is obtained from Block 2 or Block 3.

We assume for simplicity that poor residents purchase water only in Block 1. As noted above, the utility predetermines the value of P_1 through consultation with public officials regarding the price that poor residents should pay for water service. The values of P_2 and P_3 are then chosen by solving a simple optimization problem:

Minimize: net revenue = total revenue − total cost − desired investment funds

where *total revenue* is described by the first equation, above; *total cost* is the sum of the annual operation and maintenance costs of producing and delivering the volumes of water V_1, V_2 and V_3; and *desired investment funds* are the revenues required to achieve the purveyor's stated goals of expanding the service area and increasing the volume of water made available to each poor household.

The optimal value of P_2 is chosen by imposing a constraint that requires the revenue received from water sales in the second consumption block to be sufficient to pay for two cost components: (1) the operation and maintenance costs for water deliveries within Block 2, and (2) the aggregate cost of the subsidy to poor residents generated by the sale of water at a subsidized price in Block 1. In brief, the constraint requires that the subsidies generated in Block 1 are recouped through water sales in Block 2:

Revenue from Block 2 = subsidies in Block 1 + the total cost of producing and delivering the water sold in Block 2.

One additional constraint is needed to determine the optimal value of P_3. An investment target is imposed that reflects the purveyor's goal of expanding service to poor households. This is done by including a simple service-area growth function in a five-month model. For example, the purveyor might wish to expand its coverage of poor households by a selected proportion each month. A constraint is imposed that requires the purveyor to generate the revenue needed to support such expansion through the sale of water in Block 3. Thus, the optimal value of P_3 is determined by imposing the following revenue-generation constraint:

Revenue from Block 3 = revenue required to achieve the purveyor's service-area expansion goals + the total cost of producing and delivering the water sold in Block 3.

The complete model of this volume-differentiated tariff includes the objective function and the two revenue-generation constraints. The model is a simplified depiction of the market in which water buyers and sellers interact. We do not explicitly consider the factors that influence water use decisions. While it is plausible to consider choosing P_1 and V_1 to reflect social goals regarding poor residents, the optimal values of Q_2, P_2 and P_3 would normally be selected in consideration of the price elasticities of demand for water. In practice, a water purveyor might select different values of prices over time, and then measure consumer responsiveness to changes in water prices. Such information would be helpful in determining the optimal water prices, particularly if the purveyor wishes to generate revenue for investment or for expansion in service area.

An inadequate understanding of price elasticity of demand could result in a purveyor missing its revenue targets or struggling to deliver a volume of water much larger than anticipated. While recognizing the critical importance of price elasticity, we do not incorporate such estimates in our small model of water deliveries and consumption levels. Our goal is simply to demonstrate the usefulness of a volume-differentiated tariff in achieving the objectives of equity, efficiency and sustainability, while not making specific recommendations regarding water prices. Water purveyors should consider estimates of price elasticity when selecting water prices and determining the optimal sizes of consumption blocks.

Scenario analysis

Several scenarios are now constructed with which to examine the water prices, costs and revenue streams that would enable a water purveyor to maintain or expand delivery service to poor residents. In the service area considered here, 300 poor households and 200 non-poor households are connected to the delivery system. The purveyor has determined, in consultation with public officials, that the poor should be required to pay $0.12/m^3, or just 40% of the average cost of operation and maintenance, which is $0.30/m^3. The purveyor and public officials have also decided that the size of the first consumption block will reflect a minimum consumption of 50 litres per person per day (lpcd), in households with an average of 6 persons. Thus, the size of the first consumption block is set at 9 m^3 per month. Given that this is a volume-differentiated tariff, non-poor residents are not allowed to purchase water in this block.

The size of the second block reflects an average consumption of 150 lpcd by non-poor residents, in households with an average of 4 persons. Thus, the size of the second block is set at 18 m^3 per month. The purveyor does not need to determine the size of a third block, as consumers can purchase as much water as they wish at the higher price, P_3. Yet, for planning purposes, the purveyor must estimate the volume of water that will be purchased beyond Block 2. In our scenarios, the purveyor assumes that non-poor households will purchase an additional 60 lpcd at the higher price of P_3, which is equivalent to an additional 7.2 m^3 per month per household.

The optimal values of P_2 and P_3 will be higher than the average cost of operation and maintenance, which is $0.30/m^3 (Figure 2). The optimization model requires that water

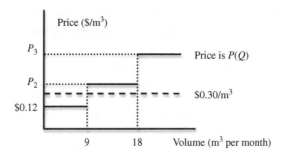

Figure 2. The water purveyor selects the initial values for the price of water in Block 1, and the sizes of Blocks 1 and 2, in view of social goals regarding minimum water requirements and the appropriate price of water for poor residents. $P(Q)$ denotes that the unit price of water increases with the volume delivered each month.

sales in Block 2 generate sufficient revenue to pay for the subsidy provided to poor households in Block 1. In addition, sales in Block 3 must generate sufficient revenue to pay for expansion of the delivery system to additional poor households.

In Scenario A, the purveyor wishes to increase the number of poor household connections by 6% per month. Assume that the average cost of establishing a connection is $100 per household, such that the sum of $1800 must be generated through water sales in Block 3 during the initial month of the scenario. That sum can be generated by selling 1440 m^3 of water at a price of $1.55/$m^3$ (Table 5, column 1). Of that price, $0.30/$m^3$ is needed to pay for operation and maintenance costs, while $1.25/$m^3$ is invested in new connections.

The purveyor also wishes to increase the amount of water made available to poor households at the same time the service area is expanded. Assume a 6% rate of increase in the volume consumed per day. Then, in the second month, poor households increase their consumption from 50 to 53 lpcd, which is equivalent to increasing the size of the first consumption block from 9.0 to 9.5 m^3 per month (Table 5).

As poor households increase their water use, the value of the subsidy provided to those households increases. If the price of water in Block 1 remains at $0.12/$m^3$, then the price of water in Block 2 must increase, so that the higher cost of providing the subsidy is recovered in water sales to non-poor households. Thus, the optimal price of water in Block 2 increases from $0.44/$m^3$ in the first month to $0.45/$m^3$ in the second month and $0.52/$m^3$ in the fifth month (Table 5). If the cost recovery and investment programme is maintained as depicted in Table 5, 79 additional households will have been connected during the 5 months of the scenario, and the average consumption of water in poor households will have increased from 50 to 63 lpcd.

Scenarios B and C examine the relationship between the subsidized price of water in Block 1 and the optimal price of water in Block 2, given the requirement that the cost of the subsidy be recovered through the sale of water in Block 2. If water is priced at $0.06/$m^3$ (rather than $0.12/$m^3$) in Block 1, the price of water in Block 2 will rise more sharply than in Scenario A. In particular, the price of water in Block 2 must increase from $0.48/$m^3$ to $0.59/$m^3$ in Scenario B to generate sufficient revenue to pay for the larger subsidy to poor residents (Table 6, Scenario B). While these prices seem high in comparison with the subsidized prices in Block 1, they are not substantially higher than the

Table 5. Simulating a volume-differentiated tariff structure in which the water purveyor collects sufficient revenue to expand service area and provide larger volumes of water to poor residents, Scenario A.

Scenario A	Month in the scenario				
Parameter	1	2	3	4	5
Price in the first block, P_1	0.12	0.12	0.12	0.12	0.12
Price in the second block, P_2	0.44	0.45	0.47	0.49	0.52
Price in the third block, P_3	1.55	1.62	1.70	1.79	1.88
Number of poor households connected (thousands)	300	318	337	357	379
Consumption by poor households (litres per person per day)	50	53	56	60	63
Size of the first block, Q_1 (m^3 per month)	9.0	9.5	10.1	10.7	11.4

Note: Prices are in US dollars per cubic metre.

Table 6. Simulating a volume differentiated tariff structure in which the water purveyor collects sufficient revenue to expand service area and provide larger volumes of water to poor residents, Scenarios B and C.

Scenarios B and C	Month in the scenario				
Parameter	1	2	3	4	5
Scenario B: The price in the first block (P_1) is set at $0.06 per m^3 in each of the five months.					
Price in the first block, P_1	0.06	0.06	0.06	0.06	0.06
Price in the second block, P_2	0.48	0.50	0.53	0.56	0.59
Scenario C: The price in the first block (P_1) begins at $0.06 per m^3 and increases by 10% each month.					
Price in the first block, P_1	0.06	0.067	0.073	0.080	0.088
Price in the second block, P_2	0.48	0.50	0.52	0.53	0.55

Notes: Prices are in US dollars per cubic metre. The numbers of households connected to the system and the litres consumed per person per day are the same as in Table 5 (Scenario A).

average cost of operation and maintenance ($0.30/m^3) and they are lower than the prices many poor residents pay to street vendors and resellers in many cities (Tables 3 and 4).

The burden placed on non-poor residents to cover the cost of the subsidy can be eased somewhat by gradually increasing the price of water in Block 1, which is equivalent to gradually reducing the size of the subsidy. If the price of water in Block 1 were increased by 10% per month from its initial value of $0.06/m^3, the price of water in Block 2 would increase only to $0.55/m^3 in the fifth month, in comparison with the price of $0.59/m^3 if the price in Block 1 is maintained at $0.06/m^3 throughout the time horizon (Table 6, Scenario C). Thus, public officials and water purveyors should consider combining complementary elements of water pricing and subsidy programmes, to increase the likelihood that economic incentives and cross-subsidization schemes will be viewed favourably by poor and non-poor residents.

Preliminary assessment

This small, monthly model of a volume-differentiated tariff structure is too simplistic to generate far-reaching implications, but the scenarios indicate the potential for covering costs and generating revenue when delivering water to both poor and non-poor households. While non-poor residents might be disallowed the option of purchasing water in the lowest price block, the price paid by the poor in that block need not be zero. As the price of water in the initial consumption block increases, the financial obligation of the non-poor residents becomes smaller. And many poor residents might be able and willing to pay a non-trivial price for water in the initial consumption block, provided they receive reliable service.

The volume-differentiated tariff provides a greater likelihood of success in achieving the goals of efficiency, equity and sustainability than does a typical increasing block-rate tariff. By disallowing non-poor residents the option of purchasing water in the lowest price block, the subsidy intended for poor households is delivered with greater accuracy and less slippage. Sharper targeting reduces the aggregate cost of providing the subsidy to those for whom it is intended. The volume-differentiated tariff also provides a keener incentive for non-poor households to use water wisely. Their initial purchases take place at a higher price, and the likelihood that they will purchase water in a third or fourth block increases. Thus, the price paid for the last units of water consumed by non-poor households is likely to be higher in the case of a volume-differentiated tariff than in the case of a uniformly applied increasing block-rate tariff.

Regarding sustainability, the volume-differentiated tariff provides helpful opportunities to generate revenues to pay for operations, maintenance and investment. As shown in the scenarios, the prices of water in higher blocks can be selected with the explicit goal of generating sufficient revenue to achieve desired levels of investment in the water delivery system. Uniformly applied increasing block-rate tariffs can provide similar opportunities, but the inherent problem of slippage in targeted subsidy payments places such tariffs at an initial disadvantage. The value of a subsidy provided to non-intended beneficiaries represents an opportunity cost, because that value might be better applied toward investments in the quality and sustainability of the delivery system.

Summing up

Many public officials responsible for managing water resources rely on water pricing to achieve the goals of efficiency, equity and sustainability. Water prices certainly can communicate information regarding incremental costs and values, and current scarcity conditions, in ways that other policy parameters cannot. Yet water prices can rarely achieve several policy objectives without assistance from other, complementary policy interventions and investments.

Increasing block-rate tariffs can be helpful in signalling a desire to provide consumption subsidies to poor households, but the effectiveness of such tariffs is limited if non-poor households are allowed to purchase water at the subsidized prices made available to poor households. Volume-differentiated tariffs provide a greater likelihood of success in targeting a subsidy to poor households, but purveyors must have the authority and the technical capability of disallowing non-poor households from purchasing water at the subsidized prices.

It is also essential to increase the proportion of households connected to municipal water systems in many cities of developing countries. Even the best-designed tariff structure cannot provide benefits to poor households that are not connected to the supply network. To this end, public officials and water purveyors should consider increasing their investments in expanding water delivery service, perhaps while also raising the per-unit price of water to assist in generating sufficient revenue to support a faster pace of investment. The prices paid to street vendors and household resellers in many developing countries suggest that poor households are able and willing to pay for water service. Subsidizing the initial cost of establishing household connections might have a greater impact on household health and welfare than subsidizing the per-unit cost of water, particularly in regions where connection rates are presently quite low.

The prospect for improving water delivery service in developing countries is brightened by the experience gained regarding water prices and tariff structures. Increasing block-rate tariffs are the norm in many settings, such that purveyors and consumers are familiar with programmes in which the price of water varies with the volume consumed. Most purveyors and consumers also understand the need to target low prices carefully, so that intended subsidies are delivered with some degree of accuracy. They would agree also that revenues must be sufficient to operate, maintain and enhance delivery service. What is needed, now, is to build upon this accumulated experience by refining water tariffs, modifying the way in which subsidies are provided, and expanding service areas to include greater numbers of poor households. The chances of success will be enhanced by also considering the important roles of institutions and complementary policies and investments in supporting appropriate water tariffs.

Acknowledgements

I appreciate very much the helpful comments and suggestions of an anonymous reviewer.

References

Angel-Urdinola, D. F., & Wodon, Q. (2012). Does increasing access to infrastructure services improve the targeting performance of water subsidies? *Journal of International Development*, *24*, 88–101.

Bakker, K. (2007). Trickle down? Private sector participation and the pro-poor water supply debate in Jakarta, Indonesia. *Geoforum*, *38*, 855–868.

Bakker, K., Kooy, M., Shofiani, N. E., & Martijn, E. (2008). Governance failure: Rethinking the institutional dimensions of urban water supply to poor households. *World Development*, *36*, 1891–1915.

Banerjee, S., Foster, V., Ying, Y., Skilling, H., & Wodon, Q. (2010). Cost recovery, equity, and efficiency in water tariffs: Evidence from African utilities. Policy Research Working Paper 5384. Washington, DC: World Bank.

Berg, S. V., & Mugisha, S. (2010). Pro-poor water service strategies in developing countries: Promoting justice in Uganda's urban project. *Water Policy*, *12*, 589–601.

Brocklehurst, C., Pandurangi, A., & Ramanathan, L. (2002). Tariff structures in six South Asian cities. Water Tariffs and Subsidies in South Asia, Paper 3. Washington, DC: World Bank.

Chitonge, H. (2011). A decade of implementing water services reform in Zambia: Review of outcomes, challenges and opportunities. *Water Alternatives*, *4*(3), 1–22.

Dahan, M., & Nisan, U. (2007). Unintended consequences of increasing block tariffs pricing policy in urban water. *Water Resources Research*, *43*(W03402), 1–10.

Diakité, D., Semenov, A., & Thomas, A. (2009). A proposal for social pricing of water supply in Côte d'Ivoire. *Journal of Development Economics*, *88*, 258–268.

Donkor, E. A. (2010). Evaluating increasing block tariff pricing policies when applied to multiple household connections. *Water International*, *35*, 748–762.

Foster, V., Pattanayak, S., & Prokopy, L. (2002). Do current water subsidies reach the poor? Water Tariffs and Subsidies in South Asia, Paper 4. Washington, DC: World Bank.

Gerlach, E. (2008). Regulating water services for Nairobi's informal settlements. *Water Policy*, *10*, 531–548.

Gerlach, E., & Franceys, R. (2009). Regulating water services for the poor: The case of Amman. *Geoforum*, *40*, 431–441.

Gerlach, E., & Franceys, R. (2010). Regulating water services for all in developing economies. *World Development*, *38*, 1229–1240.

Gessler, M., Brighu, U., & Franceys, R. (2008). The challenge of economic regulation of water and sanitation in urban India. *Habitat International*, *32*, 49–57.

González-Gómez, F., García-Rubio, M. A., & Guardiola, J. (2011). Why is non-revenue water so high in so many cities? *International Journal of Water Resources Development*, *27*, 345–360.

Hadipuro, W. (2010). Indonesia's water supply regulatory framework: Between commercialization and public service? *Water Alternatives*, *3*, 475–491.

Jansen, A., & Schulz, C. (2006). Water demand and the urban poor: A study of the factors influencing water consumption among households in Cape Town, South Africa. *South African Journal of Economics*, *74*, 593–609.

Kagaya, S., & Franceys, R. (2007). Costs of urban utility water connections: Excessive burden to the poor. *Utilities Policy*, *15*, 270–277.

Kalulu, K., & Hoko, Z. (2010). Assessment of the performance of a public water utility: A case study of Blantyre Water Board in Malawi. *Physics and Chemistry of the Earth*, *35*, 806–810.

Kanakoudis, V., Gonelas, K., & Tolikas, D. (2011). Basic principles for urban water value assessment and price setting towards its full cost recovery: Pinpointing the role of the water losses. *Journal of Water Supply: Research and Technology–AQUA, 60,* 27–39.

Keener, S., Luengo, M., & Banerjee, S. (2010). Provision of water to the poor in Africa. Policy Research Working Paper 5387. Washington, DC: World Bank.

Komives, K., Halpern, J., Foster, V., Wodon, Q., & Abdullah, R. (2006). The distributional incidence of residential water and electricity subsidies. Policy Research Working Paper 3878. Washington, DC: World Bank.

le Blanc, D. (2008). A framework for analyzing tariffs and subsidies in water provision to urban households in developing countries. Department of Economic and Social Affairs Paper No. 63. New York: United Nations.

Madhoo, Y. N. (2011). Redistributive impact of increasing block residential water rates: Some empirical evidence from Mauritius. *Water Policy, 13,* 471–489.

Mckenzie, D., & Ray, I. (2009). Urban water supply in India: Status, reform options and possible lessons. *Water Policy, 11,* 442–460.

Mkandla, N., Van der Zaag, P., & Sibanda, P. (2005). Bulawayo water supplies: Sustainable alternatives for the next decade. *Physics and Chemistry of the Earth, 30,* 935–942.

Mulwafu, W., Chipeta, C., Chavula, G., Ferguson, A., Nkhoma, B. G., & Chilma, G. (2003). Water demand management in Malawi: Problems and prospects for its promotion. *Physics and Chemistry of the Earth, 28,* 787–796.

Nleya, N. (2008). Development policy and water services in South Africa: An urban poverty perspective. *Development Southern Africa, 25,* 269–281.

Ntengwe, F. W. (2004). The impact of consumer awareness of water sector issues on willingness to pay and cost recovery in Zambia. *Physics and Chemistry of the Earth, 29,* 1301–1308.

Potter, R. B., & Darmame, K. (2010). Contemporary social variations in household water use management strategies and awareness under conditions of "water stress": The case of Greater Amman, Jordan. *Habitat International, 34,* 115–124.

Raghupati, U. P., & Foster, V. (2002). A scorecard for India. Water Tariffs and Subsidies in South Asia, Paper 2. Washington, DC: World Bank.

Rogers, P., de Silva, R., & Bhatia, R. (2002). Water is an economic good: How to use prices to promote equity, efficiency, and sustainability. *Water Policy, 4,* 1–17.

Ruijs, A., Zimmermann, A., & van den Berg, M. (2008). Demand and distributional effects of water pricing policies. *Ecological Economics, 66,* 506–516.

Smith, L. (2004). The murky waters of the second wave of neoliberalism: Corporatization as a service delivery model in Cape Town. *Geoforum, 35,* 375–393.

Venkatachalam, L. (2006). Factors influencing household willingness to pay (WTP) for drinking water in peri-urban areas: A case study in the Indian context. *Water Policy, 8,* 461–473.

Whittington, D., Boland, J., & Foster, V. (2002). Understanding the basics. Water Tariffs and Subsidies in South Asia, Paper 1. Washington, DC: World Bank.

Wyatt, A. (2010). Non-revenue water: Financial model for optimal management in developing countries. Publication No. MR-00118-1006. Research Triangle Park, NC: RTI Press.

A global survey of urban water tariffs: are they sustainable, efficient and fair?

David Zetland[a] and Christopher Gasson[b]

[a]Wageningen University, Environmental and Natural Resource Economics, Wageningen, the Netherlands; [b]Global Water Intelligence, The Jam Factory, Oxford, UK

This paper examines the relations between tariffs and sustainability, efficiency and equity, using a unique data-set for 308 cities in 102 countries. Higher water tariffs are correlated with lower per capita consumption, smaller local populations, lower water availability, higher demand and a lower risk of shortage. Aggregating to the national level, higher tariffs are correlated with higher GDP and better governance. A different country-level analysis shows that a higher percentage of the population with water service is correlated with better governance, higher GDP and a greater risk of water shortage. The relation between water prices and service coverage is statistically inconsistent.

Introduction

Residential water and wastewater tariffs are generally linked to the cost of building, operating and maintaining drinking-water and wastewater systems, but tariffs rarely recover the full cost of service. Economists define the 'full cost of service' as the cost of operations, capital replacement, system expansion and – most important – the opportunity cost of using urban water today instead of saving it for tomorrow or using it elsewhere, e.g. for the environment or irrigation. Policies that reduce the price of water below the full cost of service are likely to increase unsustainable water consumption, causing stress on supplies; dependence on outside sources of financing and the political interference that comes with it; service interruptions due to underfunding of operating and capital costs; and inequality due to limits on service to outlying, informal and newly settled areas.

These outcomes result when water managers with limited water, capital budgets and operating resources must choose whom to serve among multiple demands. The most common choice – to serve the powerful and rich over the weak and poor – is particularly acute in developing countries struggling to extend clean water service to the entire population (Segerfeldt, 2005; North, Wallis, & Weingast, 2009). The United Nations Development Programme (UNDP, 2006, pp. 2–3), for example, writes:

> In many countries scarcity is the product of public policies that have encouraged overuse of water through subsidies and underpricing. There is more than enough water in the world for domestic purposes, for agriculture and for industry. The problem is that some people – notably the poor – are systematically excluded from access by their poverty, by their limited legal rights or by public policies that limit access to the infrastructures that provide water for

Table 1. Descriptive statistics for 2011 GWI data.

Variable	Units	Observations	Mean	Std. Dev.	Min	Max
Water	USD per m^3	308	1.21	1.13	0	7.54
Wastewater	USD per m^3	248	1.02	1.07	0	5.68
Combined	USD per m^3	308	2.02	1.90	0	10.00
GDP	USD per capita	308	22,630	20,600	345	108,230
Water tariff change	percent from 2010	272	1.90	18.20	-76	136
Wastewater tariff change	percent from 2010	213	4.16	23.86	-57	279

Source: GWI (2011a).

> life and for livelihoods. In short, scarcity is manufactured through political processes and
> institutions that disadvantage the poor.

This sentiment should be borne in mind when examining the variables describing the relations among water tariffs and measures of sustainability, efficiency and equity.

Data

The primary data come from Global Water Intelligence's 2011 survey of water and wastewater tariffs for 308 cities in 102 countries (GWI, 2011a). These cities were chosen for their large populations and representative natures. GWI gathered data on tariffs and GDP per capita via phone, email and internet; converted local currencies into 2011 USD equivalents using current market exchange rates; and normalized the price of receiving one cubic metre of drinking-water or wastewater service by adding the charge for consuming 15 m^3 to the monthly fixed charge and then dividing the result by 15. This last step makes it possible to compare water prices on a standard measure, a necessary step when the cost of service in various locations depends on a mix of fixed and variable charges. Note that GWI's data do not reflect the cost of 'irregular service' to households without connections or capture the range of prices and operating practices within countries; for these, see Rygaard, Binning, and Albrechtsen (2011) and IB-NET (http://www.ib-net.org), respectively. Table 1 gives descriptive statistics for GWI (2011a).

It should be noted that 15 m^3 per year works out to about 40 litres per day, a number that most households will exceed. The World Health Organization defines 20 litres per *capita* per day (LCD) to be a minimum humanitarian standard (Howard & Bartram, 2003); Chenoweth (2008) calculates that 135 LCD is a minimum consistent with economic and social development. The presence of fixed charges means that GWI's cost per cubic metre at a consumption rate of 40 litres per day may overstate the average cost per cubic metre for a household that consumes 200 litres per day – or it may not: increasing block rates may make the average cost per cubic metre at higher consumption volumes significantly higher.

Some notes on water and wastewater tariffs

Most water utilities operate under some form of political or regulatory price control that aims at minimizing tariffs, subject to covering some or all operating and capital costs, which vary with local labour rates, the age and condition of infrastructure, the rate of infrastructure maintenance and replacement, policies on water pricing and subsidies, and water scarcity. Labour costs generally rise with GDP, but they are also affected by over- or under-staffing, public vs. private operation, union or civil-servant status, and so on. Infrastructure conditions vary with system age and extent, service mandates, management changes in the past or anticipated future, and the ebb and flow of financing. Policies that subsidize water prices, shift costs among user groups or fail to reduce theft lead to dependence on outside funding, increased debt, or reductions in maintenance. Water scarcity can affect prices by forcing a utility to spend more money on expensive sources (e.g. desalination or wastewater recovery) or by reducing the volume of water available to customers, which means that the price per unit of water sold has to rise so that total revenues cover (mostly fixed) total costs. It is very difficult to know whether or how these institutional factors affect water and wastewater prices over time, but their variety suggests that policies create a range of effects (Hanemann, 2005; Whittington, Hanemann, Sadoff, & Jeuland, 2009).

The high cost of Belgian capital and labour thus explains why water in Gent costs $7.54/m^3$ (all prices in 2011 US dollars) in the same way that cheap labour and capital might explain Cairo's cost of $0.04/m^3$, but these prices are not directly proportional to income or local costs. Belgian GDP per capita is 14 times Egypt's, but Gent's water tariff is 188 times Cairo's. Political factors can even invert prices: Ireland and Saudi Arabia are wealthier countries than Egypt, but water is free in Dublin and only $0.03/m^3$ in Jeddah. The big difference between minimum and maximum prices does not mean that most prices are roughly in the middle – the median price per cubic metre of water is $0.92. Water tariffs also vary within countries. In the countries with the most cities in the survey (USA with 27, China with 25 and India with 17) the minimum/median/maximum prices per cubic metre of water are $0.53/1.13/3.14 in the US, $0.17/0.35/0.59 in China, and $0.05/0.11/0.28 in India. There may be many reasons for prices that vary by a factor of four or more, but the lesson is clear: no country has 'average' water prices.

Wastewater charges are more complicated. Most people are willing to pay for drinking water service to their houses, but wastewater systems handle rainwater flows as well as municipal and industrial discharges. Some systems clean the water before it leaves the area, while others merely export raw sewage. These mixed 'services' make it harder to establish or set wastewater charges. Residential water is free in Cork, Dublin, Belfast, and Ashgabat; these cities – and 58 more – also do not charge for wastewater service, so they cover costs with outside funding or water sales (8 of the 10 top water tariffs are in cities that do not charge for wastewater), or they underinvest in the wastewater system.

Other policies change the price per unit of water with consumption, to induce water conservation or make water 'affordable' to some needy population. Veolia, for example, calculates water prices in Nice and Toulouse according to household characteristics; many Latin American cities set tariffs based on household income; prices in Israel depend on the source of water and the number of people in the house; and so on. GWI uses the $15\,m^3$ benchmark to make it easier to compare tariff structures in which the price per unit of water may rise with consumption (increasing block rates), fall (decreasing block rates), stay the same (a linear rate), or be zero – as when customers pay a fixed charge per month no matter how much water they use. The most common rate structure in GWI (2011a) is increasing (151 cities), followed by linear (141 cities), decreasing (9 cities) and fixed (7 cities), which includes cities that provide free water. Social equity, likewise, may explain why 'poor' customers or customers who use less water may pay less per unit of water consumed, but social tariffs sometimes benefit rich people intentionally misclassified as 'poor' instead of poor people without connections; sometimes they are not reflected in the price of water but in direct income supports.

It is therefore difficult for outsiders with limited data to know if tariffs are 'fair' or reflect the structure of water costs. Martinez-Espiñeira, García-Valiñas, and González-Gómez (2009), Ruester and Zschille (2010), and Thorsten, Eskaf, and Hughes (2009) explore the factors determining water tariffs in great detail.

GWI's Global Water Risk Index

This long discussion of the various influences on water tariffs illustrates how the complexity of a structural model of water prices will vary with parameters and variables in each of our 308 cities. Since it is not possible to know all of these structural models affecting water prices (and thus efficiency, sustainability and equity), a reduced-form model was used to understand the major influences on price and consumption data in GWI. The reduced-form model uses factors that indirectly affect prices, i.e., measurements of water availability, demand, and risk of shortage tracked in GWI's proprietary Global Water Risk Index (GWI, 2011c). The GWRI is created by combining over 200 maps, arrays and algorithms containing information about hydrology, population, economic activities, political boundaries and other natural and social factors into spatial and temporal models of supply and demand. The GWRI's $0.5° \times 0.5°$ resolution groups data into squares that are $55 \, km^2$ at the equator and smaller near the poles. These squares are assigned to cities, but they do not match municipal boundaries.

For water availability, the GWRI includes variables for water availability by river basin, storage capacity, historic volumes of rainfall and runoff, frequency of floods and droughts, and so on. Demand data are assembled for the domestic, agricultural and industrial sectors. Demand for domestic water can be met by formal or informal sources. Agricultural water demand is met by precipitation and irrigation. Industrial demand draws data from 13 major industries: power generation, oil and gas, petroleum refining, mining, chemicals, metals, automotive, food and beverages, microelectronics, pulp and paper, textiles, pharmaceuticals and biofuels. The GWRI also reflects the estimated future influences of climate change (Scenario A1B) and sectorial changes on supply and demand (IPCC 2007).

The GWRI's indexed value for risk (i.e., water scarcity) is calculated by simulating supply and demand over a range of potential futures and recording the frequency and magnitudes of instances in which demand exceeds supply. The index takes a value of 1.00 if demand exceeds supply 100% of the time and 0.00 if demand never exceeds supply. Intermediate values reflect lower frequencies and magnitudes of demand exceeding supply. Current GWRI values for risk tend to be clustered at the extremes: 240 cities face scarcity risk (i.e. 1.00 values) while 108 cities do not (0.00 values). These values may correspond to results, since management also matters. Dhaka, Mumbai, Miami and Milwaukee have 0.00 values; Sao Paulo, Paris, New Delhi, Madrid, Atlanta and New York have 1.00 values. Anyone familiar with water management in these cities knows that scarcity risk need not lead to shortage (also see Jenerette & Larsen [2006] for a complementary analysis of urban water scarcity). Table 2 has descriptive statistics for the GWRI data (all as of 2010).

Table 2. Descriptive statistics for 2010 GWRI data.

Variable	Units	Observations	Mean	Std. Dev.	Min	Max
Population	people	558	2,734,000	3,013,000	1,000,000	35,700,000
Supply	index value	558	1630	5320	-57	76,725
Demand	index value	558	160	240	0	2140
Risk	index value	558	0.54	0.47	0	1

Source: GWI (2011c)

Additional data and caveats

GWI has tariff data for 308 cities in 102 countries and GWRI data for 588 cities in 112 countries, but these two datasets overlap only for 189 cities in 88 countries. These data are augmented by other data sources such as GWI (2011a) consumption data in litres per capita per day (LCD) for 63 cities; 2008 data on urban access to piped water for 191 countries from WHO/UNICEF (2011); 2009 governance rankings for 213 countries calculated as the average of the World Bank's Governance Indicators for voice and accountability, political stability, government effectiveness, regulatory quality, rule of law and control of corruption (Kaufmann et al., 2010); and 2011 Human Development Index values for 187 countries (UNDP, 2011). Table 3 summarizes these data sources, which overlap with GWI (2011a) data for 102 countries and overlap with both GWI (2011a) and GWI (2011c) for 75 countries.

The authors make several simplifying assumptions to bring tractability to the data. First, it is assumed that tariffs in surveyed cities – a subset of all cities in each country – can be combined with national statistics for income and governance and regional statistics for water availability, risk, etc. It is thus assumed, for example, that the population-weighted tariffs of two cities in Bangladesh can be matched against a governance ranking for the whole country. Second, tariffs are examined at a consumption level of $15\,\mathrm{m}^3$ – simplifying tariff schedules that may have five or more steps of varying heights (prices per cubic metre) and widths (threshold volumes) into a single price per cubic metre. Third, the discussion of the factors affecting water and wastewater tariffs is simplified by concentrating on water tariffs and assuming that the factors affecting wastewater tariffs are similar. Indeed, water and wastewater tariffs have a 67% correlation in the 246 cities that charge for both. Correlation is lower when different organizations provide water and wastewater service, when the systems are expanding at different rates, or when tariffs are fixed for one system but based on volume in the other (most volumetric wastewater charges are based on water consumption).

The results, therefore, need to be interpreted with care. Although the regressions explore multivariate relations – an improvement on bivariate analysis – significant variables of interest are often missing (statistics on subsidies from the government or non-revenue water, for example). The multivariate analysis augments the bivariate analysis by clarifying the relative contributions of independent but overlapping variables. More important, correlations are explored among variables that are more likely to have causal relations. Water price and consumption may be correlated, for example, but causality from price to consumption is likely to be stronger. Since panel data are not available, it has been necessary to work with short-term correlations within the cross-sectional data. Causality can be assumed where short-run effects are likely to drive the relation in one direction.

Table 3. Descriptive statistics for countries.

Variable	Units	Observations	Mean	Std. Dev.	Min	Max
Access to tap water	percent (2008)	191	76	29	0	100
Governance rank	100 high (2010)	213	50	27	0	98
Human Development Index	1.0 high	187	0.66	0.17	0.29	0.94

Sources: WHO/UNICEF (2011), Kaufmann et al. (2010) and UNDP (2011).

Analysis

Although there are insufficient data on each location in GWI's survey to carry out a detailed structural investigation of the causes and effects of various water tariff regimes, it is possible to carry out a limited analysis to see whether some of the simple relations in the data conform with economic theory. Readers should consider this analysis as the first – rather than the last – word on these topics.

Sustainability – balancing demand and supply

Excess demand is the greatest threat to sustainable water service. Although demand can exceed supply because of natural causes, it is more often the result of poor management. Shortages can be addressed by increasing supply from local or imported sources (at a cost of time, money and environmental impacts) or reducing demand through changes in preferences (forgoing a lawn), adoption of high-efficiency technologies, reductions in system leakages, or price increases that dampen demand. Arbués, García-Valiñas, and Martínez-Espiñeira (2003) and Dalhuisen, Florax, de Groot, and Nijkamp (2003) have made detailed studies of the relation between water prices and demand, but higher prices can also change preferences (Ariely, 2008), incentivize technology adoption, or fund reliability improvements – see Zetland (2011). Higher prices can even benefit the poor, as discussed below.

There must, of course, be a negative relation between price and consumption if higher prices are going to reduce demand. GWI (2011a) data on water prices and average LCD consumption for 63 cities in 34 countries support this relation, as shown in Figure 1. The quality of LCD data – derived by dividing total residential consumption

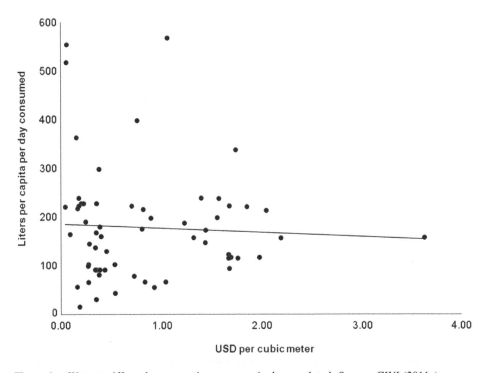

Figure 1.   Water tariffs and consumption are negatively correlated. *Source*: GWI (2011a).

volume by total population served – varies from very good (exact metering of each residence with a registered number of occupants) to poor (estimated residential consumption in an unmetered system divided by a census statistic for service area population).

Wealth also affects the demand for water, so we ran a simple OLS regression of LCD on water price per cubic metre and GDP per capita. Regression 1 (reported with other regressions in Appendix 1) identifies a negative relation between consumption and price and a positive relation between consumption and wealth. According to estimated coefficients, a $0.50/m^3 price increase from the mean price of $0.84/m^3 is correlated with a 40 LCD drop in consumption from the mean of 180 LCD, or a point-estimated price elasticity of -0.37. This elasticity compares favourably to the median price elasticity of -0.35 that Dalhuisen et al. (2003) report in their survey of 64 studies with 314 elasticities, but remember that GWI's prices are based on assumed consumption, not the actual tariff schedules households face.

Efficiency – investing in reliability

There are many reasons why water prices can be low (abundant water, low costs, subsidies, government policies, etc.), but they should not be kept low if the resulting high water consumption threatens reliability. Figure 2 affirms this idea, showing that higher tariffs are correlated with a lower risk of shortage, but causality is unclear and numerous 0 or 1 values mean this relation may not be robust.

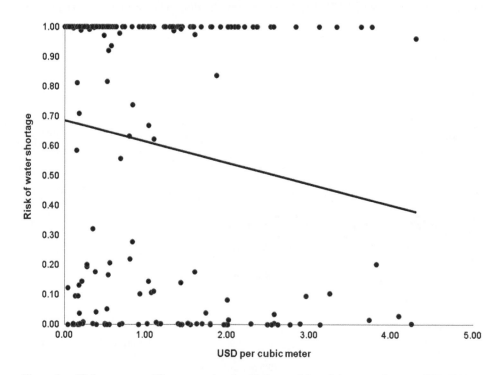

Figure 2.   Higher water tariffs are correlated with lower risks of shortage. *Source*: GWI (2011a, 2011c).

Water prices need to cover operating costs as well as capital expansion and replacement. According to the UNDP (2006, p. 85):

In many utilities tariffs are set far below the levels needed to meet the overall costs of operation and maintenance. In effect, this delivers a subsidy to all households with private tap connections. On the other side of the balance sheet, the shortfall between revenue and cost will be reflected in transfers from government, rising debt, reduced spending on maintenance or a combination of the three.

Insufficient spending leads to negative present and future impacts, but it is hardly better to fill the gap with debt and/or subsidies that create additional costs. First, they lead managers to spend more time with their financial benefactors and less time managing operations and serving customers. Second, these benefactors can distort strategic or tactical decisions, e.g. where to expand the system or whom to hire. Third, debt and subsidies are inherently volatile: they can and do change much more rapidly than the stream of customer payments. Ireland's financial struggles have led to a plan to reintroduce charges for residential water service – reversing a past populist policy but also creating logistical and financial complications (Taylor, 2010).

The data yield further insights. Regression 2 (water tariff on local population, available water, demand and risk for 189 cities in 75 countries) reveals that higher water tariffs are correlated with a lower population (diseconomies of scale, even though population density may be more relevant), less available water (dearer supplies) and a lower risk of shortage (lower consumption plus funding for reliability). These results do not change if the combined water and wastewater tariff are used or a quadratic term is added for supply that captures the problem of too much water (floods).

If GWI (2011a) city data are aggregated (giving weighs within countries by urban population) and data for service area coverage, governance and GDP per capita are added, this creates a sample of 102 countries.

Figure 3 shows that higher prices and better governance are correlated. This relation holds in Regression 3, which also shows that higher tariffs are correlated with higher GDP and a lower percentage of the urban population receiving water service; see Biswas (2010) for a critical discussion of coverage. Governance results, controlling for income, are consistent with customers paying more when they trust their money will be well spent – and with incompetent governments pursuing 'cheap water' populism. Saudi Arabia, for example, has extremely low water prices ($0.03/m^3), cheap petrol, and a habit of bribing citizens to reduce civil unrest (*The Economist*, 2011); it also has a low governance ranking of 44 – tied with Morocco and below Mozambique.

Rearranging these variables in Regression 4 (tap water coverage on governance, tariff, and per capita GDP), confirms the negative relation between coverage and price and the positive correlations between coverage and both governance and GDP. These results are consistent with more money and better governance delivering better water service. The negative correlation of prices – given the lack of coverage variation in developed countries – is consistent with limited but expensive service to urban elites or unsustainable populism in developing countries. Populism often brings poor service: customers in Saudi Arabia, India and other places pay low prices for supplies that are available only a few times per week.

Fairness – serving the poor and everyone else

Unreliable water service complicates and shortens life for people – as is known from discussions of the Millennium Development Goals, the human right to water, rates of

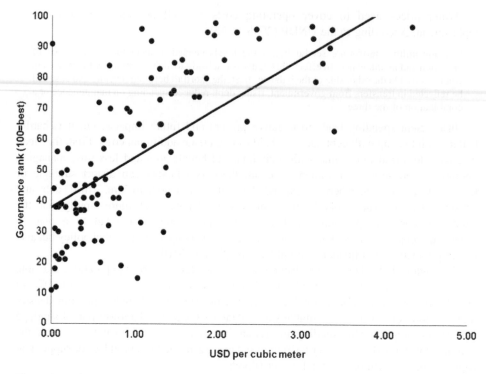

Figure 3. Higher water tariffs are correlated with higher governance ranking. *Sources*: GWI (2011a) and Kaufmann et al. (2010).

mortality and morbidity, and so on. Although some activists concentrate on lowering the price of water to underserved populations, this goal can backfire (UNDP, 2006, p. 85–86):

> Whether utility subsidies are progressive depends on the profile of households connected to the utilities: the lower the proportion of poor households connected, the less progressive the subsidy.... An obvious danger is that excessively high prices will drive users to alternative sources of provision.... Many utilities have been locked in a cycle of underfinancing, undermaintenance and underexpansion. With tariff revenues falling far short of the level needed to maintain the network, there is no money to finance expansion to unserved households on the scale required.

Underserved populations need leverage to get water service from the local water monopoly. They are unlikely to have political power, but financial leverage can work. This phenomenon is observed in the spread of mobile phone service in developing countries, where the number of mobile phone connections per 100 people exceeds the share of people who have piped water to their home, as shown in Figure 4.

Although the poor have their own ways of finding water (see Hammond, Kramer, Tran, Katz, & Walker, 2007), they are frequently 'protected' by pro-poor policies that create service obligations for low-volume customers without proportional increases in revenues. Cash-strapped utilities respond by withholding service, and the poor pay time and money for lower-quality water (Keener, Luengo, & Banerjee, 2010; Kjellén & McGranahan, 2006). It should be noted that GWI's data on social tariffs or programmes are not used to make this point. The negative relationship between normal tariffs and service area in GWI data show that lower prices are correlated with a smaller service area.

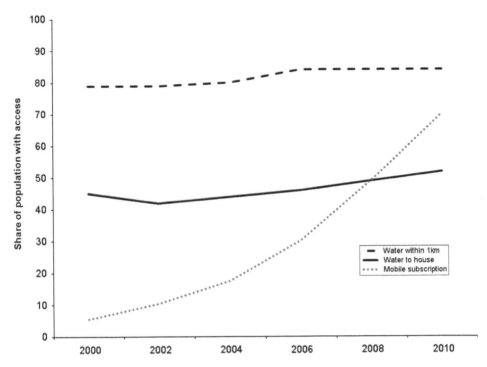

Figure 4. Mobile phones versus water services for rural and urban inhabitants in the developing world. *Sources*: Mobile phone subscriptions per 100 people from ITU (2011). Access to 'developed' or 'piped' water from annual reports at WHO/UNICEF (2011) for 2000–2008, linearly extrapolated for 2010. (These statistics are not exactly compatible because some people have more than one mobile phone.)

In Regressions 5 and 6, the factors correlated with the provision of piped urban water in 75 countries are explored. Coverage is positively correlated with good governance, risk of local water shortages (perhaps water service is more important with risk) and greater water availability (it is easier to provide service – holding risk constant – when there's more water). It is interesting to see that these regressions do not identify a correlation between water prices and service area, contra Regressions 3 and 4 that used fewer variables. That lack of result may indicate that these data do not provide enough information to clarify the complex relations among the variables.

Regression 7 illustrates this complexity by identifying a significant correlation between aggregated national data for water tariffs (the regressor), governance and GDP (per Regression 3) while failing to establish significance with population served, demand, risk, or water availability – in contrast to their significant, city-level relations in Regression 2. These results suggest that local characteristics – like local water management – may not be clear and consistent when aggregated to a national level.

Discussion

The results come with two caveats. First, the relations among water prices, sustainability, efficiency and fairness are not standardized around the world. Water prices emerge from a complex interplay of economic, political and social factors that have evolved over time. Second, the data cannot capture the complex relations among quantified and missing variables. The next few sections discuss how water prices reflect and affect governance, financial stability and affordability.

Governance

Good governance at the national level can improve local water management, but it is not a necessary condition. A water utility free of political interference or regulation can independently deliver good or bad service – depending on the principal-agent dynamics between political regulators and water managers whose interactions determine the quality of service customers receive from the water monopoly (Biswas, 2010; Zetland, 2011). It is possible to explore their interactions in a two-by-two grid in which it is clear that diligent regulators and managers deliver good service while lazy regulators and managers deliver bad service. The interesting quadrants are where good managers work in a country with poor governance or lazy managers are overseen by diligent regulators. In the good manager, bad regulator scenario, the manager with an informational advantage can deliver good service despite the regulator. In the bad manager, good regulator scenario, the manager can be replaced and/or forced to serve customers by political regulators with access to basic performance data. This example illustrates how even a partial commitment to good governance can benefit customers.

Full-cost pricing and sustainability

Although some water utilities are financially self-sufficient, the majority struggle with insufficient revenues. GWI (2011b) estimates that the current global capital spending of $173 billion per year falls short of the $211 billion per year necessary to maintain capital stock as well as being woefully short of the additional $360 billion per year necessary to bring systems up to regulatory standards.

Revenue shortfalls can be addressed in several ways. The most common is to reduce spending on new infrastructure, maintenance, or even operations. The resulting deterioration in service harms existing customers and breaches the public utility promise to provide services to all of the public, some of who turn to expensive but reliable self-sufficient solutions (Rygaard et al., 2011; UNDP, 2006). The second response is to hope for hidden and overt subsidies from politicians that can evaporate with a change of administration or financial crisis. The third response is to outsource the problem to private operators who bring finance and expertise in exchange for the political permission to raise prices, or insource the problem by giving public utilities permission to raise prices.

The findings – that higher tariffs are associated with lower consumption and lower risk of shortage – dovetail nicely with the need to invest more in drinking-water and wastewater infrastructure (UNDP, 2006). These correlations are no proof of impact, but it is hard to argue that higher prices leading to higher spending on services cannot increase reliability. The inconclusive results on the relation between higher prices and service area may be even more important, given that the biggest barrier to higher prices is the fear that they may make water too expensive for the poor.

Affordability

People concerned about water affordability make two assumptions that weaken their arguments. The first is that higher prices will harm the poor. That idea – simple in theory – does not hold when higher prices are used to extend service to people relying previously on informal water providers. GWI (2011b) discusses how citizens of Phnom Phen, Manila, and other poor areas now pay less for full-cost-recovery services that deliver better water than the expensive, unreliable and unhealthy water they purchased previously from informal sellers. The second weakness is revealed by comparing water prices to income.

The actual price of water and wastewater at a consumption rate of 20 LCD for each service is lower than the "affordability" benchmark of UNDP (2006) – 3% of income – for all of our 308 cities, but that comparison is not terribly realistic. First, GDP per capita overstates the income of an average individual and definitely fails to consider income distribution. If it is assumed there is an income equal to 25% of per capita GDP, for example, then the price of 20 LCD services exceeds 3% of *that* income in five countries, with the least affordable urban water in Ouagadougu, Kathmandu, and Kampala. Second, 20 LCD is not very much. The cost of consuming 135 LCD in services (per Chenoweth, 2008) would exceed 3% of income – again based on 25% of average GDP per capita – in 80 of 308 countries. It is for the reader decide whether tariffs are too high at those income and consumption levels.

Conclusion

This analysis of water tariff data from around the world reveals that water prices are relatively low and that low prices are correlated with higher water consumption and greater risk of shortages. Higher prices would not only reduce water consumption and the risk of shortage, they would also provide funds to operate, repair and expand water and wastewater services to people now forced to drink dirtier, more expensive and less convenient water.

Acknowledgements

The authors thank Damian Bickett, Paul Ferraro, Merton D. Finkler, Christopher Goemans, Heather Lang, Anke Leroux, Ankit Patel, Reagan Waskom, and two referees for helpful comments.

References

Arbués, F., García-Valiñas, M. A., & Martínez-Espiñeira, R. (2003). Estimation of residential water demand: A state-of-the-art review. *Journal of Socio-Economics, 32*, 81–102. doi:10.1016/S1053-5357(03)00005-2.

Ariely, D. (2008). *Predictably irrational*. New York: Harper Collins.

Biswas, A. K. (2010). Water for a thirsty urban world. *Brown Journal of World Affairs, 17*, 147–162. Retrieved from http://www.bjwa.org/.

Chenoweth, J. (2008). Minimum water requirement for social and economic development. *Desalination, 229*, 245–256. doi:10.1016/j.desal.2007.09.011.

Dalhuisen, J. M., Florax, R. J. G. M., Groot, H. K. F., & Nijkamp, P. (2003). Price and income elasticities of residential water demand: A meta-analysis. *Land Economics, 79*, 292–308. doi:10.3368/le.79.2.292.

The Economist (2011, July 14). Revolution spinning in the wind.

GWI (2011a). 2011 GWI OECD global water tariff survey. *Global Water Intelligence, 12*(9).

GWI (2011b). *Global water market 2011*. Oxford: Global Water Intelligence.

GWI (2011c). *Global water risk index*. Oxford: Global Water Intelligence.

Hammond, A., Kramer, W. J., Tran, J., Katz, R., & Walker, C. (2007). *The next 4 billion: Market size and business strategy at the base of the pyramid*. Washington, DC: World Resources Institute and International Finance Corporation.

Hanemann, W. M. (2005). The economic conception of water. In P. P. Rogers, M. R. Llamas, & L. Martinez Cortina (Eds.), *Water crisis: Myth or reality?* (pp. 61–92). Oxford: Taylor & Francis.

Howard, G., & Bartram, J. (2003). *Domestic water quantity, service, level and health.* Geneva: World Health Organization.

IPCC (2007). *Fourth assessment report: Climate change 2007.* Geneva: Inter-governmental Panel on Climate Change.

ITU (2011). *Mobile cellular subscriptions per 100 inhabitants, 2000–2010,* International Telecommunications Union. Retrieved from http://www.itu.int/ict/statistics.

Jenerette, G. D., & Larsen, L. (2006). A global perspective on changing sustainable urban water supplies. *Global and Planetary Change, 50*(3–4), 202–211. doi:10.1016/j.glopla-cha.2006.01.004.

Kaufmann, D., Kraay, A., & Mastruzzi, M. (2010). The worldwide governance indicators: Methodology and analytical issues (World Bank Policy Research Working Paper No. 5430). Retrieved from http://econ.worldbank.org.

Keener, S., Luengo, M., & Banerjee, S. (2010). Provision of water to the poor in Africa: Experience with water standposts and the informal water sector (World Bank Policy Research Working Paper No. 5387). Retrieved from http://econ.worldbank.org.

Kjellén, M., & McGranahan, G. (2006). Informal water vendors and the urban poor (Human Settlements Working Paper Series, Water, No. 3). Retrieved from http://pubs.iied.org/10529IIED.html.

Martinez-Espiñeira, R., García-Valiñas, M. A., & González-Gómez, F. (2009). Does private management of water supply services really increase prices? An empirical analysis. *Urban Studies, 46*(4), 923–945. doi:10.1177/0042098009102135.

North, D. C., Wallis, J. J., & Weingast, B. R. (2009). *A conceptual framework for interpreting recorded human history.* Cambridge: Cambridge University Press.

Ruester, S., & Zschille, M. (2010). The impact of governance structure on firm performance: An application to the German water distribution sector. *Utilities Policy, 18*(3), 154–162. doi:10.1016/j.jup.2010.03.003.

Rygaard, M., Binning, P. J., & Albrechtsen, H. -J. (2011). Increasing urban water self-sufficiency: New era, new challenges. *Journal of Environmental Management, 92,* 185–194. doi:10.1016/j.jenvman.2010.09.009.

Segerfeldt, F. (2005). *Water for sale: How business and the market can resolve the world's water crisis.* Washington, DC: Cato Institute.

Taylor, C. (2010, January 25). Water charges "to raise EUR 1 billion". *Irish Times.*

Thorsten, R. E., Eskaf, S., & Hughes, J. (2009). Cost plus: Estimating real determinants of water and sewer bills. *Public Works Management and Policy, 13*(3), 224–238. doi:10.1177/1087724X08324302.

UNDP (2006). *Human development report 2006. Beyond scarcity: Power, poverty and the global water crisis.* New York: United Nations Development Programme.

UNDP (2011). *Human development report 2011. Sustainability and equity: A better future for all.* New York: United Nations Development Programme.

Whittington, D., Hanemann, W. M., Sadoff, C., & Jeuland, M. (2009). The challenge of improving water and sanitation services in less developed countries. *Foundations and Trends in Microeconomics, 4*(6–7), 469–609. doi:10.1561/0700000030.

WHO/UNICEF (2011). Joint Monitoring Programme for Water Supply and Sanitation. Retrieved from http://www.wssinfo.org/data-estimates.

Zetland, D. (2011). *The end of abundance: Economic solutions to water scarcity.* Mission Viejo: Aguanomics Press.

Appendix 1: Regressions (data available upon request)

Regression 1: LCD on watertariff, gdp (robust standard errors)

Robust linear regression

Number of obs.=	61 cities
$F_{(2, 58)} =$	7.96
Prob > F =	0.001
R−squared =	0.248
Root MSE =	101.75

LCD	Coeff.	Std. err.	t	$P > t$	[95% conf. interval]	
watertariff	− 79.556	26.378	− 3.02	**0.004**	− 132.358	− 26.755
gdp	0.006	0.001	3.98	**0.000**	0.003	0.009
constant	181.704	23.878	7.61	**0.000**	133.908	229.501

Data source: GWI (2011a).
Note: We dropped Tblisi and Belfast because their very high LCD (1800 and 900, respectively) increased estimated coefficients by a factor of three.

Regression 2: watertariff on pop, supply, demand, risk, ro (robust standard errors)

Robust linear regression

Number of obs. =	189 cities
$F_{(4,184)} =$	4.89
Prob > F =	0.001
R−squared =	0.064
Root MSE =	0.972

watertariff	Coeff.	Std. err.	t	$P > t$	[95% conf. interval]	
pop	− 4.45e−08	2.22e−08	− 2.00	**0.047**	− 8.82e−08	− 6.69e−10
supply	− 0.000	6.92e−06	− 2.74	**0.007**	− 0.000	− 5.32e−06
demand	0.001	0.000	1.65	**0.101**	− 0.000	0.001
risk	− 0.413	0.179	− 2.30	**0.023**	− 0.767	− 0.059
constant	1.433	0.151	9.48	**0.000**	1.135	1.732

Data sources: GWI (2011a,2011c).
Note: The proponderance of 0 and 1 values for risk may lead to biased OLS estimates. A comparison of OLS and ordered probit regressions with risk as the dependent variable returns statistically significant coefficients in the same direction as Regression 2.

Regression 3: watertariff on tap_cover, gov, gdp, ro (robust standard errors)

Robust linear regression

Number of obs. =	102 countries
$F_{(3,98)} =$	26.62
Prob > F =	0.000
R−squared =	0.524
Root MSE =	0.776

watertariff	Coeff.	Std. err.	t	P > t	[95% conf. interval]	
tap_cover	− 0.004	0.002	− 1.72	**0.088**	− 0.008	0.001
gov	0.025	0.005	4.58	**0.000**	0.014	0.036
gdp	0.000	5.81e−06	2.04	**0.044**	3.08e−07	0.000
constant	− 0.214	0.221	− 0.97	0.334	− 0.652	0.224

Data sources: Kaufmann et al. (2010), GWI (2011a) and WHO/UNICEF (2011).

Regression 4: tap_cover on watertariff, gov, gdp, ro (robust standard errors)

Robust linear regression

Number of obs. =	102 countries
F(3,98) =	19.93
Prob > F =	0.000
R−squared =	0.338
Root MSE =	21.357

tap_cover	Coeff.	Std. err.	t	P > t	[95% conf. interval]	
watertariff	− 2.752	1.678	− 1.64	**0.104**	− 6.081	0.577
gov	0.548	0.137	4.00	**0.000**	0.276	0.820
gdp	0.000	0.000	1.70	**0.091**	− 0.000	0.000
constant	50.521	7.159	7.06	**0.000**	36.315	64.727

Data sources: Kaufmann et al. (2010), GWI (2011a) and WHO/UNICEF (2011).

Regression 5: tap_cover on gov, watertariff, risk, ro (robust standard errors)

Robust linear regression

Number of obs. =	75 countries
F(3,71) =	19.29
Prob > F =	0.000
R−squared =	0.495
Root MSE =	18.824

tap_cover	Coeff.	Std. err.	t	P > t	[95% conf. interval]	
gov	0.599	0.139	4.31	**0.000**	0.322	0.877
watertariff	− 1.614	3.088	− 0.52	0.603	− 7.771	4.544
risk	24.472	5.109	4.79	**0.000**	14.284	34.660
constant	37.116	8.271	4.49	**0.000**	20.624	53.608

Data sources: Kaufmann et al. (2010), GWI (2011a, 2011c) and WHO/UNICEF (2011).

Regression 6: tap_cover on watertariff, supply, demand, risk, gov, gdp, ro (robust standard errors)

Robust linear regression

Number of obs. =	75 countries
F(6,68) =	52.07
Prob > F =	0.000
R−squared =	0.519
Root MSE =	18.77

tap_cover	Coeff.	Std. err.	t	P > t	[95% conf. interval]	
watertariff	− 2.524	2.999	− 0.84	0.403	− 8.508	3.459
supply	− 0.001	0.000	− 3.56	**0.001**	− 0.009	− 0.000
demand	0.013	0.009	1.38	0.172	− 0.006	0.031
risk	20.747	5.280	3.93	**0.000**	10.212	31.282
gov	0.506	0.203	2.50	**0.015**	0.102	0.910
gdp	0.000	0.000	0.64	0.526	− 0.000	0.001
constant	41.245	9.799	4.21	**0.000**	21.692	60.798

Data sources: Kaufmann et al. (2010), GWI (2011a, 2011c) and WHO/UNICEF (2011).

Regression 7: watertariff on tap_cover, supply, demand, risk, gov, gdp, ro (robust standard errors)

Robust linear regression

Number of obs. = 75 countries
$F_{(6,68)} =$ 13.78
Prob > F = 0.000
R−squared = 0.590
Root MSE = 0.639

watertariff	Coeff.	Std. err.	t	P > t	[95% conf. interval]	
tap_cover	− 0.003	0.003	− 0.84	0.406	− 0.010	0.004
supply	− 4.76e−06	3.42e−06	− 1.39	0.169	− 0.000	2.06e−06
demand	0.000	0.000	0.80	0.426	− 0.000	0.001
risk	− 0.129	0.239	− 0.54	0.591	− 0.605	0.347
gov	0.015	0.006	2.65	**0.010**	0.004	0.026
gdp	0.000	9.11e−06	2.41	**0.019**	3.79e−06	0.000
constant	0.037	0.246	0.15	0.882	− 0.455	0.528

Data sources: Kaufmann et al. (2010), GWI (2011a, 2011c) and WHO/UNICEF (2011).

Glas Cymru: lessons from nine years as a not-for-profit public–private partnership

David Lloyd Owen

Envisager Limited, Ceredigion, UK

Glas Cymru Cyfyngedig has owned Dŵr Cymru Welsh Water, the private provider of water and sewerage in Wales, since 2001. It is run as a not-for-profit company for the purpose of minimizing customer tariffs and improving customer service and environmental sustainability. The financial model has largely been able to deliver these objectives, while lowering the cost of financing these operations. The model looks to be replicable as long as there is suitable political and regulatory support.

Introduction

This paper examines the financial, tariff and operational performance of Dŵr Cymru Welsh Water (DCWW) between 2001, when the company was transformed into a not-for-profit company held by Glas Cymru Cyfyngedig, and 2010, the end of the second regulatory cycle under its ownership. These are also compared with its peers in England, which were all privatized at the same time in 1989. This case study is based on the author following of DCWW/Hyder as an equity analyst from 1989 to 2001 and being a 'member' (unpaid stakeholder) of Glas Cymru between 2001 and 2011.

Glas Cymru, water and Wales

Wales is one of the poorer parts of the United Kingdom (South and West Wales qualified for EU Cohesion Funding in 2000–2014), while at the time of the water sector's privatization in 1989 its water and sewerage assets needed to be substantially upgraded and extended in order to meet EU environmental and public health directives. For example, in 1989, 50% of sewage was treated to secondary standard and disposed to land, 30% was treated to primary standard and disposed to sea, and 20% was untreated and disposed to sea (J. Henry Schroder Wagg & Co., 1989). At the same time, water and sewerage bills have historically been higher than the average for England and Wales. This was due to higher tariffs at the time of privatization as well as the scale of investments required to address the infrastructure deficit and the need for further quality enhancements as the development of tourism raised bathing water quality expectations along with increasing the seasonality of demand. The high tariffs and additional cost drivers have resulted in affordability issues for a number of customers.

Wales can be characterized as a de-industrializing economy since the 1980s, which lowers demand for water from industrial customers. It has high-quality inland waters, but a low population density in many areas means small treatment facilities are needed, and more distribution infrastructure. Because tourism is an important part of the economy, high-quality bathing waters are seen as a priority, with the Môr Glas ('Blue Sea') bathing waters campaign launched in 1994.

It is evident that differences in Wales's topography and geomorphology, water resources and availability and population distribution, compared the with more densely populated regions in England, are not taken into account by Ofwat's 'one size fits all' approach.

From Dwr Cymru Welsh Water, to Hyder, to Glas Cymru

The evolution of Glas Cymru came as a response to extraordinary circumstances. DCWW PLC was renamed Hyder PLC in 1996, after its acquisition of SWALEC (electricity and gas distribution in South Wales, privatized in 1991) and a number of related infrastructure service and investment activities, including water and wastewater activities in Spain, Portugal and the Czech Republic. Hyder's multi-utility strategy was based on debt rather than equity, on the assumption that savings and synergies would fund the SWALEC acquisition. This meant that Hyder had a higher level of gearing (corporate debt as a percentage of equity) than the rest of the sector and in consequence was more vulnerable to changes in government policy.

Government policy between 1998 and 2000 did not favour Hyder (Bakker, 2003). In June 1998, Hyder had to pay a 'windfall tax' of £282 million relating to the profits from its utility operations since the 1989 and 1991 privatizations, and in the year starting April 2000, its water and sewerage tariffs were cut by 13% by Ofwat at the start of the third five-year asset management period (AMP) following its privatization. At the same time, government policy ensured that capital spending in 2000–2005 would be maintained. DCWW was sold to the public for 240p per share in 1989. Its share price rose to a peak of 1048p in January 1998 and fell to a low of 179p in March 2000. The windfall tax bill and the cost of maintaining its dividends and servicing the group's debt meant that by early 2000 the company expected gearing to rise above the levels stipulated in its debt covenants by the third quarter of 2001 and there was inadequate investor support for refinancing via a rights issue.

After a contested bid running for six months, WPD, a US power utility, acquired Hyder in October 2000 and sold DCWW to Glas Cymru in May 2001. Glas Cymru's management developed the concept of a bond-financed company in 1999 with a non-shareholder model to lower DCWW's cost of capital through a single-purpose not-for-profit company designed to enhance its debt rating. Before the acquisition, Glas Cymru obtained the approval of Ofwat and the Welsh Assembly Government, which set out a series of objectives for the company to meet. DCWW was acquired for £1.85 billion in assumed debt (in effect, all of Hyder's debt) against a regulated capital value (RCV) of £2.0 billion, and Glas Cymru raised £1.91 billion in debt finance. The bond covenants were structured specifically to optimize the debt ratings by minimizing the risk attached to each bond issue (MBIA, 2001).

Between 1989 and 2001 the company was a stock market–listed PLC and in line with the other water companies placed no special emphasis on tariffs and affordability other than agreeing to the price caps as decided by Ofwat, the sector's regulator. How has this approach worked in the subsequent decade?

Political context: Glas Cymru's undertakings

On 3 November 2000, Glas Cymru made eight proposals regarding its corporate governance to the National Assembly of Wales (Glas Cymru, 2000). These are based on the National Assembly's eight areas of concern that were published in relation to the original bid for Hyder.

- Dwr Cymru will be based and managed in Wales and will retain its distinctive identity as a company serving Welsh stakeholders.
- No further lob losses over and above those already agreed will take place. In addition, a lower cost of financing and the use of outsourcing to decrease operating costs will release funding towards improving service quality and environmental enhancement measures over and above those already agreed. This builds on the current strategy that appreciates the pivotal role a pristine environment plays in encouraging tourism in Wales.
- The company will be exclusively concerned with Dwr Cymru's water and sewerage activities. This obviates the need for higher-cost capital for developing non-utility activities.
- Promoting sustainable development, as defined under Article 121 of the Government of Wales Act, will form a core priority of the company.
- Cost savings will be distributed through environmental enhancements (based upon Môr Glas, the Green Sea Partnership) and further reductions in customer bills.
- Dwr Cymru recognizes the value of water as a resource in the Welsh economy and seeks to maximize revenues for any exports outside its operating region.
- The lack of a need to pay dividends or to develop unregulated businesses means that the company can concentrate on optimizing service delivery at a low price.
- Glas Cymru recognizes that the Ofwat price limits ought to be regarded as providing scope for further savings. The company's business plans are based on delivering further price savings to customers by 2005, barring circumstances beyond the company's control.

Developing the asset base

DCWW faced three main infrastructure-related challenges in 2001: (1) to comply with the European Union's Urban Waste Water Treatment Directive (all effluent discharges from urban areas with a population of more than 2000 to be treated to at least secondary standard) by 2005; (2) to fully comply with the European Union's Bathing Water Directive (and revised standards coming into effect from 2015); and (3) to address localized issues relating to water distribution.

We can gain an insight into how the asset base has changed by using Ofwat's criteria for valuing the extant and new asset base for each of the companies and relating this to how DCWW's asset value has evolved in relation to the other nine water and sewerage companies (WaSCs) privatized in 1989.

Ofwat's 'modern equivalent assets' (MEA) measure is the cost it would take to replace the extant asset base. While DCWW's water asset base has eased as a proportion of the total for the sector, reflecting a higher security of supply and access to high-quality water resources, the sewerage proportion has nearly doubled, showing how these assets have had

Table 1. DCWW's 'modern equivalent assets' compared with the sector, 1991–2010 (£ millions, 2009/10 prices).

	DCCW			WaSCs*			DCWW's % of total		
	Water	Wastewater	Both	Water	Wastewater	Both	Water	Wastewater	Both
2009/10	8.39	15.75	24.14	92.36	188.20	280.56	9.1	8.4	8.6
2004/05	7.36	10.00	17.36	77.29	165.13	242.42	9.5	6.1	7.2
1999/00	7.24	9.54	16.78	75.61	158.93	234.54	9.6	6.0	7.2
1994/95	8.30	9.39	17.69	69.48	158.21	227.69	11.9	5.9	7.8
1990/91	5.04	7.01	12.05	63.58	148.45	212.03	7.9	4.7	5.7

*Water and sewerage companies.
Source: adapted from Ofwat (2010).

to be developed to an appreciably greater extent than for most of the sector, as seen in Table 1.

The 'regulated capital value' (RCV) – assets that, as determined by Ofwat, companies are allowed to have a return on – refers to new assets mainly developed since 1989. In Table 2, two phases of greater asset development than the rest of the sector can be noted: from 1990 to 1995 and from 2000 to 2005.

It is evident that under Glas Cymru's control DCWW has developed its asset base at a faster rate than the rest of the WaSCs. By 2010, DCWW's RCV was £2500 per customer, the second-highest amongst the 10 WaSCs. South West Water (Pennon Group) had a higher RCV per capita (£3300), reflecting the number of bathing areas it is responsible for, while the other eight WaSCs had RCVs per capita from £1400 to £2300 (Glas Cymru, 2011b).

Financial performance

In the three years prior to DCWW's sale to Glas Cymru, a deteriorating financial performance is evident, with profits falling at the operating level and being further impacted by rising interest payments. The shift from long-term (creditors over one year were £793 million in 1999 and £179 million in 2001) to short-term debt (current liabilities were £63 million in 1999 and £1288 million in 2001) also reflects increasing difficulties in securing long-term funding for the company (DCC, 2002).

The 7% difference between the assumed debt and DCWW's RCV formed the 'headroom' which allowed the bond issue to be developed. The May 2001 £1.91 billion bond issue brought down the average interest cost from approximately 9.5% to 7.0%. The refinancing lowered the net interest cost by £40–50 million per year in the first two years of operation. Finance leases were used to retire the higher coupon debt, lowering average interest to 6.3% by 2005, where they have more or less remained since. Table 3 summarizes changes in DCWW's profit and loss account. In 2009/10, average interest

Table 2. DCWW's 'regulated capital value' development in relation to the sector, 1990–2010 (year end, £ millions, 2009/10 prices)

	DCWW	WaSCs	DCWW's %
2009/10	3753	47,198	8.0
2004/05	3207	40,033	8.0
1999/00	2348	34,884	6.7
1994/95	1431	23,164	6.2
1989/90	548	11,080	4.9

Table 3. DCWW, profit and loss account (Y/E 31/03, £ millions).

	1999	2000	2001	2010
Revenues	459.3	476.9	441	688.2
Operating profit	166.4	152	131	175.8
Net interest	− 51.9	− 54.3	− 89.1	− 105.2
Pre-tax profit	115	98	41.6	70.6
Post-tax profit	106.1	99.1	46.9	67.5
Preference shares	− 14	− 14	− 14	0
Ordinary shares	− 44	− 15	0	0
Retained profit	48.1	70.1	32.9	67.5

Sources: DCC (2002), MBIA (2001), Glas Cymru (2011a).

rates fell exceptionally to 3.7%, compared with 6.6% in 2008/09 and 6.4% in 2010/11 (Glas Cymru, 2009, 2011b; MBIA, 2001).

By 2010, net debt had grown to £2669 million to finance the development of the company's asset base. Assuming the average cost of financing debt has broadly fallen from 9.5% to 6.5%, the difference was worth £80 million/y in interest saved. By 2010, the company's RCV was £1.07 billion above its net debt, with the implied gearing rate falling from 93% at the time of the bond issue to 71%. From 2011, all debt will be graded at least A/A3 as the last of the junior debt issued in 2001 was retired (Glas Cymru, 2011a, 2011b).

Ending dividend payments saved a further £58 million/y at 1999 levels for DCWW, while Hyder paid total dividends of £90 million in 1998/99 and £91 million in 1999/00. If we assume that DCWW's ordinary share dividend payments would have risen in line with inflation (as based on the Retail Price Index) they would have increased by 28% to £56 million. The combined savings from lower interest rates for debt and not needing to pay ordinary and preference share dividends looks to be in the region of £150 million/y by 2010.

Taking a look at the financial performance of DCWW and comparing it in with the water and sewerage companies as a whole between 2005/06 and 2009/10 is instructive (Table 4). Compared with the 7.1% share of net cash flow, DCWW's interest payments at 12.6% are high, reflecting the debt that Glas Cymru took on in 2001. DCWW was able to minimize its

Table 4. Cash flow for DCWW and the WaSCs, 2005/06 to 2009/10 (£ millions).

	DCWW	WaSCs	%
Net cash flow from operating activities	1903.2	26,831.5	7.1
Returns on investment and servicing of finance			
Net interest	− 663.2	− 5,249.7	12.6
Dividends paid on non-equity shares	0.0	− 115.6	0.0
Total	− 663.2	− 5,365.1	12.4
UK Corporation tax paid	− 1.2	− 1,756.7	0.1
Investing activities			
Purchase of fixed assets and subsidiaries	− 1161.5	− 16,265.2	7.1
Infrastructure renewals expenditure	− 333.8	− 3,366.3	9.9
Disposal of fixed assets	0.5	425.5	0.1
Movements on long term loans to group companies	0.0	− 1,220.4	0.0
Total	− 1494.7	− 20,425.3	7.3
Dividends paid on equity shares	0.0	− 10,037.1	0.0
Net cash flow before financing	− 256	− 10,752.6	2.4

UK Corporation Tax, and its investing activities were in line with the sector as a whole, although it was not involved in making loans to its parent company as was the case in some other companies. Most telling is the impact of not paying dividends (Ofwat, 2010).

Operating costs

By 2000, DCWW was seen as one of the poorer-performing companies in the sector when measured by Ofwat's operational criteria. Glas Cymru sought to address this, as well as holding down its operating costs (as seen in Table 5) through an outsourcing strategy whereby operations and maintenance work and capital projects were managed by third parties on multi-year contracts relating to each five-year AMP. This strategy also involved transferring contract risk to the outsourcing companies. By 2010, 85% of Glas Cymru's staff worked for outsourcing partners (Glas Cymru, 2011a, 2011b).

There has been a mixed record for service delivery, starting with poor performance as assessed by Ofwat in 2000 (eighth out of ten), which was addressed through the outsourcing contracts, resulting in being the best rated of the WaSCs between 2003 and 2005. Performance eased in subsequent years, falling to fourth in 2008/09 and seventh in 2009/10, which has resulted in a reappraisal of the outsourcing approach (Glas Cymru, 2002, 2005, 2009, 2011b).

Customer charges

As a not-for-profit company, Glas Cymru can allocate any retained profits either to customer rebates ('customer dividends') or to discretionary spending to improve service quality or environmental performance. Customer rebates worth £9 per household were made in 2003 and 2004. An £18 per customer rebate was made in 2006, a £20 rebate in 2007, £21 in 2008 and £22 in 2009, meaning that DCWW's bills were 12% above the average for the sector by 2010, against 23% above average in 2001. Table 6 shows how this is translating into real price changes in comparison with the other WaSCs. No other customer rebates were seen in the sector between 2000 and 2010 (Glas Cymru, 2011b). As noted below, the outsourcing strategy has changed since 2010 due to evolving circumstances.

In contrast, between 1989/90 and 1999/00, real prices for water services rose by 17% (33% for the sector) and by 54% for wastewater (42% for the sector) (Ofwat, 2000). As a result, the difference in average household bills has been eroded since 2000, as summarized in Table 7.

In total these rebates have cost £150 million. Discretionary spending of £50 million on environmental and service quality enhancements was made during AMP3 (2000–2005) and increased to £90 million during AMP4 (2005–2010).

Table 5. Operating expenditure, 2000–2010.

DCWW	1%
Severn Trent, Yorkshire	8%
Anglian	10%
Thames	11%
Northumbrian	19%
United Utilities	22%
Southern	25%
Wessex	26%
South West	34%

Table 6.   Real price change, 2000–2015.

DCWW	− 6%
Northumbrian, Severn Trent	− 3%
Anglian	− 2%
South West	2%
Yorkshire	3%
Southern	8%
United Utilities	11%
Thames	13%
Wessex	17%

Table 7.   Household water and sewerage bills in England and Wales, 2000/01 to 2014/15 (£ per household).

	2000/01	2010/11	2014/15
DCWW	342	399	374
WaSCs	301	365	365
Difference (£)	41	34	9
Difference (%)	14	9	2

Affordability and nonpayment

Household incomes continue to be lower in Wales than in England (Office for National Statistics, 2012), meaning that affordability remains a concern, especially amongst lower-income households, with 14% of households having a household income of less than 50% of the median in 2009 (see Table 8).

Since 1999, water companies in England and Wales are not allowed to cut off domestic supplies, and as of 2010 bad debts of £804 million have accrued by the sector. This included £22 million in write-downs by DCWW in 2009/10 and £19 million in 2008/09, equivalent to 3.2% of 2009/10 revenues. DCWW spent £2 million on implementing three customer-assistance schemes in 2009/10: Welsh Water Assist (capped bill of £228, used by 8000 households), Water Direct (£25 rebate when the bill is paid by social services, for 13,000 households) and a Customer Assistance Fund (for debt support, used by 3000 households).

Leakage reduction, water resources and the environment

Total leakage (distribution losses from DCWW's system and customer supply losses) was estimated at 446 million litres per day (J. Henry Schroder Wagg & Co., 1989) at the time of privatization. Leakage has been reduced from 410 Ml/day in 1996/97 to 226 Ml/day in

Table 8.   Household incomes in England and Wales (£ per capita).

	2000	2009
Wales	11,379	13,484
England	9,582	15,545

Table 9. Glas Cymru's water leakage, 2005–2011 (10^6 L per day).

	2005/06	2006/07	2007/08	2008/09	2009/10	2010/11
Total leakage	224	209	204	194.4	192.8	199.3
Distribution losses	192.9	182.6	177	168	161.7	156.3

2005/06 and 193 Ml/day in 2009/10, against Ofwat's targets of 225 Ml/day for 2005 and 195 Ml/day for 2010. The increase in total leakage in 2010/11 was due to exceptional winter conditions. Table 9 breaks out distribution losses from total leakage. The company anticipates reducing leakage to 184 Ml/day by 2015 (Glas Cymru, 2010, 2011a, 2011b).

The reduction in leakages means less water needs to be put into the distribution network when demand is constant. This appears to be the case, because 1143 Ml/day was distributed in 1988/89, against 1,050 Ml/day in 2000/01 and 816 Ml/day in 2009/10. Overall 327 Ml/day less water was abstracted between 1989/89 and 2009/10, with 253 Ml/day of this coming via leakage reduction.

Between 2000 and 2005, new or upgraded wastewater treatment facilities with a population equivalent of 2.56 million came into operation. In 1995, 55% of wastewater was subject to secondary or tertiary treatment, rising to 70% in 2000. By 2009, 99.8% was treated to at least secondary level and 29.6% to tertiary level. Of rivers, 78.5% were classed as being of good biological quality in 1990 by the Environment Agency, against 55.4% in England. By 2000, the proportion in Wales was static at 78.3% while rising to 69.0% in England. In 2008, the last year this testing criterion was used, 72.0% of rivers in England were classed as good and 88.0% in Wales (DCWW, 2010; Glas Cymru, 2011b; Lloyd Owen, 2011; MBIA, 2001).

In 1988, 10 of the 37 designated bathing waters failed the mandatory testing standards. Untreated effluents from a population equivalent of 690,000 were discharged into these waters. In 2010, all 81 designated bathing areas passed the EU mandatory standards, 72 also meeting the guideline standard, with 46 being awarded Blue Flag status (bathing water to EU guideline standard along with suitable recreational facilities), while a further 47 rural beaches, both designated and non-designated, were granted Green Coast status for high-quality bathing water (Glas Cymru, 2011a; J. Henry Schroder Wagg & Co., 1989).

Looking to 2015

DCWW is to deliver price reductions of £30 per customer before inflation in the current (2010–2015) regulatory period (Ofwat, 2009), calling for a 20% reduction in controllable operating spending (Glas Cymru, 2010). This means that further discretionary customer dividends will not be paid in 2010–2015. Outsourcing of operating and capital costs is falling from 85% to 60% due to two outsourcing contracts ending over future cost reductions and risk allocation. There are areas of concern, such as attempts to introduce artificial competition into the sector and 'inset appointments' whereby high-value housing developments are removed from the customer base. In addition, the continued weakness of the economy means that affordability will continue to be an issue. While the 2007–2008 banking crisis ended monoline 'wrap' insurance of debt, whereby an even higher debt rating could be obtained, as in the 2001 bond issue, the company has maintained a high-quality debt portfolio, which continues to keep financing costs down. In 2011, gearing fell from 70% to 67%, demonstrating that the model is able to respond to these challenges (Glas Cymru, 2011b).

Leakage is targeted to fall to 184 Ml/day in 2015, with carbon emissions planned to fall by 25% by 2015 and 50% by 2035. The latter will be attained by developing anaerobic digestion systems for generating energy from sewage sludge. In 2009/10, 2% of energy used was via renewable generation; this will rise to 10% from 2011 via a £100 million project for three digesters (Glas Cymru, 2011a, 2011b).

Conclusions

Despite some relative shortcomings on service delivery, it is evident that the not-for-profit model has managed to drive down operating and financing costs and customer bills faster than traditional private-sector utility management approaches, while ensuring that environmental obligations are also met. The model appears to be applicable for both private and public entities, as long as suitable finance is arranged which is related to the model's needs. Political and regulatory support is essential prior to the fund-raising and the model entering into operation. The role of outsourcing needs to be defined, especially in relation to the allocation of operating risk between the company and the third-party operators. The Glas Cymru model is not necessarily a magic bullet for the sector – it has yet to be replicated (Thomas, 2002) – but its validity has been demonstrated in this case.

Disclosure

David Lloyd Owen was a member of Glas Cymru Cyfyngedig from 2001 until his statutory retirement in 2011. Members, who are unpaid stakeholders, act as an external source of scrutiny instead of shareholders.

References

Bakker, K. J. (2003). From public to private to . . . mutual? Restructuring water supply governance in England and Wales. *Geoforum, 34*, 359–374.

DCC (2002). *Dwr Cymru Cyfyngedig: Directors' report and financial statements for the year ended 31 March 2002*. Brecon: Dŵr Cymru Welsh Water.

DCWW (Dŵr Cymru Welsh Water) (2010). *Dŵr Cymru Welsh Water June Return*. Brecon: Author.

Glas Cymru (2000) *Open letter to the First Minister*. Press release by Glas Cymru Cyf, 3rd November 2000, Glas Cymru Cyf, Brecon, Wales.

Glas Cymru (2002). *Annual general meeting*. Brecon: Glas Cymru Cyf.

Glas Cymru (2005). *Annual general meeting*. Brecon: Glas Cymru Cyf.

Glas Cymru (2009). *Annual general meeting*. Brecon: Glas Cymru Cyf.

Glas Cymru (2010). *Annual general meeting*. Brecon: Glas Cymru Cyf.

Glas Cymru (2011a). *Annual report & accounts, 2010–11*. Brecon: Glas Cymru Cyf.

Glas Cymru (2011b). *Annual general meeting*. Brecon: Glas Cymru Cyf.

J. Henry Schroder Wagg & Co (1989). *The Water Share Offers, Pathfinder Prospectus*. London: Author.

Lloyd Owen, D. A. (2011). *Pinsent Masons water yearbook 2011–12*. London: Pinsent Masons.

MBIA (2000). *Information memorandum: Multicurrency programme for the issuance of up to £3,000,000,000 guaranteed asset-backed bonds*. Paris: Imprima Group.

Office for National Statistics (2012). Regional gross disposable household income NUTS1 regional GDHI 1997–2010, (Excel sheet 25-Apr-2012). Retrieved from http://www.ons.gov.uk/ons/taxonomy/index.html?nscl=Regional+Gross+Disposable+Household+Income.

Ofwat (2000). *Water and sewerage bills, 2000–01*. Birmingham: Author.

Ofwat (2009). *Future water and sewerage charges 2010–15: Final determinations*. Birmingham: Author.

Ofwat (2010). *Financial performance and expenditure of the water companies in England and Wales 2009–10: Supporting information*. Birmingham: Author.

Thomas, C. (2002). Welsh Water: Role model or special case? *Utilities Policy, 10*, 99–114.

A critical examination of models and projections of demand in water utility resource planning in England and Wales

Gareth Walker

School of Geography and Environment, University of Oxford, United Kingdom

Demand modelling plays a vital role in water resource management yet has rarely been critically reviewed. This paper adopts a critical realist framework for a historical analysis of demand modelling practices and their role in long-term water resource management in England and Wales from 1945 to 2010. It then focuses on recent domestic demand models in the English and Welsh private water sector. A critique of scientific realist assumptions regarding demand models is presented and the role of the current regulatory environment in encouraging a highly strategic use of demand models is discussed. Policy recommendations toward more effective modelling practices are made.

Demand models and resource planning policy

Models and projections of demand form an essential component of long-term resource planning in water utilities. Supply-oriented planning has traditionally employed large, long-term, sunk investments which rely upon the accuracy of demand forecasts to ensure economic efficiency and security of supply. Policy has tended to regard such models of demand as scientific and objective in nature, their assumptions and projections remaining an uncontested basis for legitimizing supply projects. In more recent years, demand-side management has gained traction in resource management policy. Demand-side measures call for the use of increased efficiency in the consumption and allocation of water resources in securing a supply–demand balance and therefore represent demand as a system subject to analysis and manipulation, rather than passive prediction. The transition to demand management policy therefore comprises a change in the epistemic status of demand and its models. Policy must accept the contentious nature of demand models and projections; it must be aware of their discursive role in presenting a specific interpretation of demand which in turn prescribes specific approaches to demand management. Where this is not openly acknowledged and integrated into the planning process, there is a risk of demand models being employed to serve the strategic interests of their originators, rather than to reach socially optimal outcomes.

This paper employs a school of philosophy called 'critical realism' to analyze the structure, content, and strategic context of demand models and projections in resource planning in England and Wales from 1945 to 2010. Through critiquing the status of models as objective and scientific, the analysis demonstrates how models have been employed strategically as discursive tools to legitimize resource management strategies. Simultaneously, the role of institutional structures in reinforcing specific approaches to demand modelling as well as shaping power and information asymmetries between stakeholder groups in resource planning is outlined. The paper concludes by discussing the need for new approaches which openly acknowledge the uncertainty inherent in demand models and their role in wider resource planning governance procedures. Specifically, UK policy must address the conflicting incentives and strong information asymmetries which privatization and its regulatory environment have generated.

Models of demand as scientific knowledge

Boyd (1983) outlines 'scientific realism' as assuming that (1) a model's theoretical terms are understood to refer to relatively similar observable and non-observable external objects and forces; (2) models are confirmed as true through a process of scientific observation and methodological processes; (3) the historical progress of models is a case of successively more accurate approximations to the truth; and (4) the reality which models describe is largely independent of the scientist's thoughts or theoretical commitments.

Constructivist objections to scientific realism as applied to models of consumption point to their diverse and often incommensurable assumptions, observing that they do not form a consistent epistemic body of research (Sharp et al., 2011). The independence of knowledge derived from models is also questioned through observing their prescriptive nature; models of consumption are situated within a spectrum from economic-atomistic to structural-cultural models which often reflect the so-called 'deep versus light green' debate surrounding sustainable consumption (Fuchs & Lorek, 2005). Furthermore, projections and scenarios may not only endorse one course of events (Midttun & Baumgartner, 1986; Nielsen & Karlsson, 2007) but also make others inconceivable (Slaughter, 2004). A positivist–post-positivist debate emerges, in which the need for rational scientific enquiry is pitted against a need to make the biases and vested interests inherent in models explicit (Patomäki & Wight, 2000).

Critical realism makes the case that the positivist–post-positivist debate stems from a failure to separate questions of a reality independent of the observer (ontology) and the observer's socially embedded, restricted knowledge of that reality (epistemology). The scientific process is understood to be partially socialized and therefore fallible, but still relating to an external material reality and therefore subject to the scientific rationale of hypothesis testing and instrumental reliability. Social systems are argued to be 'open' or non-stationary in behaviour, generating events and temporary tendencies which emerge for periods of time, and which are in turn subjectively experienced. Scientific enquiry into such systems is therefore a constant process of abduction and hypothesis testing in which partially socialized models are employed to explain temporary regularities (Bhaskar, 1986).

The research presented employs critical realism to examine demand modelling in England and Wales in two stages. In the first, a historical analysis of the practice of long-term water resource planning and the role of demand models in England and Wales from 1945 to 2010 is carried out. The models employed in the industry are assessed in terms of the commensurability of their mathematical form, their proposed generative mechanisms, and their quantitative accuracy in projection. To test the socialized nature of models, a critical discourse analysis (Fairclough, 2003) is applied to documents which site or generate water demand data from 1945 to 2010. Sources include national resource planning strategies, water company plans, industry regulatory reports, water policy documents, independent research body outputs, and non-governmental group lobbying documents. Specific documents are referenced throughout the article, and a complete list of documents reviewed is available from the author upon request. Having presented historical evidence for the vulnerability of long-term projections to unexpected shifts in demand and the socialized nature of demand modelling, the paper then addresses the specific case of domestic per capita modelling in contemporary water resource planning in England and Wales. A survey of the production, distribution and consumption of demand forecasts in water resource planning is presented, as well as data from 20 semi-structured interviews with key informants within the water industry, research bodies, and regulators. The interviews addressed, in order of discussion: (1) the structure and performance of demand models and the influence of regulation; (2) the impacts of (1) on approaches to demand management; (3) the role of demand model outputs in the negotiation of future resource scenarios with regulators; and (4) an open ended discussion. Interview anonymity was assured and so identities cannot be disclosed. A copy of the interview structure is available from the author.

Results

Research outcomes are summarized below and are followed by sections detailing research findings through a historical analysis of demand modelling and resource planning in England and Wales. The historical analysis is split into three periods of reconceptualization and explores how new models are actively selected and retained by a wider context of rules, social norms, institutions, laws and policies, collectively referred to as the 'mode of regulation' (Benassy, Boyer, & Gelpi, 1979; Lipietz, 1986). The analysis then focuses on the specific case of domestic demand modelling in order to expose the impact of conflicting incentives and institutional arrangements on the demand modelling process.

A striking outcome of the quantitative analysis of long-term (5 to 10 years) national demand projections in England and Wales from 1945 to 2010 was the lack of any significant improvement in accuracy. Instead, a period of increased error in projection corresponded to a period of rapid socio-economic restructuring in the 1970s, highlighting the vulnerability of traditional demand forecasting to unexpected and complex social change (Figures 1 and 2). This period of high error coincided with a crisis in policy concerning the legitimacy of demand models and the resource strategies they prescribed. In response, the mathematical structure of models and the causal mechanisms evoked to explain demand were radically revised and replaced, suggesting a degree of incommensurability between models (see "Endorsed methods" and "Ways of representing" in Figure 3). In the last decade (2000–2010), water policy in the England and Wales has attempted to address the vulnerability of longer-term projections to complex social and climate change issues through moving away from 'models as predictions' and towards 'models as scenarios'. This has required a new form of demand modelling which explicitly acknowledges uncertainty and addresses diverse stakeholder perceptions. However, this is undermined by current institutional arrangements.

In terms of institutional design, the analysis confirms the significance not only of changes in the structure and theoretical grounding of models, but also in the context in which they are produced and shared. Wider discursive institutional structures define the conditions under which models are considered to produce legitimate knowledge (see "Epistemic frameworks" in Figure 3) and the channels through which models are produced, distributed and consumed (see "Discourse practices" in Figure 3). Major changes in model structure and practice coincided with the institutional restructuring of the water industry, suggesting a significant influence of institutional design on the successful uptake of new modelling approaches. This has significant policy implications for demand modelling in the

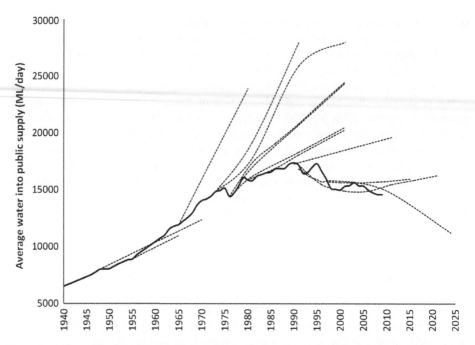

Figure 1. Selected projections of water into supply (dashed) vs. reported (solid), England and Wales. Notes: Pre-1955 "water into supply" data based on industry surveys acknowledged as incomplete and hence likely to be underestimates. Post-1955 data based on standardized industry reporting. Projection sources displayed (in chronological order of origin) are: Ministry of Health (1949); CAWC (1959); industry opinion as quoted in Skeat (1965); "locally based" industry projections from WRB (1973); "alternative" government projections from WRB (1973); CWPU (1976); "upper" projection from CWPU (1977b); NWC (1982); composite of water company projections from NRA (1992); "managed" "most likely" projection from NRA (1993); composite company projections from Ofwat (1994b); "delta" scenario from EA (2001); composite of water company business plan projections submitted to Ofwat in 2009.

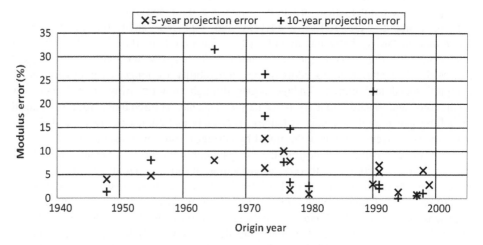

Figure 2. Modulus error for 5- and 10-year projections, sorted by year of origin. Note: Errors calculated on discrepancy between "water into supply" and projected values. Data sources listed under Figure 1.

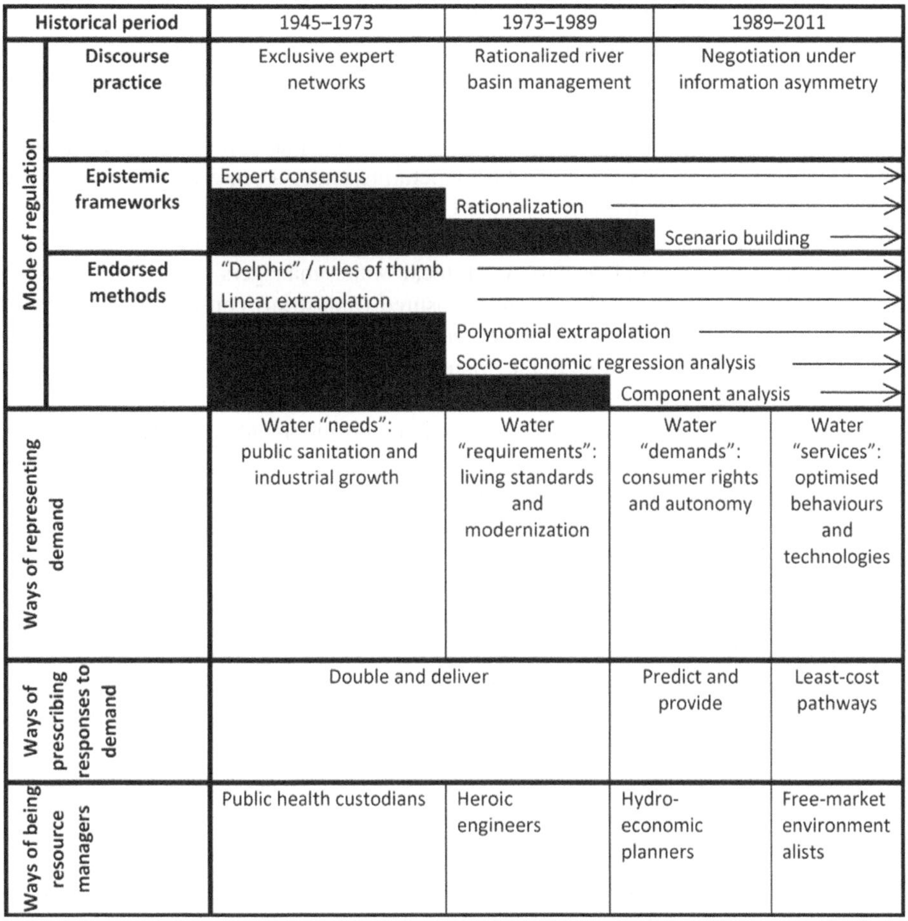

Historical period		1945–1973	1973–1989	1989–2011	
Mode of regulation	**Discourse practice**	Exclusive expert networks	Rationalized river basin management	Negotiation under information asymmetry	
	Epistemic frameworks	Expert consensus ⟶			
			Rationalization ⟶		
				Scenario building ⟶	
	Endorsed methods	"Delphic" / rules of thumb ⟶			
		Linear extrapolation ⟶			
			Polynomial extrapolation ⟶		
			Socio-economic regression analysis ⟶		
				Component analysis ⟶	
Ways of representing demand		Water "needs": public sanitation and industrial growth	Water "requirements": living standards and modernization	Water "demands": consumer rights and autonomy	Water "services": optimised behaviours and technologies
Ways of prescribing responses to demand		Double and deliver		Predict and provide	Least-cost pathways
Ways of being resource managers		Public health custodians	Heroic engineers	Hydro-economic planners	Free-market environment alists

Figure 3.   Representations and practices surrounding demand modelling across time.

context of the current privatized water industry, as standardized regulatory reporting tends to resist experimentation and innovation in demand modelling methods.

Finally, models not only provide projections of future conditions, but specific representations of demand and endorsed responses which are shaped by wider socio-political contexts (see "Ways of representing", "Ways of prescribing" and "Ways of being" in Figure 3). A historical analysis shows many instances of demand models being employed discursively as a mechanism to underpin coordinated action in resource planning. Models provide a shared, intersubjective rationalization and explanation of observed demand patterns and prescribe and legitimize resource planning decisions (Jessop, 2004). As such, they are powerful strategic tools which often reflect the interests and strategies of their originators. This is of particular relevance to the current institutional context of privatized resource planning, where principal-agent problems drive a strategic use of modelling in transferring financial and political risk between government, regulators, and private companies.

1945 to 1973: the age of experts and no surprises

Post-war water resource planning in Britain was heavily influenced by a remit of rehousing and economic development and carried out by a self-governed group of engineers and experts, later formalized in 1963 through establishment of the Water Resource Board (WRB) which took on a central advisory role for all resource planning in England and Wales (Guy & Marvin, 1995; McCulloch, 2006). Operating under a sense of stewardship over public health and with the authority of expert knowledge, successive committees assessed current and future water consumption at a national scale. Each assessment consisted of a fairly informal and incomplete survey of local water managers' "best estimates" of unmeasured (domestic and leakage) and measured (industrial) consumptions, and each described a vaguely linear increase of net water into supply and per capita consumption (PCC).[1] Each attributed this trend to the "rising standards of health and personal hygiene" (Ministry of Health, 1949) which had seen dramatic increases through the nineteenth century as well as the period of post-war economic development and growth in industry (CAWC, 1959, 1962; Hassan, 1998; Ministry of Health, 1949). This interpretation cemented the view that there was "no reason to suppose that this increase will not continue" (CAWC, 1959). Water demand was essentially a black box, external to the industry, linear in behaviour, and to be accommodated; hence resource planners "should not themselves determine the pattern of development" (CAWC, 1971, p. 45).

The consensus generated through successive advisory committees and later through the WRB meant that a rigorous examination of the assumptions driving demand forecasts was unnecessary where a cautious, business-as-usual, linear extrapolation would suffice. Herrington (1973, p. 30) summarizes the dominant process for legitimizing demand forecasts at the time:

> A forecast based on something little more advanced than a hunch (usually extrapolation) may be quoted over and over again, and often come to be uncritically accepted by those charged with the prediction of demands.

Any suggestion that projections were overestimates was deemed an unnecessary risk, and attempts to influence consumption were strictly limited by concerns of public health and economic production. In commenting on the possibility of demand management, the Ministry of Health (1949) stated, "it is not within the national interest to attempt to restrict the consumption of water put to legitimate use" and warned that "the task of providing homes for all with modern sanitation will take many years to complete". Similarly, any attempt to influence industrial consumption "might do serious damage to individual industries" (Herrington, 1973, p. 3) and in any case it was "beyond the powers of any single water undertaking to decide what was appropriate in each case and to refuse to supply any more" (HLG, 1963, p. 3).

As housing and industrial growth accelerated over the 1960s, resource planners altered their trend-based approach to include exponential projections of growth in consumption, and by 1973, the Water Resources Board estimated that water into supply would effectively double, from 14,000 ML/day in 1973 to 28,000 ML/day in 2001 (Figure 1: WRB, 1973, the highest projected consumption for year 2000).

1974 to 1989: restructuring and rationalization

The practice of demand modelling and its place within water resource planning shifted dramatically in the period from 1974 to 1989. While the WRB had achieved consensus in representations of demand and its projection, it was at most an advisory body (McCulloch, 2006). The government argued for an authority able to manage competing demands and coordinate development at the river basin scale (CAWC, 1971; WRB, 1973), and in 1973 the industry was consolidated into 10 river basin authorities and 24 water supply companies. The National Water Council (NWC) and Central Water Planning Unit (CWPU) were established as a means of standardization in measurement and reporting across water authorities. The CWPU keenly observed in its annual report that reorganization provided "the opportunity for rationalising the administrative mechanisms by which the industry formulates its forwards demands" (CWPU, 1976, p. 18). In contrast to the expert-driven forecasts of the WRB, the legitimacy of demand forecasts was now defined by the formalized approaches embodied in this new institutional structure.

> Until 1974 responsibility for demand forecasting lay with a large number of mostly small water supply undertakings and sewerage and sewage disposal authorities. Only since 1974, when 10 large Water Authorities were created, has there been much interest in the formal modelling of water demands and discharges. (CWPU, 1977c, p. v)

This drive for a standardized approach coincided with a dramatic change in the behaviour of demand. From 1975 onwards, economic recession struck and industrial demand not only changed pace, but began to reverse (Figure 4). Similarly, a period of unusually low rainfall in 1975–76 and subsequent restrictions on consumption saw the first observed case of a decrease in domestic consumption (visible in Figure 4 as a dip at 1976), triggering the first genuine discussions concerning the potential of public communications and efficiency measures to contribute to security of supply (NWC, 1978). Linear projections fell out of favour on both their empirical and philosophical merits. The CWPU put forward an almost Humean criticism of the inductive logic which had previously supported trend analysis:

> Even where the past trend has been stable and is easy to identify there is no guarantee that the trends will not change in the future, and for this reason projections of past trends cannot be regarded as forecasts in the strict sense of the word. (CWPU, 1977b, p. 3)

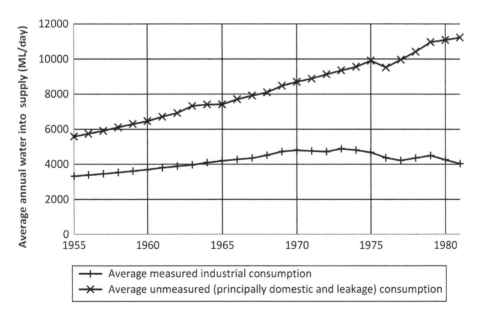

Figure 4.   Reported average measured and unmeasured consumption of water in public supply in England and Wales, 1955–1981. Data sources: CAWC (1959); CWPU (1977b); WSA (1990).

Figure 5. Measured industrial consumption and industrial production in England and Wales, 1955–1990. Data sources: Index of industrial production ONS (2012); Measured industrial water consumption (CAWC 1959); CWPU (1977b); WSA (1990).

Extrapolation and trend analysis were ill-equipped for the task of explaining a complex system such as consumption because they made "no attempt to understand why consumption is rising or falling" (CWPU, 1976). Planners were forced to re-evaluate the mathematical structure of their models and the causal mechanisms they enlisted. Multiple studies investigating the predictive power of socio-economic variables in both metered (industrial) and unmetered (domestic and leakage) demand were carried out. The results were not encouraging; a movement of employment away from manufacturing to the service sector had dissociated economic growth from metered demand (CWPU, 1977b; Figure 5). Studies which attempted more complex trend analysis or the use of socio-economic factors in explaining unmeasured domestic consumption revealed little more than a strong relation to occupancy and multiple possible trends (CWPU, 1978a, 1978b). As a result, water planners began to speculate that the assumed mechanism of increasing basic services and economic growth no longer agreed with observation, and that in turn the "scope for additional uses is limited" (CWPU, 1977b, p. 24). Ultimately this left planners with the unsettling conclusion that trends in future demand "will be attributable to different factors from those which have been important in the past" (CWPU, 1977b, p. 3).

The loss of legitimacy in industry demand projections coincided with a growing resistance to large capital projects, and as a result demand forecasts became a key battleground for competing philosophies of resource management. Kielder Reservoir, approved in 1973 (prior to the shift in demand behaviour), was becoming an increasingly obvious example of the vulnerability of large irreversible capital investments to inaccuracies in demand projections. By the time of its completion in 1982 at a cost of £150 million, it was evident that most of the water would not be required and was earmarked for transfer schemes (NRA, 1995a). This sense of economic evaluation driving the scrutiny of demand projections was summarized by the Monopolies and Mergers Commission in their review of water authority economic efficiency:

> Given its high capital intensity, avoidance of undue premature provision of facilities is a matter of importance to cost containment and budgeting. [...] the fixed capital resources involved in the supply or provision of water services are buried or otherwise immovable. Hence forecasts must relate not simply to total demand but to demand in particular areas and localities if the right service is to be provided at the right location at the right time. (MMC, 1981, p. 166)

In 1976, only three years after the approval of the Kielder Water Scheme, plans drawn up by the Southern Water Authority to flood 700 acres of farmland at Broad Oak were rejected on the basis of their use of linear projections in demand forecasting, as well as a lack of emphasis on water conservation in the form of leakage control (NRA, 1995a). A similar enquiry into raising the levels of Ennerdale Reservoir would later (in 1980) be rejected entirely on the basis of failing to take control of leakage into consideration (NRA, 1995a).

In response to the need to reclaim authority over demand projections, the water industry was forced to begin picking apart the "unmeasured" component of demand which for so long had been considered a black box of linear consumption and which, by then, represented the majority of water being placed into supply. The incidence of domestic monitoring programmes steadily increased from reorganization onwards (Figure 6), and with this increase in data came the need to develop new models of consumption. This led to the establishment of an informal network of water planners, engineers and economists who began meeting regularly under the banner of the Water Use Studies Group with a remit to propose new modelling approaches (NWC, 1982, p. 5). By 1981, the group was formalized. It included all regional water authorities, and further members from the CWPU and NWC, and became the channel through which information and best practices concerning demand modelling in the industry were communicated.

In light of the failure of top-down modelling approaches, the group began to emphasize bottom-up, reductionist approaches which explicitly sought to identify the causal mechanisms driving demand.

> Ultimately from the point of view of the development of demand forecasting models, it is causation which is of greater interest, and regression analysis, however successful it may appear, can never be considered the final word. (CWPU, 1978b, p. 13)

A "component" approach to demand forecasting was promoted which aimed to isolate domestic consumption from leakage and then further reduce domestic PCC into its

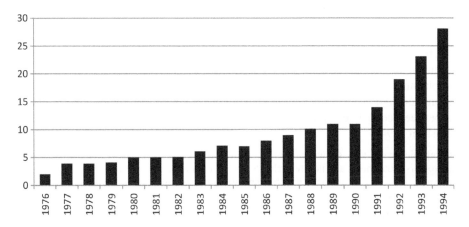

Figure 6. Number of domestic consumption monitors running in given year. Digitized copy of graph in NRA (1995b).

constituent components of appliance ownership, frequency of use, and volume per use (CWPU, 1975b). The group hoped to "construct a series of 'universal equations' for per capita household demand" (CWPU, 1975b, p. 2) which would serve alongside empirical data as a basis for demand forecasting. In reality, the approach did not represent a causal model, but served to provide a vocabulary through which to express uncertainties regarding the drivers of demand. While great effort had been put into quantifying the causal factors and providing an objective means of projection, the industry once again resorted to a consensus amongst experts as its main means of projecting consumption, albeit on a more informed and detailed platform.

> Medium-term forecast makes use of an economic analysis of past patterns of demand. Beyond five years the reliability of historically based equations is considered to be limited and a more judgmental approach is used. A Demand Forecasting Group within SWA arrives at a consensus on the longer-term forecast taking into account projections of various types of consumption and peak levels of demand. (MMC, 1986, p. 93)

By the 1980s, the component approach was widely endorsed as a replacement for trend-based and socioeconomic projections. Discussion began in earnest to establish a "national consumption monitor" which would provide component-based information. However, as the prospect of privatization became more obvious, the collaborative culture of the Demand Studies Group came into question. As one former member of the group observed:

> As privatisation approached there was a mood that "why should water authorities who had invested a great deal of work share the findings?" The group was broken up by privatization although there was some contact between individual companies. (Interview subject, 2011)

1989 to 2005: regulatory games and strategic constructs

The privatization of the water industry in 1989 critically changed the distribution of information within the industry and the channels through which it was shared. As Shapiro and Willig (1990) observe, a key aspect of privatization is that it "gives informational autonomy to a party who is not under public control". Where private water company and societal objectives were misaligned, regulatory intervention became necessary and regulators were tasked with clawing back information from companies to inform policy. Under these conditions of misaligned incentives and asymmetric information distribution, a principal-agent problem ensued in which demand projections became a part of a "game" between companies and regulators.

Tasked with addressing a lack of competition and incentives for economic efficiency within the industry, the Water Services Regulatory Authority (Ofwat) employed a price-cap mechanism which required companies to report on projected costs and revenues over a five-year planning period. An unintended consequence was that forecasts for measured consumption significantly affected projected revenue and in turn represented a contested area between companies and Ofwat. As Ofwat noted in its initial analysis of demand forecasts in 1994:

> Companies have also shown caution in their forecasts of water delivered to measured customers (households and non-households) in order not to be optimistic over future levels of revenue, hence causing some understatement of the future level of demand for water. (Ofwat, 1994a, p. 11)

As domestic meter penetration began to grow, so too did the influence of demand projections on projected revenue. Ofwat repeatedly cited this misalignment of incentives in periodic reviews and tended to revise measured demand projections upwards in approved company business plans (Ofwat, 1999, 2000). However, privatization also tasked the National Rivers Authority[1] (NRA) with a duty to assess "actual and prospective demand for water" to inform environmental protection and national resource planning. Contrary to Ofwat's view of demand as an indicator of revenue, the NRA interpreted demand under a new philosophy of "demand management".

> In the past, it has generally been practice to develop new resource to keep ahead of the rise in demand. Now, however, it is considered appropriate to identify what steps can be taken to control demand to see if new developments are really essential. (NRA, 1993)

By 1989, unmeasured demand, which included both leakage and domestic consumption, represented 72% of water placed into supply and so became the focus of the NRA's new management philosophy. Increasing unmeasured consumption was reconceptualized from an indicator of increased health and modern living standards to one of a consumer-driven demand for new levels of services embodied in high-consumption goods combined with redefined standards of "comfort, cleanliness and convenience" (Shove, 2003). Government policy redrew the boundaries of efficiency in line with this new model of consumption; beyond leakage reduction, efficiency was now to include economic principles of demand control through expanded domestic metering, the regulation and incentives towards efficiency improvements in products, and the provision of information to consumers in support of informed economic decision making. As the Department of Environment (DOE) outlined in its policy document *Using Water Wisely*:

> In order for ordinary citizens to make the maximum contribution to greater efficiency, not only in droughts but all year round, they need to have authoritative and comprehensive guidance readily available about preventing waste, and what are the most efficient ways of using water, and the relative costs. (DOE, 1992, p. 7)

A Pareto definition of optimized consumption defined not only what demand management was, but also what it wasn't. In particular, the autonomy of the consumer was not to be questioned, and any actions to address the drivers of demand for these services themselves were to be avoided.

> These uses are legitimate and necessary for the continuance of our way of life. Sometimes they are of positive benefit as in the case of a properly treated discharge, helping to supplement how the river flows. (NRA, 1993, p. 4)

This perspective continues to this day in the oft-quoted slogan of the leading water-efficiency body in the UK: "the key to water efficiency is reducing waste, not restricting use" (Waterwise, 2012).

These new concepts of demand led the NRA to interpret the calculation of "prospective demand" as a representation of its own policy aspirations rather than a summary of company forecasts. Arguing that measures to impact leakage and domestic efficiency were easily achievable, NRA forecasts became a form of coercive argument in resource planning. As the NRA noted in its consultation document at the time:

> It is considered that the "managed" forecast represents a realistic basis for the focus of the development strategy work as it is believed that it incorporates realistic assumptions of growth together with easily available measures in relation to demand management. (NRA, 1993, p. 3)

While it was recognized that NRA and water company demand projections might not align, it was not considered to be a pressing issue because they were initially in vague agreement (NRA, 1993). However, discrepancies in regulatory and water company understandings of the role of demand forecasting in resource planning would become more apparent as resource planning was progressively "reregulated" (Bakker, 2003). Successive droughts, in particular that of 1995, resulted in water shortages that drove unprecedented public hostility towards the privatized water industry and sparked a series of reviews and regulatory interventions. In particular, the new definition of waste was on the agenda. While customers were urged to reduce wasteful behaviour and outdoor use, water companies were in return accused of not addressing leakage (POST, 1995).

Over the following years, regulation's influence on demand forecasting and reporting grew, and with it the competition between companies and regulators to shape the discourse surrounding demand. Demand was no longer exogenous to resource planning – to be objectively predicted and responded to; instead, projections took on a hybrid form of policy aspiration, economic planning and resource management. This left the identity of projections somewhat ambiguous and brought forward the risk of losing the shared rationalization of demand which was so important for collaborative planning. Having been granted a consultative role in the development of water company 25-year resource plans,[2] the Environment Agency[3] (EA) became increasingly aggressive in promoting demand projections as a reflection of the government's policy aspiration of driving down consumption. In 2005, an independent body (Waterwise) was established by industry with a remit to reduce the upward trend in PCC by 2010, and a government-supported network of water companies, regulators, local government bodies and building research bodies was formed with a specific remit to "reduce per capita consumption in households". Similarly, the government Department for Environment, Food and Rural Affairs (Defra) established an "aspirational aim" of reducing PCC to 130 litres by 2030 (Defra, 2008) and gradually introduced new regulations for newly built properties to limit water consumption to approximately 125 litres. Meanwhile, Ofwat interpreted demand management in economic terms of increased metering and tariff reform, combined with a framework of "least cost planning" which assessed "economic levels" of leakage reduction and demand management. In both cases, the need to regulate leakage and domestic consumption led to renewed emphasis on the need to differentiate between their relative contributions to unmeasured demand – an issue repeatedly identified as a weakness in regulation (HOCCPA, 2007; Ofwat, 1996, 1997). In the absence of universal metering, the component approach promoted prior to privatization was adopted as a means of calculating leakage and domestic consumption separately (Herrington, 1996; UKWIR, 1995, 1997). The EA began to require companies to project component trajectories up to 2035 in their resource plans, establishing the approach as the principle means of regulating and measuring the impact of policy mechanisms and aspirations on future domestic demand.

To address the problem of information asymmetry, regulators began to rely more heavily on inter-company comparisons of PCC and leakage figures as indicators for "reasonable" estimates. Unfortunately, a growing picture of high spatial variance in PCC emerged, which the industry struggled to explain, and once again the problem of providing a causal model for demand re-emerged in the privatized context; studies repeated the search for explanatory variables in socio-economic data and once again failed (Chambers, 2005; EA, 1998). A tension was developing between the need to standardize and compare demand projections, the seemingly unexplainable spatial variance of demand patterns across water companies, and poorly defined boundaries between economic, resource-planning and policy interpretations of demand projections.

A case study of domestic demand modelling

Domestic demand represents the majority component of water into supply and as a result PCC has become the focus of many of the issues in demand projection and regulation

Table 1.   Sources cited for observed demand in England and Wales.

Sources cited for observed demand	Not used/ mentioned in document	Primary observation	Demographic analysis	Referenced third-party bodies				
				UK Water Industry Research (UKWIR)	Market Transformation Programme (MTP)	Water Research Council (WRC)	Waterwise	National Policy Targets
Household demand	0%	84%	12%	0%	0%	4%	4%	4%
Per capita demand	4%	52%	16%	0%	0%	0%	0%	4%
Micro component values	28%	56%	0%	12%	24%	16%	36%	12%

Notes: Percentage based on: "household demand" or "per capita demand" or "micro component values". Based on complete sample of draft Water Resource Management Plans submitted to the E.A.Only sources which occurred in more than 5% of water resource management plans sampled in January and February of 2011 are included. Resource planning documents do not represent a complete summary of data used by companies, and are therefore only an approximate measure of the relative role of information sources.

Table 2.   Sources cited for projected domestic demand in Enlgand and Wales.

Sources cited for projected demand	Not used	Demographic analysis	Meter impacts	Referenced third-party bodies							
				UKWIR	MTP	WRC	Waterwise	CCDEW study	Herrington (1999)	EA	National Policy Targets
Household demand	0%	0%	32%	8%	0%	4%	0%	16%	0%	0%	32%
Per capita demand	4%	12%	20%	12%	0%	12%	0%	40%	4%	8%	56%
Micro component values	24%	0%	4%	4%	32%	16%	16%	16%	16%	20%	12%

See notes for Table 1.

reviewed above. Having identified multiple and conflicting conceptualizations and incentives relating to demand modelling, as well as the limited performance of long-term demand projections, the research focused specifically on the construction of PCC projections. A review of resource plans (see Table 1 notes for details), reveals that current and projected domestic PCC figures are constructed through several distinct epistemic frameworks. Estimates of current domestic demand are a hybrid of primary observation through company metering, surveys and monitoring programmes; demographic analysis; referenced third-party sources; and national average policy values (Table 1). Projected demand also represents a mixture of economic and demographic extrapolation and modelling; referenced third-party projections; and government policy aspirations (Table 2). This mixture of empiricism, consensus and aspiration as the driving frameworks for legitimizing knowledge concerning demand in turn creates tensions and conflicts in the interpretation of final figures.

In observed demand, the need to accurately describe local variance in domestic consumption patterns conflicted with the widespread practice of circular referencing, in which isolated studies would continually be re-referenced until they were gradually accepted as "standard", an issue previously identified by Herrington in the 1970s. In projected demand, the status of model outputs as scientific "projections" conflicted with both circular referencing and the inclusion of government policy targets. For example, while many companies project new properties to conform to a building code standard of 125 litres per head per day, original documents outlining the use of those building codes specifically stated:

> It [the Building Code estimate of water consumption] is also not capable of calculating the actual potable water consumption of a new dwelling. Behaviour and changing behaviour can also have an effect on the amount of potable water used throughout a home. (CLG, 2009, p. 5)

A further prominent example was the government "aspiration" of achieving a PCC of 130 per day by 2030 (Defra, 2008), which over the course of the resource planning process gradually assumed the form of a target (in the perception of many of the interviewees). While a broad expectation was placed on companies to demonstrate progress towards this figure as well as a mandatory water efficiency target of one litre per property per day (Ofwat, 2007), the aspiration will ultimately be missed under current industry projections (Figure 7). Demand projections therefore struggled to reflect local variances while simultaneously accounting for homogeneous national average targets employed by policy and regulation. This relatively murky process of constructing PCC figures was noted by Portsmouth Water in its resource plan:

> The Environment Agency collected micro component data from the water companies for the Draft Water Resources Management Plans (May 2008). This data was not published by the Environment Agency and some of the companies radically altered their pcc forecasts for the Final Water Resources Management Plan. Radical changes in pcc would have required a major revision to the micro components. There does not appear to have been any public debate about the logic of such major changes to micro component. (Portsmouth Water, 2009, p. 3)

Triggers and alarm bells

The impact of modelling demand without expressing uncertainty or epistemology became particularly obvious in cases where projections were scrutinized by regulators. Demand projections were often described in interviews as setting off "triggers" or "alarm bells" with regulators under specific conditions. One trigger was a projected but narrow supply–demand deficit, in which companies were considering resource options such as reservoirs. As seen in earlier cases prior to privatization, the environmental and social concerns surrounding such developments triggered a scrutiny of demand forecasts as a means of contesting their legitimacy. In the case of South East Water (one of three companies brought to public enquiry over their 2006 resource plans), the EA's statement of case outlined that:

> Resource (and in particular reservoir) developments appear to feature heavily in South East Water's selected options and more so than seems necessary, particularly if demand forecast and demand management assumptions are critically examined. (EA, 2010, p. 5)

The EA correctly observed the large uncertainty surrounding future demand forecasting assumptions and the possibility of alternative trajectories of demand. However, the debate surrounding the grounds for generating future projections emphasized the possible, the probable and the reasonable interchangeably, and as a result the final conclusions of the planning inspector simply accepted that under conditions of high uncertainty, a competition over the "correct" forecasts was futile:

> Water resources plan-making is principally based on the forecasting of water demand and water supply over the planning period of 25 years. Forecasting is not an exact science. It cannot predict future levels of water supply or water demand with certainty, and it does not purport to produce the 'right' answer. The statutory language recognizes this, hence, for example, the Act requires the plan to contain '*the water undertaker's estimate*' of the quantities of water required to meet its obligations, and the '*likely*' sequence and timing of final plan options. Differences of opinion will arise as to what assumptions or judgments should or should not have been made, as to the reliability and interpretation of data upon which forecasts are based, and so on. These inevitable uncertainties increase as the forecasting period runs into the future. (Planning Inspectorate, 2010, p. 11)

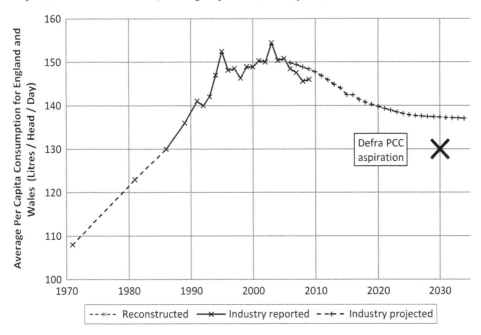

Figure 7. Reconstructed, reported, and projected average per capita consumption (PCC) for England and Wales. Per capita consumption data sources: Reconstructed: 1971, 1981, Herrington (1996); Industry reported: 1986, 1989, WSA (1990); 1991, Ofwat (1992); 1992–1994, Ofwat (1993–1995); 1995–2000, Ofwat (1997–2001); 2000–2006, Ofwat (2003–2007); 2006–2008, Ofwat (2011). Industry projected: sourced from "Normal Year 2006/07 Baseline" projections in draft Water Company Resource Management Plans submitted to E.A. in 2007 (weighted by population).

The second "alarm bell" sprang from the use of comparative regulation in assessing demand forecasts. Where companies were identified as being outliers, their projections were often challenged and recalculated to be in better agreement with neighbouring company assumptions. However, the industry still struggles to explain the remaining variance in demand projections (Figure 8), and, partially in response, an informal network of water resource planners has developed to share information and generate consensus over a legitimate means of generating demand forecasts. This Demand Forecasting Group shows a striking similarity in function and provenance to the Water Use Studies Group of the 1970s. However, comparative regulation bears the risk of artificially normalizing projections; consensus may be reassuring when arrived at independently, but when artificially generated it may simply represent an endorsed narrative or "majority rules" opinion.

Demand models and the transfer of risk

The lack of transparency in the generation of demand forecasts and their uncertainty, the conflicting incentives of various actors involved in the modelling process, and the asymmetry of information between them have combined to turn demand forecasting into a form of risk negotiation (Figure 9). Demand forecasts become intensely contested narratives of future events, each legitimizing different objectives, each relying on very different epistemic frameworks. These risks are broadly divided between short-term economic and long-term resource planning, and between private company and regulatory incentives.

In resource planning, the risk of policy failure is negotiated against risk to security of supply. As Bristol Water observed, any failure of government policy concerning demand would directly affect supply–demand balances. This issue was particularly evident in the most recent public enquiries. In Thames Water's recent experience, per capita projections formed a component (but not a dominant one) of the debate surrounding the legitimacy of their plan. Thames Water's resistance to assuming complete ownership of domestic demand trends is summarized in a commissioned report presented in their resource plans:

> At this moment in time, Thames Water are justified in their statement that achieving the vision is particularly high risk for companies with a supply demand deficit. The vision should be aimed for, but there is considerable uncertainty in the outcomes and timescales of achieving this and therefore, planning on the basis of 130 l/h/d is potentially high risk. (Artesia Consulting, 2008)

Similarly, in the Planning Inspector's report on South East Water's public enquiry, it was concluded that:

> The demand forecasts in a water resources management plan should be "realistic", rather than purely aspirational. This is because the consequences of having too little water supply are greater than those of having too much. As a generality, it can be said that it is easier to defer a planned new resource should demand at some point in the future turn out to be lower than expected than it is to accelerate a new resource if demand is higher than expected. (Planning Inspectorate, 2010, p. 9)

Demand forecasts at a resource planning level therefore began to represent a proxy through which government and the water industry negotiated the relative importance of risk in policy failure versus risk in security of supply, albeit in an indirect, non-transparent way.

A similar negotiation arose between economic and resource-planning objectives. Internal to the companies, a number of resource planners interviewed noted that projections of domestic consumption sometimes conflicted with economic planning within the company. Interviewees noted that uncertainties surrounding demand management options may translate to uncertainties in revenue streams and that in other cases forecasts

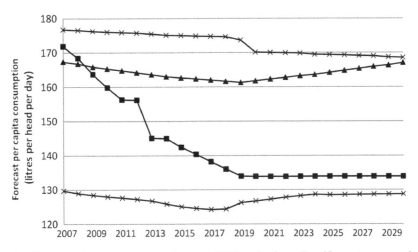

Figure 8. Four sample water company dry year PCC projections. Specific water companies not stated for neutrality purposes. Data sourced from projections in draft Water Company Resource Management Plans submitted to E.A. in 2007.

which were deemed too high were believed to result in lower price allowances from Ofwat. These negotiations are carried out in separate 5-year economic plans, resulting in a potential mismatch in projected demand. Instances of measures to influence demand (in particular metering and water efficiency) in water company resource management plans confirmed by the EA but rejected by Ofwat on the grounds of economic efficiency were frequently cited by interview subjects. By September 2009, the head of the industry's representative body commented on the observed discrepancy between the plans by stating it was "hard now to say whether companies, Ofwat and the government are still going down the same track" (*Utility Week*, 2009).

Conclusions

The adoption of demand management principles in resource planning requires a new interpretation of the knowledge derived from demand models and the institutional structures which channel it. Demand modelling must move away from a purely predictive practice and instead become a means for actively learning and re-evaluating our understanding of consumption while discussing possible trends of socio-technical change. Where the challenges facing water resource planning involve complex socio-ecological systems, it will often be the case that shared problem perceptions are not initially aligned. New approaches to modelling must attempt to facilitate collective learning and the development of shared problem perceptions in the modelling process. This reflects a wider need for participatory policy design in water resources (Pahl-Wostl, 2005).

In the case of the English and Welsh water sectors, the regulatory process plays an essential role in shaping the generation and dissemination of demand projections. Current institutional structures introduce conflicting incentives between agents involved in the modelling process, and as a result the EA, Ofwat, water company resource planners, water company financial planners and other external stakeholders approach demand modelling in resource planning from a highly strategic, competitive vantage point. Models are often pitted against one another and compete for legitimacy. As a result, transparency in the generation of knowledge from demand models is undermined; the inherent uncertainties of model projections are not expressed, the conflicting incentives and biases of the agents

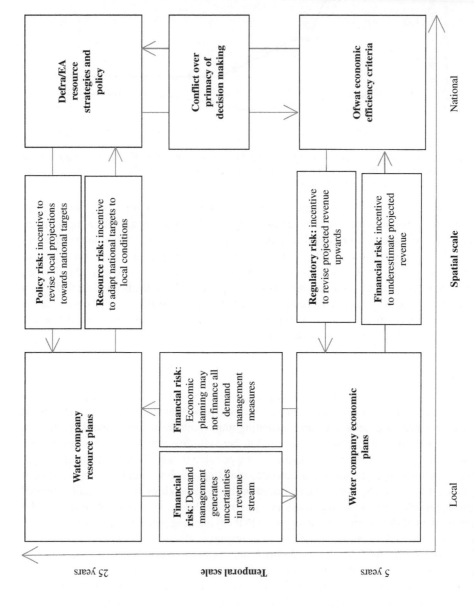

Figure 9. Conceptual model of transfer of risk.

involved remain unacknowledged, and the risk of models being used as a form of discursive power is overlooked. To mitigate such behaviour and support a more learning-based approach, UK policy must seek a means of removing demand modelling from the 'regulatory game' which is played out between companies and regulators.

To this end, the critical realist interpretation of scientific enquiry as a partially socialized process becomes an appropriate position for theoretical analysis. The critical realist hypothesis of social systems as *open systems*, governed by underlying generative mechanisms which may be inactive or interactive processes, argues that what is observed is in fact only a set of temporary regularities. This has significant implications not only for the status of long-term demand projections, but also for any effort to predict the outcomes of efforts to alter water users' behaviour. A historical analysis argued that the process of demand modelling is one in which temporary regularities are observed and mathematical models are hypothesized. These models are underpinned by assumed but only partially observed causal mechanisms. Following unexpected shifts in demand behaviour, radically new conceptualizations of demand are proposed which tend to be incommensurate with their predecessors. With respect to the critical realist claim concerning the socialized nature of models, the paper has cited multiple examples of how models of demand are inherently value-laden and employed strategically to legitimize actions. It is therefore important to recognize this as an issue not only of policy but, at a more fundamental level, of epistemology.

Acknowledgements

While this paper does not reflect their opinions, I would like to acknowledge Paul Herrington of Leicester University, Philip Turton of the UK Environment Agency, and an anonymous reviewer for their generous support and helpful suggestions in developing this paper. Thanks are also owed to Sue Hubbard of the Hertford Waterworks Museum for support in accessing archived documents.

Notes

1. Later the Environment Agency.
2. Reinforced in later years by the 2003 Water Act, which made the consultation and publication of these plans a statutory requirement.
3. Having taken over responsibility for environmental regulation from the NRA in 1996.

References

Artesia Consulting (2008). *Defra's vision for new and existing household per capita consumption: Study for Thames Water*. Bristol: Artesia Consulting.

Bakker, K. J. (2003). *An uncooperative commodity: Privatizing water in England and Wales* (1st ed.). New York: Oxford University Press.

Benassy, J. P., Boyer, R., & Gelpi, R. M. (1979). Régulation des économies capitalistes et inflation. *Revue Économique, 30*(3), 397–441.

Bhaskar, R. (1986). *Scientific realism and human emancipation* (1st ed.). London: Verso.

Boyd, R. N. (1983). On the current status of the issue of scientific realism. *Erkenntnis, 19*, 45–90.

CAWC (Central Advisory Water Committee). (1959). *Sub-committee on the growing demand for water (interim report)*. London: Her Majesty's Stationery Office.

CAWC. (1962). *Sub-committee on the growing demand for water (final report)*. London: Her Majesty's Stationery Office.

CAWC. (1971). *The future management of water in England and wales*. London: Her Majesty's Stationery Office.

Chambers, V. K. (2005). *Increasing the value of domestic water use data for demand management: Summary* (Summary Report No. P6805). Swindon: WRc.

CLG (Communities and Local Government). (2009). *The water efficiency calculator for new buildings*. London: Communities and Local Government Publications.

CWPU. (1975). *Household use of water*. London: Her Majesty's Stationery Office.

CWPU. (1976). *Annual report 1975/1976*. London: Her Majesty's Stationery Office.
CWPU. (1977). *Public water supply in 1975 and trends in consumption*. London: Her Majesty's Stationery Office.
CWPU. (1977b). *Modelling of water demands and waste-water discharges in England and Wales*. London: Her Majesty's Stationery Office.
CWPU. (1978a). *Long term trends in per capita consumption from public supplies*. London: Her Majesty's Stationery Office.
CWPU. (1978b). *Impact of social and economic factors on consumption from public water supplies*. London: Her Majesty's Stationery Office.
Defra (Department for Environment, Food and Rural Affairs). (2008). *Future water: The government's water strategy for England*. London: Her Majesty's Stationery Office.
DOE (Department of Environment). (1992). *Using water wisely*. London: Her Majesty's Stationery Office.
EA (Environment Agency). (1998). *Review of selected water company reports on the estimation of unmeasured household per capita consumption*. London: Her Majesty's Stationery Office.
EA. (2001). *Water resources for the future: A strategy for England and Wales*. Bristol: Her Majesty's Stationery Office.
EA. (2010). *Environment agency statement of case: Inquiry in connection with a draft water resources management plan prepared by South East Water PLC*. London: Her Majesty's Stationery Office.
Fairclough, N. (2003). *Analysing discourse: Textual analysis for social research*. London: Routledge.
Fuchs, D. A., & Lorek, S. (2005). Sustainable consumption governance: A history of promises and failures. *Journal of Consumer Policy, 28*(3), 261–288.
Guy, S., & Marvin, S. (1995). *Planning for water: Space, time and the social organisation of natural resources* (Working Paper No. 55). Newcastle Upon Tyne: University of Newcastle.
Hassan, J. (1998). *A history of water in modern England and Wales*. Manchester: Manchester University Press.
Herrington, P. (1973). *Water demand study*. Leicester: University of Leicester.
Herrington, P. (1996). *Climate change and the demand for water*. London: Department of Environment.
HLG (Housing and Local Government). (1963). *Conference on water resources in the north west*. London: Her Majesty's Stationery Office.
HOCCPA (House of Commons Committee of Public Account). (2007). *Ofwat: Meeting the demand for water. Twenty-fourth report of session 2006–07*. London: Her Majesty's Stationery Office.
Jessop, B. (2004). Critical semiotic analysis and cultural political economy. *Critical Discourse Studies, 1*(2), 159–174.
Lipietz, A. (1986). Behind the crisis: The exhaustion of a regime of accumulation. A "regulation school" perspective on some French empirical works. *Review of Radical Political Economics, 18*, 13–32.
McCulloch, C. S. (2006). The Kielder Water Scheme: The last of its kind? In *Improvements in reservoir construction, operation and maintenance: Proceedings of the 14th conference of the British Dam Society at the University of Durham from 6 to 9 September 2006* (pp. 196–210). Durham: University of Durham.
Midttun, A., & Baumgartner, T. (1986). Negotiating energy futures: The politics of energy forecasting. *Energy Policy, 14*(3), 219–241.
Ministry of Health. (1949). *Committee on causes of increase in consumption of water (interim report)*. London: Her Majesty's Stationery Office.
MMC (Monopolies and Mergers Commission). (1986). *A report on water supply and distribution services of the authority and the companies: Forecasting and leakage control*. London: Her Majesty's Stationery Office.
MMC. (1981). *A report on water services supplied by the authority and the companies*. London: Her Majesty's Stationery Office.
Nielsen, S. K., & Karlsson, K. (2007). Energy scenarios: A review of methods, uses and suggestions for improvement. *International Journal of Global Energy Issues, 27*(3), 302–322.
NRA (National Rivers Authority). (1993). *National water resources development strategy: Water company consultation paper*. London: Her Majesty's Stationery Office.
NRA. (1995a). *Measures to safeguard public water supplies*. London: Her Majesty's Stationery Office.
NRA. (1995b). *Domestic consumption monitoring survey* (DMC Project 5). London: Demand Management Centre.

NWC (National Water Council). (1978). *The 1975–76 drought: A report*. London: Her Majesty's Stationery Office.

NWC. (1982). *Components of domestic demand*. London: Her Majesty's Stationery Office.

Ofwat. (1992). *Water delivered report: An analysis of information reported by water companies for the year 1990/1991*. Birmingham: Her Majesty's Stationery Office.

Ofwat (1993–1995). *Annual report: The cost of water delivered and sewerage collected*. Birmingham: Her Majesty's Stationary Office.

Ofwat. (1994a). *Future charges for water and sewerage services*. Birmingham: Her Majesty's Stationery Office.

Ofwat. (1994b). *Future levels of demand and supply*. Birmingham: Her Majesty's Stationery Office.

Ofwat. (1996). *Report on recent patterns of demand for water in England and Wales*. Birmingham: Her Majesty's Stationery Office.

Ofwat. (1997). *1996–1997 report on leakage and water efficiency*. Birmingham: Her Majesty's Stationery Office.

Ofwat (1997–2001). *Annual report: Report on leakage and water efficiency*. Birmingham: Her Majesty's Stationary Office.

Ofwat. (1999). *Prospects for prices*. Birmingham: Her Majesty's Stationery Office.

Ofwat. (2000). *Final determinations*. Birmingham: Her Majesty's Stationery Office.

Ofwat (2003–2007). *Annual report: Security of supply, leakage, and the efficient use of water*. Birmingham: Her Majesty's Stationary Office.

Ofwat. (2007). *Water efficiency targets* (RD 15/07). Birmingham: Her Majesty's Stationery Office.

Ofwat (2011). *Summary of performance report*. Birmingham: Her Majesty's Stationary Office.

ONS (Office of National Statistics). (2012). Seasonally adjusted index based on all industrial production industries in England and Wales (Data series "CKYW"). Retrieved from http://www.statistics.gov.uk on 05/03/12.

Pahl-Wostl, C. (2005). Participative and stakeholder-based policy design, evaluation and modelling processes. *Integrated Assessment*, *3*, 3–14.

Patomäki, H., & Wight, C. (2000). After postpositivism? The promises of critical realism. *International Studies Quarterly*, *44*(2), 213–237.

Planning Inspectorate. (2010). *Report to the Secretary of State for Environment, Food, and Rural Affairs: Enquiry into the South East Water Resource Management Plan 2010–2035* (APP/WRMP/09/02). London: Her Majesty's Stationery Office.

Portsmouth Water. (2009). *Updated Water Resources Management Plan*. Appendix 25: Microcomponents. Portsmouth: Portsmouth Water.

POST (Parliamentary Office of Science and Technology). (1995). *The 1995 drought*. Technical Report 71. London: Her Majesty's Stationery Office.

Shapiro, C., & Willig, R. D. (1990). On the antitrust treatment of production joint ventures. *Journal of Economic Perspectives*, *4*(3), 113–130.

Sharp, L., McDonald, A., Sim, P., Knamiller, C., Sefton, C., & Wong, S. (2011). Positivism, post-positivism and domestic water demand: Interrelating science across the paradigmatic divide. *Transactions of the Institute of British Geographers*, *36*, 501–515.

Shove, E. (2003). *Comfort, cleanliness and convenience: The social organization of normality*. New York: Berg.

Skeat, W. O. (1965). Trends in water engineering in Great Britain. *Journal of American Water Works Association*, *57*(7), 824–830.

Slaughter, R. (2004). *Futures beyond dystopia: Creating social foresight*. London: Routledge.

UKWIR (United Kingdom Water Industry Research). (1995). *Demand forecasting methodology* (95/WR/01/1). London: UKWIR.

UKWIR. (1997). *Forecasting demand components* (97/WR/07/1). London: UKWIR.

Utility Week. (2009, 16 September). Water sector seeks clarity from Ofwat over long-term strategic plans.

Waterwise. (2012). Save water: Be water wise. Retrieved from http://www.waterwise.org.uk/pages/save-water.html.

WRB (Water Resources Board). (1973). *Water resources in England and Wales*. London: Her Majesty's Stationery Office.

WSA (Water Services Association). (1990). *Waterfacts*. London: Water Services Association.

The dynamics of privatization and regulation of water services: a comparative study of two Spanish regions

Germà Bel[a], Francisco González-Gómez[b] and Andrés J. Picazo-Tadeo[c]

[a]Departament de Política Econòmica, Universitat de Barcelona, Spain; [b]Departamento de Economía Aplicada, Universidad de Granada, Spain; [c]Departament d'Economia Aplicada II, Universitat de València, Spain

As in other economic activities, privatization of water delivery has not resulted in the retreat of the public sector, but rather a change in the way in which the government intervenes in the water industry. This paper illustrates this situation by comparing urban water services in two Spanish regions, Andalusia and Catalonia. Water service delivery is structured very differently in these two regions with respect to private involvement, the degree of market concentration and, as a result, problems in competition. The characteristics of the two regions' respective regulatory agencies reflect the different paths taken to privatization: in Catalonia private firms have much more tradition and operate throughout the region; in Andalusia their introduction has been much more recent and limited in scope.

Introduction

Public delivery of water services has been frequent since most countries municipalized water distribution in the late nineteenth and twentieth centuries. In the last quarter of the twentieth century, however, privatization has increasingly been used as a policy instrument to reform water service management and delivery. Even though the water service has not been as subject to privatization as other services (solid waste collection, for example), many municipalities and other tiers of government have privatized delivery in countries that include, among others, Spain and France. In England and Wales privatization has also included water resources. Privatization has reduced the importance of public delivery in many public services over the last few decades. However, as in other economic activities, transferring water delivery to the private sector has not resulted in the retreat of the public sector, but rather a change in the way in which the government intervenes in the water industry, especially when private producers have substantial market power.

Since the seminal works by Majone (1990, 1994) and Vogel (1996), the understanding that privatization leads to more detailed and prescriptive regulation has become widely accepted. Indeed, ownership and regulation may constitute alternative forms of government intervention. The idea that governments choose between regulation and government ownership when intervening in public services with monopoly characteristics is clear in the contractual approach to government intervention promoted by Gómez-Ibáñez (2003). This link between privatization and more detailed regulation means that governments can shift their focus from managing the inputs and processes in the delivery of public services to regulating the performance of the firms that produce these services. Hence, public delivery is not the sole alternative available for guaranteeing public control.

This paper examines the relation between privatization and regulation in the water sector. The paper illustrates this situation by studying urban water services in two regions in Spain. In this country, municipalities are responsible for the water distribution service, while its regional governments hold responsibilities for the regulation of the water sector in each region. We compare the structure and dynamics of water distribution in Andalusia and Catalonia. These two regions are the most populated in Spain, accounting for one-third of the total population of the country. The characteristics of water service delivery in Andalusia and Catalonia differ with respect to private involvement, degree of market concentration and, as a result, problems in competition. Consequently, their regional regulators have very different institutional characteristics and behaviours. This reflects different paths of privatization, much broader in Catalonia and much more recent and limited in scope in Andalusia.

We compare private involvement, market concentration and empowerment of the regulatory agency in both regions. Relatively few urban water services (by Spanish standards) have been privatized in Andalusia and institutionalization and the functions performed by its regional regulatory authorities are quite weak. By contrast, the degree of urban water service privatization in the region of Catalonia is the highest in Spain. The regional regulatory authority in Catalonia enjoys strong institutionalization and empowerment, exerting tighter control on the water sector. Our comparative analysis shows that public ownership and regulation are used as alternative tools for government intervention, and that privatization triggers more stringent regulation.

The rest of the paper proceeds as follows. The next section provides a brief background on privatization in the water sector. After that, we undertake a study of the two cases of Andalusia and Catalonia. Then we discuss the lessons and implications that can be drawn from the comparative analysis.

Background: water delivery privatization

The end of the 1970s and early 1980s witnessed a wave of privatization in the USA and the UK that would soon spread to the rest of the world. At the time, one of the main rationales used to justify privatization was that it improved efficiency. The theoretical foundations of this argument can be found in the theories of public choice and property rights. The more pragmatic neo-institutional theory interprets privatization as a reaction to the lack of capacity of the public sector to face its obligations within a context of limited financial resources (Feigenbaum & Henig, 1997).

In the last few decades, privatization has spread to almost all economic activities, including the delivery of water services in urban areas. Nevertheless, unlike other sectors, governments have been more cautious regarding the decision to privatize this service. In fact, there are countries whose regulations do not even consider the possibility of privatizing water services. Keeping the management of the service in public hands has been seen as a way of guaranteeing access to water.

Table 1 displays the percentage of population served by private water companies in OECD countries. In most countries, local governments are responsible for urban water delivery, so decisions regarding the form of delivery are made at the local level. One major exception is that of England and Wales, where the Water Act of 1989 privatized the whole

Table 1.   Participation of the private sector in water supply in OECD countries (percentage of the population served by private firms).

Low or nonexistent (less than 10%)	Austria, Belgium, Canada, Denmark, Finland, Iceland, Ireland, Japan, Luxembourg, Netherlands, New Zealand, Norway, Poland, South Korea, Sweden, Switzerland, Turkey
Moderate (between 10% and 30%)	Australia, Germany, Hungary, Mexico, Portugal, Slovakia, United States
High (between 30% and 50%)	Greece, Italy, Spain
Major (between 50% and 70%)	Czech Republic
Predominant (over 70%)	France, England and Wales

Source: Pérard (2009).

water industry. Some of the reasons that can lead local governments to transfer the water service to private firms are the latter's ability to obtain financial resources and to take advantage of know-how based on their experience in the sector and their greater flexibility to introduce and apply innovations in service delivery. In addition to this, some developing countries have implemented privatization of water services within the framework of programs of economic reform promoted by the World Bank and the International Monetary Fund. Critical views on the social effects of this exogenously induced privatization include Esteban-Castro (2008) and Spronk (2010).

The reason behind the relatively low rate of privatization of water services, compared to that of other sectors, is embedded in the characteristics of the sector itself. See Bel and Fageda (2007, 2009) for reviews of the empirical literature on factors explaining public service privatization, with special emphasis on water. The water sector is structured around local monopolies, which makes it extremely difficult to introduce competition. It is, therefore, a clear case of an industry in which private companies can take advantage of market power. However, the high level of transaction costs involved in water privatization negatively affects the expectations of local governments of obtaining benefits from transferring delivery to private firms and reinforces the market power of private firms.

The caution expressed as regards privatization of water services has been shown to be appropriate. Comparative analyses conducted in this industry suggest that public and private delivery do not show systematic differences in terms of efficiency, contrary to the theories which claim greater efficiency for private delivery (Bel, Fageda, & Warner, 2010; Bel & Warner, 2008; González-Gómez & García-Rubio, 2008). In fact, the relationship between ownership and efficiency is more complex than initially considered, and issues such as types of private ownership, corporate governance, access to know-how and markets, and the legal and institutional system are important for firm restructuring and performance (Estrin, Hanousek, Kocenda, & Svejnar, 2009).

In some instances, the renationalization or remunicipalization of water services has occurred because contracts have been cancelled or because of disagreements between the government and the private firms. The cases discussed in the literature include those of Buenos Aires (Baer & Montes-Rojas, 2008; Dagdeviren, 2011; Laborde, 2005) and Cochabamba (Assies, 2003; Nickson & Vargas, 2002). In other instances, on the expiration of the contract, the local government has decided to return to in-house delivery of water services. This has occurred in Paris, Atlanta and some Spanish cities as well (González-Gómez, Guardiola, & Ruiz-Villaverde, 2009; Ruiz-Villaverde, García-Rubio, & González-Gómez, 2010). Reverse privatization has occurred in other local public services, as shown by Warner (2008) and Chen (2009).

A further type of reform aimed at overcoming the shortfalls of water privatization has been the creation of regulatory agencies in the sector that are empowered to monitor the behaviour of private companies. Examples of such agencies include the Office of Water Services (Ofwat) in England and Wales, the Regulatory Agency for Water and Solid Waste Services (*Entidade Reguladora dos Serviços de Águas e Resíduos*, ERSAR) in Portugal and the Superintendence of Health Services (*Superintendencia de Servicios Sanitarios*) in Chile. These agencies have been created with the purpose of protecting public interests in the water sector and are designed to promote efficiency in the companies operating in the sector, to ensure that the prices approved for the service are consistent with the costs incurred and that investments meet the requirements for improving the services.

Given this background to water privatization, we proceed to analyze the cases of privatization and regulation in the Spanish regions of Andalusia and Catalonia.

Water privatization and regulation in Andalusia and Catalonia

The regions

Andalusia is in the south of Spain and is administratively divided into eight provinces. It is the most populated region in Spain, with 8.4 million inhabitants in 2010 (almost 18% of the total Spanish population), and the second-largest, at $87,268\,km^2$ (17% of the total surface area of Spain). According to data on GDP per capita and adjusted disposable family income per capita (purchasing power parity) provided by the Foundation of Savings Banks (Fundación de las Cajas de Ahorros – FUNCAS, 2011), the GDP per capita of Andalusia is around €18,000. Hence, Andalusia is at the bottom of economic indicators (including GDP and income) in Spain. GDP per capita is 74.7% of the national average and the region is ranked 15th out of 17 Spanish regions. Adjusted disposable income per inhabitant (purchasing power parity) is 87.7% of the national average, ranking 16th. In comparative terms, agriculture and services are relatively important in the regional productive structure. Its climate and 1100 km of coastline make Andalusia one of the main tourist destinations in Spain, particularly for visitors from European Union countries such as the United Kingdom, Germany and France.

Catalonia is in the north-east of Spain and is divided into four provinces. It is the second-most populated region in Spain, behind Andalusia, with 7.5 million inhabitants in 2010 (16% of the total Spanish population), and has a surface area of $32,106\,km^2$ (6% of the total surface area of Spain). With a GDP per capita of around €28,000, Catalonia is above the Spanish average in terms of GDP and income. GDP per capita is 117.6% of the national average and the region is ranked 4th out of the 17 Spanish regions. Adjusted disposable income per inhabitant (purchasing power parity) is 102.2% of the national average, ranking 9th. In comparative terms, industry and services are important in the regional productive structure. Alongside Andalusia, Catalonia is a top regional destination for tourism, with tourists coming from the rest of Spain and a variety of other countries.

The structure and dynamics of urban water delivery

Andalusia

Since the 1980s, there has been a gradual externalization of the urban water services in Andalusia. In 2009, more than 50% of Andalusian municipalities had externalized the management of the water service. If we consider population served, municipalities where the service has been externalized account for 89% of the total population of the region.

Table 2. Structure and dynamics of water service delivery in Andalusia, 2003 and 2009 (percent).

	2003		2009	
	Municipalities	Population	Municipalities	Population
Direct public delivery	56	16	49	11
Public firm	21	44	28	50
Public-private firm	10	16	10	15
Private firm	13	24	13	24
TOTAL	100	100	100	100

Source: own elaboration based on two surveys of municipalities in Andalusia.

Direct public delivery is the most common form of delivery among Andalusian municipalities, being used by around 50% of them (recall though that the population served by direct public delivery – 11% – falls well below this percentage). Government-owned firms (or public firms subject to commercial law; see Warner & Bel [2008] for a detailed explanation of the types of organizational forms for water delivery in Spain) have been the most frequent tool used to externalize water delivery: 28% of Andalusian municipalities use this type of public firm for service delivery (serving half the regional population). Moreover, 10% of municipalities use mixed public-private firms for service delivery, and in 13% of the municipalities, the service is contracted out to a private firm. Table 2 displays the structure of water service delivery by form of delivery in the region.

Over the past decade, while direct public delivery has lost some ground, public firms have gained market share. By contrast, the market shares of mixed public-private firms and private firms have remained remarkably stable, both in terms of municipalities as well as the population served. Indeed, when comparing data for 2003 and 2009, it is readily apparent that direct public delivery decreased from 56% to 49% of municipalities (16% to 11% of the population), while delivery by means of public firms increased from 21% to 28% of municipalities (44% to 50% of the population). As mentioned previously, in that period the representation of mixed companies and private firms remained stable.

Catalonia

Private delivery of water has a long tradition in the region of Catalonia. Indeed, delivery has been private in the largest city in the region, Barcelona, since the nineteenth century. By the end of the last decade, private delivery was by far the most popular form of delivery in the region. Of the municipalities with a population of more than 2000 inhabitants, almost 80% (containing over 80% of the population) were served by private firms. At some distance, public firms served 11% of municipalities and slightly less than 10% of the population. Mixed firms had an even lower market share, serving 7% of municipalities and 6% of the population, while the share of direct public delivery was residual, both in terms of municipalities as well as of population. Table 3 presents the structure of water service delivery by type of organization in the region.

Over the past decade, private delivery has gained market share, extending its presence particularly in smaller municipalities. Mixed firms have also expanded moderately, while direct delivery and public firms have lost market share. When data for 2003 and 2009 are compared, we see that public delivery (direct plus public firms) decreased from 21% to 14% of municipalities (15% to 11% of the population), while the presence of private firms increased.

Table 3.   Structure and dynamics of water service delivery in Catalonia, 2003 and 2009 (percent).

	2003		2009	
	Municipalities	Population	Municipalities	Population
Direct public delivery	5	5	3	3
Public firm	16	10	11	8
Public-private firm	5	4	7	6
Private firm	74	81	79	83
TOTAL	100	100	100	100

Source: own elaboration based on two surveys of Catalonian municipalities. Data refer only to municipalities with a population of more than 2000. This includes more than 95% of the population of the region.

Structure of the private market for water delivery

Andalusia

As can be seen in Table 2 above, private firms deliver the urban water services in 13% of Andalusian municipalities, covering about a quarter of the population. Two firms – Aqualia and Aquagest Andalucía – have more than half of the private concessions, covering almost 80% of the total population served by private firms. Aqualia is the water division of multiservice provider FCC, one of the leading Spanish firms in public service delivery and a major international player in the private market for public services. Aqualia manages concessions in 40% of Andalusian municipalities with private delivery, and serves half of their population.

The ownership of Aquagest Andalucía is shared by two regional savings banks, Unicaja (35%) and Caja Granada (15%), along with the firm Agbar, a major international player in the water sector, which owns 50% of the firm. In turn, Hisusa Holding de Infraestructuras y Servicios Urbanos owns 99.44% of Agbar. It is worth noting that Suez Environnement España (a subsidiary of the French multinational, Suez Environnement, the leading private company in the water sector worldwide) owns 75.74% of Hisusa, while the local partner Caixa Holding owns the remaining 24.26%. Aquagest Andalucía manages concessions in 15% of Andalusian municipalities with private delivery, and serves more than a quarter of their population.

Besides these two firms, another three still enjoy a significant share of the private market for water delivery: Gestagua (12% of municipalities and 9% of the population), Agua y Gestión (12% of municipalities and 5% of the population) and Acciona Agua (11.5% of municipalities and 5% of the population).

The market for private water delivery in Andalusia shows moderate oligopolistic characteristics. As indicated, the two leading firms, Aqualia and Aquagest Andalucía, serve 55% of municipalities with private delivery and almost 80% of the population served by private firms. Market concentration has increased in terms of population served in the last decade, as shown by the concentration scores in Table 4 (where Concentration ratio 1 is the market share of the leading firm, Concentration ratio 2 the aggregate market share of the two leading firms, and so forth).

The Herfindahl-Hirschman Index (HHI) has become the standard concentration measure for antitrust enforcement purposes (Yoo, 2002). The HHI is defined as the sum of the squares of the market shares: $HH = \Sigma Q_i^2$ ($i = 1$ to n), where Q_i is the ith firm's market share and n is the total number of firms in the field. Its advantage over simple

Table 4. Market concentration of private delivery of urban water in Andalusia, 2003 and 2009.

	2003		2009	
	Municipalities	Population	Municipalities	Population
Concentration ratio 1	0.45	0.49	0.40	0.51
Concentration ratio 2	0.57	0.69	0.55	0.79
Concentration ratio 3	0.69	0.79	0.67	0.88
Concentration ratio 4	0.79	0.83	0.79	0.93
Herfindahl-Hirschman Index	0.244	0.298	0.231	0.355

Source: own elaboration based on surveys of municipalities in Andalusia.

concentration ratios consists in its ability to take into account both the number of firms and the differences between them, since large firms are given greater weight than small firms.

The Herfindahl-Hirschman Index of concentration has remained stable for municipalities, but has increased for population: the HHI value for 2009 is 0.355, indicating the existence of an oligopolistic market. This suggests that the leading firms follow a strategy of obtaining concessions in highly populated municipalities.

Catalonia

As shown in Table 3 above, private firms deliver urban water services in about 80% of the Catalonian municipalities with a population of more than 2,000 inhabitants, and these municipalities account for almost 85% of the total population of the region. One firm, Agbar, clearly dominates the Catalan market for the private delivery of water: by 2009, Agbar had been awarded two-thirds of the concessions in municipalities with private delivery, which covered close to 90% of the total population served by private firms. While the company has a strong presence throughout the region, Agbar is omnipresent in the metropolitan area of Barcelona, which includes the city of Barcelona and the other most-populated cities in the region, including l'Hospitalet de Llobregat and Badalona.

While in practice Agbar enjoys a regional monopoly in Catalonia, two other firms have several concessions: this is the case for Aqualia (6% of municipalities and 4% of the population) and Companya d'Aigües de Sabadell (CASSA, 6% of municipalities and 6% of the population). CASSA is a regional company whose main concession is that of the city of Sabadell (about 200,000 inhabitants). Table 5 presents information about the market concentration in the private delivery of urban water in Catalonia. The concentration indices show that the smaller municipalities that contracted out water

Table 5. Market concentration in the private delivery of urban water in Catalonia, 2003 and 2009.

	2003		2009	
	Municipalities	Population	Municipalities	Population
Concentration ratio 1	0.66	0.85	0.67	0.86
Concentration ratio 2	0.79	0.91	0.73	0.92
Concentration ratio 3	0.88	0.95	0.79	0.97
Concentration ratio 4	0.90	0.97	0.81	0.98
Herfindahl-Hirschman Index	0.465	0.730	0.454	0.736

Source: own elaboration based on surveys of Catalonian municipalities.

delivery during the first decade of the new millennium tended to choose small, local firms for the service, and as a result market concentration ratios for the municipalities have fallen. However, the market concentration indices for the population served have remained highly stable. All in all, the structure of the private market seems to be especially constant in the region. The Herfindahl-Hirschman Index of concentration (see definition above) has remained quite stable for municipalities as well as for population. In any case, values of 0.454 (municipalities) and 0.736 (population) clearly confirm the monopolistic nature of the private market in Catalonia.

Regulatory institutions

Andalusia

The regulatory agency of the water sector in Andalusia has had an ephemeral life. The Andalusian Agency for Water (*Agencia Andaluza del Agua*, AAA) was created by regional law on 1 January 2005. It was conceived as an agency dependent on the Regional Department of Environmental Affairs. It was made responsible for the coordination of regional powers regarding water and water works. From the outset, it was conceived as the water administration of the regional government of Andalusia (Junta de Andalucía).

As regards urban service delivery, the AAA was made responsible for the planning and regulation of water supply to urban systems, as well as sewage systems and the cleaning of urban wastewater. Moreover, it was made responsible for the prevention of floods. However, a regional law passed on 30 July 2010 dramatically changed the characteristics of water regulation. Responsibilities previously assigned to the AAA were transferred to the Regional Department of Environmental Affairs and the Agency of Environment and Water. The latter, however, plays only a minor role in water regulation – a responsibility that has in practice been taken back by the general administration of the regional government.

The functions related to the supervision of the management of urban water services have been transferred to the Water Observatory (*Observatorio del Agua*), a consultancy attached to the Regional Department of Environmental Affairs. The Water Observatory was created recently (autumn 2011). Its main function will be to generate and disseminate information on the water service to the regional administrative bodies in charge of water policy and regulation. The hope is that the Water Observatory will work as an effective tool for increasing transparency in all matters related to urban water delivery (Consejería de Medio Ambiente, 2011).

Catalonia

The Catalan Agency for Water (*Agència Catalana de l'Aigua*, ACA) is a public firm owned by the regional government of Catalonia and attached to the Regional Ministry of Territory and Sustainability. It was created in 2000 to act as the water administration of Catalonia, responsible for executing regional government water policy. The ACA is a specific legal entity. The basic regulation of the ACA was established in 2003 by regional decree. The ACA is responsible for many functions, of which the most important are:

a) Planning water policy – this includes planning global water delivery in the region, as well as any other water resources.
b) Management of reservoirs in Catalonia.

c) Control and supervision of the core network of water supply, including the basic Ter-Llobregat system.

d) Preparing the planning proposal for wastewater treatment in Catalonia and implementing planning, including both infrastructure replacement and improvement. Moreover, the ACA also performs functions in public sewage systems. In this regard, it is responsible for promoting, building and operating waterworks that are under the jurisdiction of the regional government.

e) Tax and revenue functions – the ACA manages, collects, administers and controls the revenues accrued by the agency.

f) Designing the projects and actions associated with the water cycle, including infrastructure and environmental improvements.

Besides these functions, the ACA has created the Catalan Water Price Observatory (*Observatori del Preu de l'Aigua a Catalunya*). The observatory is designed as a tool for raising public awareness of the essential elements that make up water prices in the different areas and municipalities of the region, including those related to urban water delivery. Reports have been published since 2008; the information presented in them is obtained from municipal tax regulations on water supply price and from regional taxes on water. The price structures specified in the decrees of the Committee on Prices in Catalonia are another important source of information. Note that this committee is dependent on the regional ministry with responsibility for consumer-related affairs, while any changes in tariffs and the prices of various public services – urban water delivery among them – need to be approved by the committee in line with the decision made (in the case of water urban delivery) by the local governments.

Discussion and policy implications

Local governments are responsible for urban water delivery in Spain, and the regions are responsible for regulating the water sector, water delivery outside urban areas and wastewater treatment. Considerable regional differences in the management of urban water services exist in Spain, as the two cases studied in this paper show. In Andalusia, around 50% of municipalities have externalized water delivery (recall that externalization includes public firms operating under commercial law as well as private firms), which accounts for around 90% of the population. In Catalonia, direct (bureaucratic) public delivery is minimal and almost all municipalities with more than 2,000 inhabitants (i.e. virtually all the population) have externalized the service. Differences between the two regions in terms of the delivery of water service by means of contracting out to private firms are far more significant. In Andalusia, fully private firms deliver water to just 13% of municipalities (representing a quarter of the population), whereas around 80% of the Catalan municipalities with more than 2,000 inhabitants have private firms delivering their water service. Privatization of urban water services in Catalonia is well above the Spanish average, which is around 40% (see Bel, 2006). Privatization is much less frequent in Andalusia than in Catalonia and well below the Spanish average as well.

The private market for water delivery in Andalusia has an oligopolistic structure, with three firms controlling around two-thirds of the market if we consider municipalities with private delivery, and around 80% of the market if we consider population. In the case of Catalonia, the market is heavily controlled by one firm, which delivers water services in two-thirds of municipalities, accounting for nearly 90% of the population. Basic concentration ratios and the Herfindahl-Hirschman Index in both regions clearly show these characteristics. In short, privatization is much more important in Catalonia than in Andalusia, and concentration in the private market, while significant in Andalusia, is far more important in Catalonia.

Water supply is considered a public "service of general interest" in the European Union (EU, 2004). Consequently, the public sector needs to ensure the provision of high-quality and affordable water service to all citizens. While Catalonia has taken significant steps towards developing an institutional framework that exerts regulatory functions in this sector to protect the interests of users, Andalusia has yet to instigate such reforms. This absence of institutional initiatives in Andalusia is difficult to justify if we consider that following the regulatory changes made since the end of the 1980s, privatization has become the chosen form for managing the water service in a growing number of cities.

The transfer of public services declared as being of general interest, as is the case for water, into the hands of private operators does not mean governments can opt for a totally laissez-faire approach. Given the nature of the water industry, prone to competition failures and characterized by high transaction costs, it is recommended that the public sector monitor the behaviour of firms closely.

Therefore, municipalities typically retain regulatory functions after externalizing the service, particularly if this externalization implies the transfer of management to private firms. After all, the city is ultimately responsible for the provision of water in its jurisdiction. However, the control exerted by city councils is often insufficient: first, because council staffs lack the specific expertise and knowledge, and, second, because of problems of asymmetric information.

Our main policy recommendation is the creation of regulatory agencies within the regional government organization or, ideally, of independent regulatory agencies. Whatever the case, such agencies must be assigned powerful tools to oversee the sector. The ability to exercise control from a broader regional perspective allows comparative analyses of different business units to be undertaken. As such, behaviours that deviate from the mean can be identified more readily. Moreover, the mere existence of a supra-municipal regulator can be expected to provide an incentive for companies in the industry to behave more efficiently.

Acknowledgements

The authors are grateful for the financial support from the Spanish Ministry of Economy and Competitiveness (projects ECO2012-32189, ECO2012-38004, ECO2009-06946/ECON and ECO2009-08824/ECON). Germà Bel also acknowledges funding from the Autonomous Government of Catalonia (project SGR2009-1066) and ICREA Academia. Andrés J. Picazo-Tadeo appreciates the financial support from the Autonomous Government of Valencia (project PROMETEO/2009/098). Francisco González-Gómez acknowledges financial support from the Junta de Andalucía (project P11-SEJ-7039). A preliminary version of this paper was presented at a 2011 workshop in Granada on water pricing and the roles of the public and private sectors in efficient urban water management, organized by the Universidad de Granada and Global Water Intelligence. Comments by anonymous reviewers and by Cecilia Tortajada have been very useful.

References

Assies, W. (2003). David versus Goliath in Cochabamba: Water rights, neoliberalism, and the revival of social protest in Bolivia. *Latin American Perspectives, 30*, 14–36, doi:10.1177/0094582X03030003003

Baer, W., & Montes-Rojas, G. (2008). From privatization to re-nationalization: What went wrong with privatizations in Argentina? *Oxford Development Studies, 36*, 323–337, doi:10.1080/13600810802264456.

Bel, G. (2006). *Economía y política de la privatización local* [Economics and politics of local privatization]. Madrid: Marcial Pons.

Bel, G., & Fageda, X. (2007). Why do local governments privatize public services? A survey of empirical studies. *Local Government Studies, 33*, 517–534. doi:10.1080/03003930701417528

Bel, G., & Fageda, X. (2009). Factors explaining local privatization: a meta-regression analysis. *Public Choice, 139*, 105–119. doi:10.1007/s11127-008-9381-z.

Bel, G., Fageda, X., & Warner, M. (2010). Is private production of public services cheaper than public production? A meta-regression analysis of solid waste and water services. *Journal of Policy Analysis and Management, 29*, 553–577. doi:10.1002/pam.20509.

Bel, G., & Warner, M. (2008). Does privatization of solid waste and water services reduce costs? A review of empirical studies. *Resources, Conservation & Recycling, 52*, 1337–1348, doi:10.1016/j.resconrec.2008.07.014.

Chen, C. A. (2009). Antecedents of contracting-back-in: A view beyond the economic paradigm. *Administration & Society, 41*, 101–126. doi:10.1177/0095399708330258.

Consejería de Medio Ambiente (2011). *Medio ambiente en Andalucía. Informe 2010* [Environment in Andalusia: 2010 report]. Seville: Junta de Andalucía.

Dagdeviren, H. (2011). Political economy of contractual disputes in private water and sanitation: Lessons from Argentina. *Annals of Public and Cooperative Economics, 82*, 25–44. doi:10.1111/j.1467-8292.2010.00428.x.

Esteban-Castro, J. (2008). Neoliberal water and sanitation policies as a failed development strategy: Lessons from developing countries. *Progress in Development Studies, 8*, 63–83. doi:10.1177/146499340700800107.

Estrin, S., Hanousek, J., Kocenda, E., & Svejnar, J. (2009). The effects of privatization and ownership in transition economies. *Journal of Economic Literature, 47*, 699–728. doi:10.1257/jel.47.3.699.

EU (2004). Communication from the Commission to the European Parliament, the Council, the European Economic and Social Committee and the Committee of the Regions: White paper on services of general interest. COM/2004/0374 final.

Feigenbaum, H. B., & Henig, J. R. (1997). Privatization and political theory. *Journal of International Affairs, 50*, 338–355.

FUNCAS (2011). *Balance económico regional (autonomías y provincias). Años 2000 a 2009* [Regional economic report (autonomous regions and provinces). Years 2000 to 2009]. Madrid: Fundación de las Cajas de Ahorros.

Gómez-Ibáñez, J. A. (2003). *Regulating infrastructure: Monopoly, contracts and discretion.* Cambridge, MA: Harvard University Press.

González-Gómez, F., & García-Rubio, M. A. (2008). Efficiency in the management of urban water services: What have we learned after four decades of research? *Hacienda Pública Española / Revista de Economía Pública, 185*, 39–67.

González-Gómez, F., Guardiola, J., & Ruiz-Villaverde, A. (2009). Reconsidering privatization in the governance of water in Spain. *Municipal Engineer, 162*, 159–164. doi:10.1680/muen.2009.162.3.159.

Laborde, L. (2005). Intitutional framework for water tariffs in the Buenos Aires Concession, Argentina. *International Journal of Water Resources Development, 21*, 149–164. doi:10.1080/0790062042000316866.

Majone, G. (1990). Introduction. In G. Majone (Ed.), *Deregulation or reregulation? Regulatory reform in Europe and United States* (pp. 1–6). New York: St. Martin's Press.

Majone, G. (1994). Paradoxes of privatization and deregulation. *Journal of European Public Policy, 1*, 53–69.

Nickson, A., & Vargas, C. (2002). The limitations of water regulation: The failure of the Cochabamba concession in Bolivia. *Bulletin of Latin American Research, 21*, 99–120. doi:10.1111/1470-9856.00034.

Pérard, E. (2009). Water supply: Public or private? An approach based on cost of funds, transaction costs, efficiency and political costs. *Policy and Society, 27*, 193–219. doi:10.1016/j.polsoc.2008.10.004.

Ruiz-Villaverde, A., García-Rubio, M. A., & González-Gómez, F. (2010). Analysis of urban water management in historical perspective: Evidence from the Spanish case. *International Journal of Water Resources Development, 26*, 653–674. doi:10.1080/07900627.2010.519497.

Spronk, S. (2010). Water and sanitation utilities in the Global South: Re-centering the debate on "efficiency". *Review of Radical Political Economics*, *42*, 156–174. doi:10.1177/0486613410368389.

Vogel, S. K. (1996). *Freer markets, more rules: Regulatory reform in advanced industrial countries*. Ithaca, NY: Cornell University Press.

Warner, M. E. (2008). Reversing privatization, rebalancing government reform: Markets, deliberation and planning. *Policy and Society*, *27*, 163–174, doi:10.1016/j.polsoc.2008.09.001.

Warner, M., & Bel, G. (2008). Competition or monopoly? Comparing privatization of local public services in the US and Spain. *Public Administration*, *86*, 723–735, doi:10.1111/j.1467-9299.2008.00700.x.

Yoo, C. S. (2002). Vertical integration and media regulation in the new economy. *Yale Journal on Regulation*, *19*, 171–300.

Public choice of urban water service management: a multi-criteria approach

Alberto Ruiz-Villaverde[a], Francisco González-Gómez[a] and Andrés J. Picazo-Tadeo[b]

[a]Department of Applied Economics and Water Research Institute, University of Granada, Spain;
[b]Department of Applied Economics II, University of Valencia, Spain

Local policy makers in developed countries have to make decisions in increasingly complex scenarios. Consequently, they should use all the tools available when deciding which management option is the most suitable for urban water service, given how important that service is and the variety of criteria involved in making such a decision. This article employs 'analytic hierarchy process' techniques to perform an *ex post* analysis of the decision to transfer the management of the urban water service in Granada (in southern Spain) to a public-private partnership. The main conclusion is that the decision was rational, in that it was the best possible alternative considering the hierarchy of preferences at the time. Furthermore, confronting the serious financial difficulties faced by the local government took clear precedence over other aspects when the decision was taken.

Introduction

In most countries, local governments are the branch of the public administration that is closest to citizens. Following the principles of good governance, city councils should provide public services in pursuit of greater efficiency and universal orientation (Goldsmith, 1992). However, the scenario in which local governments make their decisions is becoming increasingly complex. Several factors contribute to this complexity in medium-sized and large cities. The first is population growth worldwide (Antrop, 2004), fostered by the change in production structure toward industry and services, which has led to a gradual migration from rural areas to cities. Secondly, the local governments in most developed countries are taking on more responsibilities (Martínez-Vázquez & Timofeev, 2009). A few decades ago it was unthinkable that city councils would provide childcare for their workers, social assistance for the elderly and disabled, or organized leisure activities for their citizens.

In this increasingly complex scenario, one important decision that local governments face in many countries is how the public services under their jurisdiction should be managed. The liberalization and deregulation of economic activity that have occurred in most industrialized economies since the 1980s have led to greater responsibility and more autonomy in local decisions (Goldsmith, 1992). Since then, the choice of management for providing public services has become a recurring debate that has aroused the interest of both policy makers and researchers.

On the one hand, public interest theories based on market failures hold that when markets fail to achieve optimum economic well-being, governments must intervene by providing certain goods and services. This would be the case in densely populated and congested metropolitan areas, where a simple market structure might not be enough to guarantee overall well-being. Conversely, in sparsely populated rural areas, the local government is often the only supplier willing to provide certain public services, which highlights the serious limitations of market mechanisms where public services are concerned (Warner, 2006; Warner & Hefetz, 2003).

On the other hand, private interest theories linked to public choice theory claim that public management often results in overproduction and inefficiency when politicians and bureaucrats monopolize public services. In this sense, the political system would work like a market in which the stakeholders – politicians and bureaucrats – interact to achieve their own personal interests instead of the social objectives that politicians enunciate rhetorically (Friedman & Friedman, 1980). This approach is based on three main hypotheses (Boyne, 1998): firstly, service contracting implies a lower level of spending on the services that are provided by means of an external agency; secondly, competitive tendering is associated with an improvement in the technical efficiency of service provision; and finally, a substantial part of any efficiency gained through contracting out a service will be retained by the local government. Accordingly, incorporating *ex ante* competition into public service markets by way of public tenders would make it possible to increase technical efficiency in the provision of the service while also reducing costs.

Whatever the case may be, municipal governments must decide on the best option for managing local services. Should councils manage local services by themselves? Should they establish independent public bodies? Should they privatize the management of certain local services? These are just some of the relevant questions to be answered.

Public choice regarding the management of the urban water service is particularly important. The large initial investment and high fixed costs of maintenance and renewal of infrastructure, in addition to the existence of economies of scale and economies of density (network effect), justify the fact that the water industry is structured around local natural monopolies, making it highly sensitive to public regulation and political control. As a result, intuition or political and ideological debate should never be considered sufficient to justify decision making. Local governments must rely on management tools that enable them to make rational and not just political or ideological decisions.

It is also important to bear in mind that decision-making processes are not usually based on a single criterion, but rather on several criteria that need to be accounted for jointly. In this framework, multi-criteria analysis (MCA) is useful in two different ways. On the one hand, it makes it possible to perform *ex ante* analyses and therefore incorporate analytic rationality into decision making. On the other hand, *ex post* analyses can also be carried out, making it possible to test whether past decisions were rational. In this sense, the analysis in this paper leads us to understand rationality as reflecting upon and assessing different alternatives, depending on one or several pre-established objectives and under the criteria of optimization and consistency – that is, opting for the best alternative possible without any of the established preferences contradicting each other.

This work contributes to the existing literature in this field of research by demonstrating the usefulness of MCA as a tool that might help local policy makers choose how to manage urban water services. More specifically, the so-called 'analytic hierarchy process' (henceforth AHP) is used to carry out an *ex post* analysis of the decision made in 1997 by the local government of Granada, a southern Spanish city, to transfer the management of urban water service to a public-private partnership. To do so, this paper employs data from the minutes of the plenary sessions of the Granada City Council, data from technical reports compiled by a special commission of experts created ad hoc to help councillors in the voting and decision-making processes, and finally, the results of a questionnaire completed by a group of five experts from the Water Research Institute of the University of Granada. The main conclusion of the research is that, based on the information available at the time the decision was made, incorporating a private partner into the management of the urban water service in the city of Granada was a rational move. Furthermore, confronting the serious financial difficulties faced by the local government took clear precedence over other considerations, such as the social interests of the municipality, when the decision was made.

The rest of the paper is organized as follows. The next section provides an overview of the management of urban water services and the reasons that might influence the choice of one management option or another. The third section describes the application of the AHP to the case study of Granada. The fourth section comments on the results, and the fifth section concludes.

Management of urban water services

Legal aspects in Spain

The legal framework that regulates the management of municipal services in Spain is constituted by Law 7/1985 of 2 April (BOE, 1985), regulating the *Terms and Conditions of Local Government*, and Law 57/2003 of 16 December (BOE, 2003), on *Local Government Modernization Measures*. Article 25 of Law 7/1985 stipulates that local governments are responsible for the provision of urban water services. However, local policymakers have the power to decide how the water service should be managed. In the first place, they may choose to manage the service themselves or to outsource it. Secondly, and in the case of the urban water service being outsourced, management can be transferred to an entirely public company, an entirely private company or to a mixed public-private partnership. It is worth highlighting that only the management of the urban water service can be privatized; the infrastructure will always remain public property. The company that is awarded the concession is responsible for running the service and maintaining the infrastructure for the duration of the contract. Figure 1 shows the distribution of the type of management of water services in 2008 according to population supplied in Spain.

As regards the duration of contracts, when the service is transferred to a public company or is managed by the city council itself, the decision can be reviewed at any time. Conversely, when the urban water service is completely or partially outsourced to a private company – by means of either a concession awarded after a public tender or a public sale of shares – contracts can remain valid for up to 50 years when they involve infrastructure work as well as service operations, or 25 years when they solely involve operations. At the end of the contract, local governments may again choose the alternative they deem the most suitable for the management of the urban water service.

Theoretical background

The introduction highlighted the debate regarding government regulation and intervention in economic issues and the position of theories based on market failures versus theories which place more emphasis on government failures. This section goes one step further and focuses on other approaches within the realms of 'industrial organization theory', which

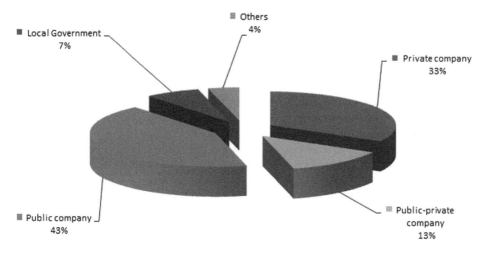

Figure 1.   Percentage of the population in Spain served by different types of urban water service management in 2008. Source: AEAS (2010).

focuses more on how governments intervene and the relationship between incentives and ownership.

'Agency theory' contemplates a principal-agent problem of moral hazard and conflict of interest that arises as a result of separating the ownership and control of an organization, placing emphasis on managers' discretion to use assets belonging to the organization for their own benefit. In the context of this research, processes involving the outsourcing or privatization of public services encourage the separation of principals (public authorities) from agents (private managers). The problem is how to ensure that social interests prevail over private interests, bearing in mind how difficult it is to design a contract that promotes dynamic competition and reduces the probability of monopolistic practices (Bolton & Dewatripont, 2005). In this sense, the idea is to implement supervisory and control processes that may help reconcile the objectives of public authorities and service managers.

According to the foregoing reasoning, the debate regarding the public choice of local service management would be centred on whether it is better to 'make' or 'buy'. In order to assess the advantages and disadvantages of privatizing public services, both government organization and market structure must be taken into account. In this sense, researchers recognize the importance of transaction costs in such processes – costs that must be considered from two different perspectives (Hefetz & Warner, 2007).

On the one hand, in terms of bureaucracy, markets may work better and more efficiently under public regulations, but with limited direct provision on behalf of governments (Savas, 2000). On the other hand, from a market perspective, transaction costs are higher when the management of a service is privatized, because of the complexity of contract specification and the processes involved in controlling and supervising private activity (Brown & Potoski, 2003). As a result, the costs linked to controlling and supervising private activity must be taken into account and play a decisive role in the success or failure of a privatization process. However, the extant empirical evidence on the subject states that privatizing urban water service does not generate cost savings (Bel & Warner, 2008), because of the high transaction costs involved and the specific configuration of the water industry and its market (Warner & Bel, 2008).

Applied research

Several papers have attempted to identify the factors behind the decisions made by local governments in relation to the management of local public services. Recent literature reviews (Bel & Fageda, 2007, 2009) summarize the main factors influencing local privatization of municipal services such as urban water supply. These factors can be grouped into three main categories: pragmatic, political and ideological. The authors' research in this paper focuses on the pragmatic factors, such as local government financial constraints and the quest for efficiency.

In the first place, it is worth highlighting the financial restraints that city councils have endured since 1975. The economic crises suffered since the 1970s have raised doubts about the effectiveness of the mechanism employed to finance the expansion of the 'social welfare state'. Many developed countries have restricted increases in tax as a means to finance growth in government spending. This has affected city councils in two ways: firstly by reducing their ability to generate their own revenue, and secondly by considerably depleting the financial transfers received from higher levels of government.

As regards the search for efficiency, some authors suggest that privatization is a good way of improving the management of certain municipal services, in that economies of scale can be used to better effect (Donahue, 1989). Early empirical studies seemed to provide evidence that outsourcing to private companies reduced the cost of providing water service (Crain & Zardkoohi, 1978; Morgan, 1977), but later studies revealed that there were no significant differences in cost between private and publicly run water companies (Feigenbaum & Teeples, 1983). Some authors even reached the conclusion that publicly run water companies incurred lower costs (Bruggink, 1982). However, more recent studies (Bel, Fageda, & Warner 2010) suggest that the reduction in costs associated with privatization depends on the characteristics of the service and that in the particular case of the water industry, which revolves around a natural monopoly with highly specific assets, privatization is unlikely to achieve significant cost savings.

In general, the research on urban water management confirms what usually happens in other local public services: essentially pragmatic reasons explain local-government decisions. There is empirical evidence for France (Mènard & Saussier, 2000), the USA (Pérard, 2009), and Spain (Bel & Fageda, 2010; González-Gómez & Guardiola, 2009; González-Gómez, Picazo-Tadeo, & Guardiola, 2010; Guardiola, González-Gómez, & García-Rubio, 2010; Miralles, 2009) to this effect. These studies perform *ex post* analyses, largely applying different discrete choice techniques, aimed at investigating the factors behind the privatization of urban water service since 1975. Aside from the study of these factors, other objectives are also important for some researchers – for instance, how can research help local policy makers select the best form of management for urban water services? What criteria should be taken into account when considering the full or partial privatization of urban water service? To what extent do social criteria influence this type of decision making? AHP methods are, as shown in the next section, a powerful tool for answering these and other related questions.

The choice of management for urban water services in Granada: an application of the analytic hierarchy process

Based on an eminently positive approach, different multi-criteria analysis (MCA) techniques aim to solve decision-making problems by considering a set of objectives in conflict and attempting to achieve a final or overall goal associated with these objectives (Hajkowicz & Collins, 2007). Bearing in mind the characteristics of the decision problem studied in this research, we have opted for the analytic hierarchy process (AHP), which is a discrete-choice MCA model (Saaty, 1977, 1980, 1990).

The AHP method was chosen from a series of discrete-choice MCA techniques because it is capable of handling uncertain, imprecise and subjective data, it is robust in solving practical ranking problems and, moreover, it is clear and simple, in methodological and mathematical terms, respectively (Deng, 1999). Essentially, the AHP consists of determining the relative preference of a given set of alternatives in relation to a predetermined goal, taking into account a number of pre-established appropriate criteria and, if necessary, sub-criteria.

In practice, and to introduce analytical thinking into a decision-making process, the AHP method is based on three basic principles: the principle of constructing hierarchies, the principle of establishing priorities and the principle of logical consistency. The first phase in applying the AHP involves designing the decision-making process by establishing a proper hierarchical structure of the elements involved in the decision. In a second phase, priorities are estimated on the basis of the information and assessments available, taking into account the logical consistency of the process for each hierarchical level.

Design of the analytic hierarchy process for the case study (Phase 1)

In 1997, the local government of Granada, a southern Spanish city of 498,365 inhabitants (including the metropolitan area), decided to incorporate a private partner into the shareholding of the municipal company managing the urban water service. As a result, the original public company was transformed into a public-private partnership.

To perform an *ex post* analysis, using the AHP method, of how rational this decision was, three main sources of information are employed: first, the minutes from the Government Commission of the City of Granada related to the *Record of Management Change of Public Water and Sewage Services, 24/96* between 1996 and 1997; second, both legal and economic technical reports and also documentation taken into account by the corporate members of the City Council of Granada during the voting process and decision making; and third, the results from a study based on a questionnaire completed by a group of five experts from the Water Research Institute of the University of Granada (results of this questionnaire are available from the authors upon request). In reference to the questionnaire, we must point out that to avoid influencing their responses, the experts were not informed of the ultimate goal of the research (to analyze the rationality of the decision making). Similarly, the questions were asked in random order.

Finally, it is necessary to design an analytical hierarchy framework using three definitions as a basis: a global objective; a series of necessary criteria on which to base the analysis of decision making; and a set of alternatives to choose from, taking into consideration the foregoing aspects.

The global objective

The first step consists of defining the global objective. Bearing in mind that we are performing an *ex post* analysis of rationality in a decision-making process, the global objective is *to choose the most appropriate form of management for the urban water service in the city of Granada.*

The criteria

The second step consists of determining the criteria for making assessments. This was achieved using information from technical reports prepared by special committees of experts to assist the corporate members of the City Council in voting processes and decision making. As a result, the following criteria were established.

- *Criterion 1 (C1): Financial situation.* This refers to the financial capacity to take charge of the management of the service. The integrated water cycle, as mentioned previously, requires large investments to maintain and renew infrastructure. In this sense, the financial situation of the organization (public or private) that is going to take charge of running the service is an essential factor when assessing the various management alternatives.
- *Criterion 2 (C2): Technical and economic organization capacity.* This refers to the use of economies of scale, management capacity and flexibility, and the ability to undertake investments to improve the service, among others. When analyzing the contracting-out of local services in economic terms, it is important to assess the management alternatives available in relation to aspects such as: creating an incentive system to motivate workers; designing action and awareness procedures to evaluate the results of management and work; and the possibility of claiming ownership of innovations.
- *Criterion 3 (C3): Service improvements for citizens.* The provision of the integrated water cycle service generates significant positive externalities for the general public. Therefore, governments should take into account these externalities and the improvements in the quality of the service that each management alternative offers when making their choice.
- *Criterion 4 (C4): Improvements in the economic and social development of the city.* When choosing how to manage urban water services, it is also important to consider the incentives and motivations that the management alternatives may offer in relation to favouring the social and environmental development of cities – environmental aspects, preservation of city historical quarters, etc.

The alternatives

As a third step, we must define the alternatives for the decision-making process. Bearing in mind the Spanish legislation described earlier, the following four alternatives were considered.

- *Alternative 1 (A1): Direct management through a local (public) entity.* In this management alternative, the city council itself is responsible for directing, managing and monitoring the service. The advantage of direct management is that the local government has strong control over the service, although the restrictions imposed by legislation on the economic activities carried out by different levels of government in Spain make it less flexible than a private enterprise.
- *Alternative 2 (A2): Public company.* This option consists of creating a public company, the main features of which are that it is not governed by the principle of profit and management and does not consider exclusively economic criteria, as is the case with private companies. The main disadvantage of this management alternative is the lack of competition, which takes away any incentive to improve the management of the service or implement innovations.
- *Alternative 3 (A3): Private company.* This alternative implies effectively transferring the management of the service to a private company, although such a move does not involve a change of ownership. Delegating management to specialized companies endowed with comparative advantages in terms of technical, financial and

organizational capacities can increase confidence in improving management. One disadvantage of this alternative is, nevertheless, that the city council relinquishes control of the management of the service and transaction costs increase.

— *Alternative 4 (A4): Mixed public-private partnership.* In this legal form, capital is shared between a private partner and a public partner, the latter usually being the city council. Usually, this option results in the private partner managing the service, while the presence of the public partner safeguards the social interests of the municipality. This formula allows the city council to benefit from the know-how of the private company, while maintaining more direct control, which is in the interest of citizens. One additional advantage this option has is that it reduces transaction costs by decreasing the cost of supervising the management of the service.

The hierarchical structure of our decision-making process is summarized in Figure 2.

Estimation of priorities (Phase 2)

Having established the hierarchical structure of the decision-making process, let us begin with the first hierarchical level, where the relative importance of the criteria is compared in regard to the goal.

Hierarchical Level 1: Criteria assessment in regard to the goal

Following the AHP and considering the information obtained from the assessment made by our group of experts, we obtain the matrix of criteria comparisons in regard to the goal displayed in Table 1.

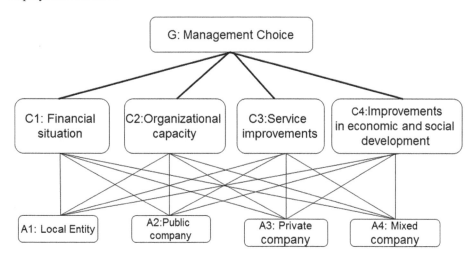

Figure 2.   Hierarchy for the case study of Granada.

Table 1.   Matrix of criteria comparisons in regard to the goal.

In regard to goal	C1	C2	C3	C4
C1	1	3	6	7
C2	0.333	1	4	5
C3	0.167	0.250	1	3
C4	0.143	0.200	0.333	1

Table 2.   Priorities of criteria comparisons (EM: eigenvector method; GMM: geometric mean method).

	Priorities (EM)	Priorities (GMM)
C1: Financial situation	0.571	0.571
C2: Technical and economic organization capacity	0.274	0.274
C3: Service improvements for citizens	0.102	0.101
C4: Improvements in economic and social development	0.054	0.053
Inconsistency		(0.060)

To estimate the relative importance of each criterion in regard to the goal, we implement both the principal right eigenvector method (Saaty, 1980) and the geometric mean method (Barzilai, Cook, & Golany, 1987; Crawford & Williams, 1985). The results obtained by the two methods are practically identical and are displayed in Table 2.

Hierarchical Level 2: Alternative assessment in regard to the criteria

At this level, we perform a pairwise comparison between the available alternatives in regard to each of the criteria. As a result, a total of four matrices are generated (one for each criterion). The results are presented in Table 3.

Table 3.   Comparison of alternatives in regard to criteria.

In regard to C1	A1	A2	A3	A4	Priorities
A1	1	0.333	0.200	0.200	0.070
A2	3	1	0.500	0.500	0.193
A3	5	2	1	1	0.368
A4	5	2	1	1	0.368
Inconsistency					(0.002)

In regard to C2	A1	A2	A3	A4	Priorities
A1	1	0.333	0.200	0.250	0.072
A2	3	1	0.333	0.333	0.151
A3	5	3	1	2	0.466
A4	4	3	0.500	1	0.311
Inconsistency					(0.040)

In regard to C3	A1	A2	A3	A4	Priorities
A1	1	0.500	0.333	0.200	0.085
A2	2	1	1	0.333	0.179
A3	3	1	1	0.250	0.184
A4	5	3	4	1	0.552
Inconsistency					(0.020)

In regard to C4	A1	A2	A3	A4	Priorities
A1	1	1	3	1	0.294
A2	1	1	3	2	0.349
A3	0.333	0.333	1	0.250	0.091
A4	1	0.500	4	1	0.266
Inconsistency					(0.040)

Table 4.   Estimation of global priorities.

	C1 (0.571)	C2 (0.274)	C3 (0.101)	C4 (0.053)	*Global priorities*
A1	0.070	0.072	0.084	0.294	0.084
A2	0.193	0.151	0.179	0.349	0.188
A3	0.368	0.466	0.185	0.091	0.361
A4	0.368	0.311	0.552	0.266	0.366
Overall inconsistency					(0.040)

Finally, after obtaining the comparison matrices of alternatives with their associated priorities, the global priorities are displayed in Table 4.

Results and discussion

In June 1997, the City Council of Granada approved the partial privatization of the municipal water company, Emasagra S.A., with 15 votes for and 12 against. A total of 49% of the shares of the municipal company were sold to Aquagest, which belongs to the Agbar Group, a large holding company that operates in all fields related to community services. In exchange, the management of the service was transferred for a period of 25 years. The shares were sold for more than €241 million, a sum that provided partial relief for the ailing accounts of the City Council at the time.

On the basis of the information available, the main reason for privatizing the service was strictly financial. According to the various reports consulted, the Granada City Council had recorded a deficit since 1992 that was seriously endangering the sustainability of the municipal accounts. In light of the fact that the other measures adopted to reduce spending were clearly insufficient, a financial rationalization plan was approved in November 1996, which included, among other measures, a reduction in spending and an increase in tax burden, while also contemplating the possibility of transferring assets to obtain extraordinary income. Financial criteria prevailed when it came to selecting one of the three private companies that participated in the auction for shares. More specifically, the financial situation of the bidding companies and the highest bid for the shares were the two most highly valued criteria. However, the City Council did not decide to fully privatize the service, despite the fact that doing so would have gone much further toward solving the financial problems it was suffering at the time. This clearly shows that the decision regarding how to manage urban water service is complex and involves not only financial, but also technical, organizational, economic and social aspects. Furthermore, the legislation does include a wide range of legal management options, which increases the interest and importance of analyzing this type of decision-making processes.

From the technical, economic and organizational perspectives, selling all the shares of the public company would have seen the City Council lose all control over the management of the service, with all the monitoring problems and transaction costs this would have entailed. From a social viewpoint, full privatization might have met strong opposition from the employees of the public company and from citizens in general, a situation that politicians seek to avoid at all costs. The main reason for this is that urban water service privatization processes are normally associated with layoffs, wage cuts and price increases that affect citizens; in Spain there is empirical evidence of a positive relationship between water prices and private management of the service (Martínez-Espiñeira, García-Valiñas, & González-Gómez, 2009).

As regards the evaluation of the group of experts in relation to the various criteria considered in our decision-making process, the first noteworthy result refers to the

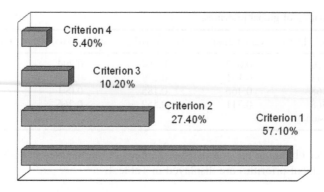

Figure 3.   Relative importance of criteria.

assessment of the criteria. It is interesting to note that the financial situation (Criterion 1) is the most important in relative terms, with 57.10% (see Figure 3). This is interesting because while the financial situation of the city council determines the decision regarding how to manage urban water services, local governments will prefer to either fully or partially privatize management. In fact, privatization has historically become a highly recurrent resource for city councils when their financial situation has not been favourable (González-Gómez, Guardiola, & Ruiz-Villaverde, 2009; Ruiz-Villaverde, García-Rubio, & González-Gómez, 2010). This issue has been extensively referred to in previous research, which points out that the main factors taken into account in local privatization decisions are essentially pragmatic (Bel & Fageda, 2007, 2009, 2010; González-Gómez & Guardiola, 2009; González-Gómez et al., 2010), financial constraints being a decisive factor.

The second noteworthy result is the striking similarity of results between Alternative 3 (private company) and Alternative 4 (mixed company). According to the final result, local governments only slightly prefer public-private partnerships to private companies (36.59% to 36.17%). We observe that private companies are slightly preferred to mixed companies under Criterion 2 (capacity of technical and economic organization). However, regarding Criterion 3 (service improvements for citizens) and Criterion 4 (improvements in economic and social development), mixed companies receive a more favourable assessment. Let us highlight, however, that Criteria 3 and 4 are less important in relative terms than Criterion 2, which is why the difference between the two alternatives in the overall result is hardly significant (see Figure 4).

The fact that a mixed company receives such a high score in relation to Criterion 3 needs to be explained. This option makes it possible to take advantage of the know-how of private management in day-to-day activities without the public partner having to relinquish its direct control over social interests. In addition, public-private partnerships have lower transaction costs than private companies do. In fact, Spanish cities have opted for this type of management to a greater extent in recent years (González-Gómez et al., 2009; Ruiz-Villaverde et al., 2010). When mixed companies are controlled effectively by a local government, they are more likely to pay attention to social objectives compared to the goal of maximizing profits (Matsumura, 1998). In addition, under this management regime it is possible to considerably reduce the problems derived from incomplete contracts in the long term (Bel & Fageda, 2010). In the same vein, Schmitz (2000) found that partial privatization can result in an optimum combination of incentives to reduce costs and increase quality, in comparison to purely public or purely private forms of management.

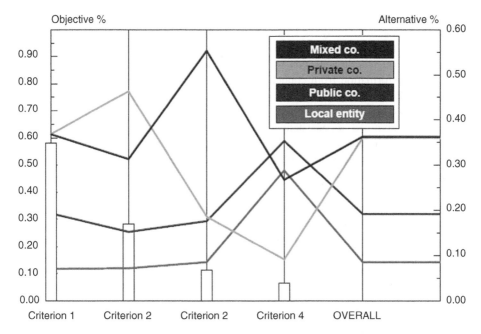

Figure 4.   Performance sensitivity for nodes.

Similarly, it is worth mentioning that Alternatives 1 (local entity) and 2 (public company) receive a favourable assessment with respect to Criterion 4, even improving on the score recorded by private and mixed companies. However, as indicated previously, Criterion 4 is less important than the others, which affects the overall results of these alternatives.

As regards overall priorities, the preferred alternative is a mixed public-private partnership, which leads us to the conclusion that, on the basis of the information available at that time, the decision made in the 1990s by the City Council of Granada was rational. That is to say, when a local government is experiencing serious financial problems, as was the case then, the alternative of complete or partial privatization is seen as a necessary move to solve such problems. Nevertheless, when criteria other than strictly financial aspects are assessed, public-private partnerships emerge as the best option.

Concluding remarks

The tendency of the population to concentrate in urban areas and new demands on behalf of citizens in developed countries have forced local governments to make more and more decisions in an increasingly complex environment. In these scenarios, politicians are expected to make rational decisions, and for them to do so, researchers are expected to provide them with the necessary tools for analysis. One important decision that local governments must address, in nations where the law provides, is how urban water service should be managed. The difficulty involved in making this decision is usually due to local governments having to consider several criteria simultaneously. In such cases, various multi-criteria analysis techniques can facilitate decision making.

This work employed the 'analytic hierarchy process' to perform an *ex post* analysis of the decision made in 1997 by the City Council in the southern Spanish city of Granada to sell part of the municipal water company's shares to a private company. Four alternatives and four decision criteria were considered in the design of the decision-making process. Furthermore, information from council meeting minutes and technical reports compiled throughout the decision-making process were used, in addition to the evaluations of a panel of five experts from the University of Granada.

The result obtained is consistent with the literature that explains decisions made by municipal governments concerning how to manage local public services. A pragmatic reason, high local debt, is the decisive factor when explaining the decision to incorporate a private partner into urban water service management in the case of Granada. Partial privatization, besides obtaining better leverage for the contribution of know-how, helps to alleviate the poor state of public finances. Nevertheless, further research in this direction is required to determine whether or not full or partial privatization should be considered as a means for funding for the local government. According to the results of this study, a public company is perceived as the most appropriate alternative for the social and economic interests of the municipality. However, when a city council faces serious financial difficulties, solving those problems takes precedence over others, including the social interests of the municipality.

It is also clear that more attention must be paid to the decision-making process in regard to the way urban water service is managed; it is complex and combines technical aspects, managerial concerns and social issues. There is even a possibility that the most important problems are not directly related to the management of the service; issues such as the territorial organization of the country, the distribution of responsibilities among the different levels of government, and the public financing system should be reconsidered. However, until a thorough reform of the current legislation is undertaken, local managers will continue to have to make decisions in highly adverse situations, for which reason studies such as this can help to improve the results of complex decision-making processes.

In view of the results obtained, it is worth investigating to what extent the financial situation of a municipality should be a decisive factor when choosing a management option for a public service such as the water supply. The local government must protect the interests of its citizens by offering high-quality and efficient services. It would therefore be desirable for service quality and efficiency, rather than other factors, to be the determinants of local government decisions. In Spain, implementing mechanisms to raise the budget capacity of municipalities and controlling budget deficits would lead local governments to pay less heed to the financial criterion in decision-making processes. That criterion determined the partial privatization of the management of the water service in the case of Granada. We do not intend to raise doubts about private participation in the management of urban water service, but rather question the fact that the financial aspect determines the final decision made by local governments.

Finally, some policy recommendations can be made on the basis of the results of this research. On the one hand, citizens' opinions should be taken into account as much as possible in this kind of decision-making process. It should not be forgotten that the decision to privatize in Granada was approved by a narrow majority and that urban water service management is now committed until 2047, following the renewal of the contract in 2005. On the other hand, it is highly recommendable to conduct studies aimed at exploring which management alternatives are the most efficient and why. In this sense, service efficiency and quality criteria should be assigned more importance when considering decisions such as privatizing urban water service.

Acknowledgments

The comments and suggestions from the referees are gratefully acknowledged. The authors also acknowledge financial support from the Junta de Andalucía (Project P11-SEJ-7039) and the Ministry of Economy and Competitiveness (Projects ECO2009-08824/ECON and ECO2012-32189).

References

AEAS (2010). *Encuesta sobre el suministro de agua potable y saneamiento en España* [Survey on water supply and sanitation in Spain]. Madrid: AEAS.

Antrop, M. (2004). Landscape change and the urbanization process in Europe. *Landscape and Urban Planning, 67*, 9–26. doi:10.1016/S0169-2046(03)00026-4.

Barzilai, J., Cook, W. D., & Golany, B. (1987). Consistent weights for judgements matrices of the relative importance of alternatives. *Operations Research Letters, 6*, 131–134. doi:10.1016/0167-6377(87)90026-5.

Bel, G., & Fageda, X. (2007). Why do local governments privatize public services? A survey of empirical studies. *Local Government Studies, 33*, 517–534. doi:10.1080/03003930701417528.

Bel, G., & Fageda, X. (2009). Factors explaining local privatization: A meta-regression analysis. *Public Choice, 139*, 105–119. doi:10.1007/s11127-008-9381-z.

Bel, G., & Fageda, X. (2010). Partial privatization in local services delivery: An empirical analysis on the choice of mixed firms. *Local Government Studies, 36*, 129–149. doi:10.1080/03003930903435856.

Bel, G., Fageda, X., & Warner, M. E. (2010). Is private production of public services cheaper than public production? A meta-regression analysis of solid waste and water services. *Journal of Policy Analysis and Management, 29*, 553–577. doi:10.1002/pam.20509.

Bel, G., & Warner, M. E. (2008). Does privatization of solid waste and water services reduce costs? A review of empirical studies. *Resources, Conservation & Recycling, 52*, 1337–1348. doi:10.1016/j.resconrec.2008.07.014.

Bolton, P., & Dewatripont, M. (2005). *Contract theory.* Cambridge, MA: MIT Press.

BOE (Official State Gazette) (1985) Law 7/1985, of 2 April, regulating the *Terms and Conditions of Local Government*, BOE No. 80, 3 April 1985. (In Spanish).

BOE (Official State Gazette) (2003) Law 57/2003, of 16 December, on *Local Government Modernization Measures*, BOE No. 301, 17 December 2003. (In Spanish).

Boyne, G. A. (1998). Bureaucratic theory meets reality: Public choice and service contracting in U.S. local government. *Public Administration Review, 58*, 474–484. http://www.jstor.org/stable/977575

Brown, T. L., & Potoski, M. (2003). Managing contract performance: A transaction costs approach. *Journal of Policy Analysis and Management, 22*, 275–297. doi:10.1002/pam.10117.

Bruggink, T. H. (1982). Public versus regulated private enterprise in the municipal water industry: A comparison of operating costs. *Quarterly Review of Economics and Business, 22*, 111–125.

Crain, W., & Zardkoohi, A. (1978). A test of the property-rights theory of the firm: Water utilities in the United States. *Journal of Law and Economics, 21*, 395–408. http://www.jstor.org/stable/725239

Crawford, G., & Williams, C. (1985). A note on the analysis of subjective judgement matrices. *Journal of Mathematical Psychology, 29*, 387–405. doi:10.1016/0022-2496(85)90002-1.

Deng, H. (1999). Multicriteria analysis with fuzzy pairwise comparison. *International Journal of Approximate Reasoning, 21*, 215–231. doi:10.1016/S0888-613X(99)00025-0.

Donahue, J. (1989). *The privatization decision: Public ends, private means.* New York: Basic Books.

Feigenbaum, S., & Teeples, R. (1983). Public versus private water delivery: A hedonic cost approach. *Review of Economics and Statistics, 65*, 672–678. http://www.jstor.org/stable/1935940.

Friedman, M., & Friedman, R. D. (1980). *Free to choose: A personal statement.* San Diego, CA: Harcourt.

Goldsmith, M. (1992). Local government. *Urban Studies, 29*, 393–410. doi:10.1080/00420989220080501.

González-Gómez, F., & Guardiola, J. (2009). A duration model for the estimation of the contracting-out of urban water management in Southern Spain. *Urban Affairs Review, 44*, 886–906. doi:10.1177/1078087408329274.

González-Gómez, F., Guardiola, J., & Ruiz-Villaverde, A. (2009). Reconsidering privatisation in the governance of water in Spain. *Municipal Engineer, 162*, 159–164. doi:10.1680/muen.2009.162.3.159.

González-Gómez, F., Picazo-Tadeo, A. J., & Guardiola, J. (2010). Why do local governments privatise the provision of water services? Empirical evidence from Spain. *Public Administration, 89*, 471–492. doi:10.1111/j.1467-9299.2010.01880.x.

Guardiola, J., González-Gómez, F., & García-Rubio, M. A. (2010). Is time really important for research into contracting out public services in cities? *Cities, 27*, 369–376. doi:10.1016/j.cities.2010.05.004.

Hajkowicz, S., & Collins, K. (2007). A review of multiple criteria analysis for water resource planning and management. *Water Resources Management, 21*, 1553–1566. doi:10.1007/s11269-006-9112-5.

Hefetz, A., & Warner, M. (2007). Beyond the market vs. planning dichotomy: Understanding privatisation and its reverse in US cities. *Local Government Studies, 33*, 555–572. doi:10.1080/03003930701417585.

Martínez-Espiñeira, R., García-Valiñas, M. A., & González-Gómez, F. (2009). Does private management of water supply services really increase prices? An empirical analysis. *Urban Studies, 46*, 923–945. doi:10.1177/0042098009102135.

Martínez-Vázquez, J., & Timofeev, A. (2009). A fiscal perspective of state rescaling. *Cambridge Journal of Regions, Economy and Society, 2*, 85–105. doi:10.1093/cjres/rsn027.

Matsumura, T. (1998). Partial privatization in mixed duopoly. *Journal of Public Economics, 70*, 473–483. doi:10.1016/S0047-2727(98)00051-6.

Mènard, C., & Saussier, S. (2000). Contractual choice and performance: The case of water supply in France. *Revue d'Économie Industrielle, 92*, 385–404. doi:10.3406/rei.2000.1058.

Miralles, A. (2009). A duration model analysis of privatization of municipal water services. *Revista de Economía Aplicada, 17*, 47–75.

Morgan, W. (1977). Investor owned vs. publicly owned water agencies: An evaluation of the property rights theory of the firm. *Water Resources Bulletin, 13*, 775–781. doi:10.1111/j.1752-1688.1977.tb02061.x.

Pérard, E. (2009). Water supply: Public or private? An approach based on cost of funds, transaction costs, efficiency and political costs. *Policy and Society, 27*, 193–219. doi:10.1016/j.polsoc.2008.10.004.

Ruiz-Villaverde, A., García-Rubio, M. A., & González-Gómez, F. (2010). Analysis of urban water management in historical perspective: Evidence from the Spanish case. *International Journal of Water Resources Development, 26*, 653–674. doi:10.1080/07900627.2010.519497.

Saaty, T. L. (1977). A scaling method for priorities in hierarchical structures. *Journal of Mathematical Psychology, 15*, 234–281. doi:10.1016/0022-2496(77)90033-5.

Saaty, T. L. (1980). *The analytic hierarchy process.* New York: McGraw Hill.

Saaty, T. L. (1990). How to make a decision: The analytic hierarchy process. *European Journal of Operational Research, 48*, 9–26. doi:10.1016/0377-2217(90)90057-I.

Savas, E. S. (2000). *Privatization and public–private partnerships.* New York: Chatham House.

Schmitz, P. W. (2000). Partial privatization and incomplete contracts: The proper scope of government reconsidered. *FinanzArchiv, 57*, 394–411. Retrieved from http://mpra.ub.uni-muenchen.de/13447/.

Warner, M. E. (2006). Market-based governance and the challenge for rural governments: US trends. *Social Policy and Administration, 40*, 612–631. doi:10.1111/j.1467-9515.2006.00523.x.

Warner, M. E., & Bel, G. (2008). Competition or monopoly? Comparing privatization of local public services in the US and Spain. *Public Administration, 86*, 723–735. doi:10.1111/j.1467-9299.2008.00700.x.

Warner, M. E., & Hefetz, A. (2003). Rural–urban differences in privatization: Limits to the competitive state. *Environment and Planning C: Government and Policy, 21*, 703–718. 10.1068/c008r.

Adopting versus adapting: adoption of water-saving technology versus water conservation habits in Spain

Roberto Martínez-Espiñeira[a] and María Á. García-Valiñas[b]

[a]Department of Economics, Memorial University of Newfoundland, Canada; [b]Oviedo Efficiency Group, University of Oviedo, Spain, and LERNA, Toulouse, France

Issues of water scarcity can be ameliorated through household adoption of water-saving technologies and by adaptation of consumption behaviour. In this paper the determinants of the adoption of water-efficient devices and of water-saving habits in Spain are analyzed using data from 27,000 households. This includes information on choices about self-reported conservation habits and decisions about the adoption of water-saving equipment. The findings show that educational campaigns have a strong positive effect on both decisions to undertake investments and decisions to adapt habits. These results also allow campaigns to be aimed at certain socio-economic groups identified in the econometric analysis.

Introduction

In developed countries the demand for water is rising at a rate that outpaces the development of traditional supply sources, leading, in many areas, to crises of water management. In response, a range of solutions have been proposed, although water suppliers are increasingly looking to conservation to reduce demand, rather than to supply-based solutions, when dealing with shortages. Even in regions that in principle enjoy an abundant water supply, there is an increased interest in demand-side management measures aimed at promoting residential water conservation. The situation is worse in developing countries, where serious problems related to scarcity and quality have a strong impact on hygiene and health (WHO/UNICEF, 2008).

In Spain, although industry and agriculture account for the bulk of water demand, domestic water use still represents a substantial proportion of total water consumption, with showering and toilet flushing representing almost 60% of total domestic water use (Sauri, 2003). Therefore, important savings can be achieved by adopting water-saving technologies, including water-efficient washing machines and showerheads, as well as dual-flush toilets.

Although pricing policies have received a lot of attention in the literature dealing with water demand management (e.g. Arbués, García-Valiñas, & Martínez-Espiñeira, 2003; Dalhuisen, Florax, de Groot, & Nijkamp, 2003; Worthington & Hoffman, 2008), policies aimed at promoting the installation of water-efficient or water-saving equipment have seldom been considered by economists. Noteworthy exceptions are Renwick and Archibald (1998), Renwick and Green (2000), and Millock and Nauges (2010), who have studied adoption of water-efficient equipment at the household level.

Water-use habits are the target of other forms of non-price policies, such as public information campaigns. However, only a few studies (for instance Domene and Sauri [2006], who found that households who have strong indoor water conservation habits reduce their consumption between 4.3 and 4.6 litres per capita per day during the winter season) have shown the impact of water-saving habits on residential water consumption.

The main aim of this paper is to fill this gap, by studying the determinants of the adoption of water-efficient devices and the adaptation of water-use habits by households. We use a large data-set resulting from a survey of close to 27,000 Spanish households conducted by the Spanish Statistical Institute (INE, 2008).

Starting from a series of individual binary variables that indicate self-reported choices about conservation habits and decisions on the adoption of water-saving equipment, we build two ordinal indices for each household. We then use a bivariate ordered probit model to model the values taken by these indices. This allows us to account for the correlation within a given household between the two types of decisions.

Modelling households' water conservation habits

Increasing focus is being placed on water conservation in the home – habits such as turning off the tap when brushing one's teeth or waiting until there is a full load before using a washing machine or dishwasher. The effect of habits on water demand is key, because it could explain a good proportion of the differences observed between the short-run and long-run price elasticities of water demand (e.g. Arbués et al., 2003; Martínez-Espiñeira, 2007; Musolesi & Nosvelli, 2007; Worthington & Hoffman, 2008). In fact, the persistence of water-use habits has been identified as a potential reason why, below a certain level of use, households might fail altogether to respond in the short run to water price changes (Gaudin, Griffin, & Sickles, 2001; Martínez-Espiñeira & Nauges, 2004).

The questions remain as to the extent that these water conservation habits and practices relate to other activities generally termed 'environmental actions' and whether different types of households are more likely to acquire water conservation habits (Gilg & Barr, 2006). Information and education are likely to be necessary but not sufficient components of any program for behaviour change, because a combination of factors is needed to promote water-saving behaviour. Influencing the habits of the less responsive users requires a better understanding of what shapes water conservation behaviours. However, gaining this understanding is a rather complex task, because the possible interactions of non-price campaigns with other policy instruments make it difficult to evaluate their separate effectiveness, as pointed out by Syme, Nancarrow, and Seligman (2000).

Most domestic water-related activities are often performed in time-space coordination with other activities (Elizondo & Lofthouse, 2010; Krantz, 2006). It has also been suggested that households are generally unaware of their own water consumption and that individual perceptions of changes in water-use behaviours are constrained by habit and a lack of knowledge about what types of adaptations can be made and how (Clark & Finley, 2008; Doron, Teh, Haklay, & Bell, 2011).

Clarke and Brown (2006) surveyed 2600 households in a study of the drivers of water conservation in Melbourne, Australia. They focused on three water-use behaviours and appliances, finding that 6% of respondents had a rainwater tank, 52% had a water-efficient showerhead, and 5% reused greywater. They found that water-use changes depended upon the capacity of individuals to acquire and apply water-saving and reuse measures. The authors also report that the key barriers to a widespread practice of conservation and alternative water use include difficulty of implementation, cost, and being a renter rather than owner of one's dwelling, rather than issues of attitudes and lack of awareness.

More recently, Dolnicar and Hurlimann (2010) showed that Australians generally have positive attitudes towards water conservation and water-saving appliances but that these positive attitudes do not consistently translate into actual behaviour (as Jensen [2008] had also found using Danish data). The main barriers to adoption of water conservation behaviours identified were the perception of inconvenience and impracticality and the costs associated with purchasing water-saving equipment. The authors suggest that these findings reveal a substantial potential in Australia for exploiting further water conservation measures.

Economic model

Several works have now examined the effect of different variables on water conservation habits and investments. Generally speaking, research on the determinants of pro-environmental attitudes and behaviours is divided into two major areas: studies focusing on economic and socio-demographic factors, and studies focusing on values, attitudes and beliefs (Dietz, Stern, & Guagnano, 1998). Olli, Grendstad, and Wollebaek (2001) found that socio-demographic factors explained a small percentage of pro-environmental acts. Nevertheless, it is important to include these factors because they have a significant role as control variables related to the cost of participating in the protection of the environment (Torgler, García-Valiñas, & Macintyre, 2010).

When it comes to the hypothesized effect of household income on choices about water conservation, two countervailing tendencies are at play. On the one hand, better-off households can more easily afford to invest in water-saving technologies. On the other hand, a diminishing marginal utility of income means that wealthy households will feel less of an incentive to conserve water and face a higher opportunity cost in the time needed for installation of new technology (Millock & Nauges, 2010). Lam (2006) found that richer households stated that they were more inclined to retrofit to conserve water, but this study did not observe actual conservation choices. The theoretical prediction of the effect of income is less ambiguous when it comes to water-saving habits. Assuming as usual that the opportunity costs of time are higher for richer users, they would find it more costly to adopt habits involving greater time investments in water-using activities; lower-income households would be expected to adapt their behaviour more readily in order to conserve water.

Regarding education, the results offered by the literature are ambiguous. On the one hand, both the adoption of water-saving technology and the adaptation of behaviours require that the nature of water shortages and water-saving options be understood, as well as that household members believe they can implement at least some of the water-saving options available and that their conservation efforts will not be exploited by others. Since the first three conditions are likely to be positively related to education, better-educated households will be more likely to conserve water. Indeed, De Oliver (1999) found education to be positively related to water conservation. However, education showed no effect on the behavioural intention to conserve water in Lam (2006).

Other socio-demographic features have been considered as control factors. Millock and Nauges (2010) found a positive and significant relationship between household size and the adoption of water-saving technologies. Although women are usually found more to be likely to adopt pro-conservation behaviours (Torgler et al., 2010), when analyzing intentions to save water, Lam (2006) unexpectedly found that gender did not exert a significant effect.

Gender effects may well differ depending on the environmental behaviour in question (OECD, 2008).

Additionally, the direction of the effect of age appears ambiguous across behaviours and studies, with some studies also showing only a non-significant effect (Trumbo & O'Keefe, 2001). Lam (2006) found a significant age effect only when other predictors were ignored.

Regarding ownership status, it is rational to think that those individuals who own the dwelling are more willing to invest in some pro-environmental appliances. Home owners find it worthwhile to invest in durable goods that will help them reduce their water bills in the future, or to take advantage of having the investment capitalized in the price of the house when selling it, while renters have less of the first incentive and none of the second. More importantly, owners are also entitled to make a wider variety of changes (e.g. plumbing changes) in the dwelling, while renters are more constrained. In fact, some authors have found a positive and significant relationship between ownership and the adoption of water-efficient equipment (Gilg & Barr, 2006; Millock & Nauges, 2010). However, some studies have detected the opposite effect (Renwick & Archibald, 1998). Moreover, there is no empirical evidence of the effect of this variable on water conservation habits. It has also been found that some dwelling characteristics are important when explaining adoption and adaptation behaviours. Thus, households with lawns, gardens and pools were found more likely to undertake conservation practices (Millock & Nauges, 2010). The age of the dwelling also matters. For example, Millock and Nauges (2010) found that the older the building, the less likely the adoption of water-efficient equipment.

Additionally, those households with pro-environmental predispositions, concerns and behaviours are more likely to engage in water-saving practices, whether through the adoption of efficient technology or through the adaptation of behaviour. To show the impact of these kinds of factors on the adoption of water-saving technologies, Millock and Nauges (2010) considered several variables to measure environmental concern in several fields. In all cases, they found a positive and significant relationship with water conservation investments. Other studies have shown similar findings (Gilg & Barr, 2006; Lam, 2006).

Data

This research is based on data (18,953 observations) from the 2008 survey *Households and Environment* (INE 2008), which investigated Spanish households' habits and attitudes towards the environment. The survey covered all the autonomous communities in Spain and included questions about water use, energy use, waste, noise and bad smells, transportation and mobility, and consumption habits. (For further details, consult INE [2009].) In each household, two people were asked to answer the survey questionnaire. A *reference person* (the person older than 18 who was living at home and was the owner or tenant of the apartment/house, and, if the residence ownership or the rent was shared, the person with the highest income) answered most questions about household equipment and appliances. The *selected person* was selected from all the household members older than 16 and asked several questions about habits, attitudes, and opinions concerning the environment.

Starting from a series of binary indicators of self-reported choices about conservation habits and adoption of water-saving equipment, two ordinal indices were built for each household. Seven self-described pro-environmental behaviours or habits linked to water use were included in the habits index, *sco_habit*. Four different appliances were considered to build the investment index, *sco_inves*. Since all the variables capturing habits and investments are binary, all their individual values were summed to calculate each index.

Table 1.   Variables for water conservation habits (1 if the description is true, 0 otherwise).

Variables	Description
habit_1	Household recycles water
habit_2	Household has water in the fridge to avoid having to run water from the tap to get cold water
habit_3	Household defrosts food in advance (not with tap water)
habit_4	Household fills the sink before washing dishes
habit_5	Household fills the washing machine and the dishwasher
habit_6	Household closes the stopcock to reduce water flow
habit_7	Household has a paper bin in the bathroom to avoid using water as a paper bin

Source: own elaboration from INE (2008)

Tables 1 and 2 show the variables capturing the habits and investments considered to calculate each index, while Tables 3 and 4 show the average values of different habits and investments variables depending on the region where the household resides. They also present the values of the two indices by region. In Spain, the regional governments ('autonomous communities') have different competences on environmental issues. Therefore, they have autonomy in applying environmental public policies. Additionally, there are significant differences among them with respect to income and climate, among other features.

In general, more than 80% of the households in our sample usually defrost food in advance instead of using tap water, and fill the washing machine and the dishwasher before each use. Additionally, a substantial percentage of households keep water in the fridge to avoid running water from the tap until it is cold, and have a paper bin in the water closet to avoid using the toilet as a paper bin. Finally, there are some habits which do not appear to be very popular, such as recycling water and closing the stopcock to reduce water flow. By regions, we observe that Andalucía, Aragón, Baleares, Canarias, Cataluña, Comunidad Valenciana and Madrid present values higher than the national average. In general, households in those regions seem to be more careful with water in terms of habits. It is worthwhile to mention the high values registered in the islands (Baleares and Canary Islands), where a culture of water conservation is well established.

When it comes to investment choices, we observe that most Spanish households have installed a single-handled tap and a water-efficient washing machine. However, the frequency of adoption is very low in the case of flow-control devices and dual-flush toilets. Some regions, particularly Aragón, Castilla-La Mancha and Comunidad Valenciana, exhibit values of the investment index (*sco_inves*) much higher than the national average.

To investigate the drivers behind the values of the two water conservation indices, we specified an explanatory model based on three broad groups of independent variables. First, we consider a set of socioeconomic characteristics of the households, which we expect to

Table 2.   Variables for water conservation investments (1 if the description is true, 0 otherwise).

Variables	Description
invest_1	Household has single-handle tap
invest_2	Household has at least one flow-control device
invest_3	Household has a water-efficient toilet
invest_4	Household has a water-efficient washing machine (A, A + or A++)

Source: own elaboration from INE (2008)

Table 3. Water conservation habits by autonomous community.

Autonomous community	habit_1	habit_2	habit_3	habit_4	habit_5	habit_6	habit_7	sco_habit
Andalucía	0.3169	0.6471	0.8726	0.3357	0.7760	0.2576	0.7426	3.9485
Aragón	0.2205	0.7028	0.9449	0.3465	0.8760	0.2953	0.4055	3.7913
Asturias	0.0388	0.5673	0.7510	0.3224	0.7163	0.2633	0.1857	2.8449
Baleares (Islas)	0.1991	0.8055	0.8924	0.7414	0.8970	0.3043	0.6087	4.4485
Canarias	0.2593	0.6102	0.8466	0.2011	0.6878	0.6314	0.8536	4.0899
Cantabria	0.1175	0.6110	0.9373	0.2402	0.8825	0.2689	0.6371	3.6945
Castilla y León	0.1556	0.5042	0.8306	0.4250	0.8368	0.2181	0.3729	3.3431
Castilla-La Mancha	0.1509	0.7869	0.9129	0.4930	0.8569	0.2706	0.5692	4.0404
Cataluña	0.2602	0.5082	0.8245	0.5076	0.8020	0.3251	0.5067	3.7342
Comunidad Valenciana	0.2106	0.7387	0.9124	0.3602	0.9163	0.2111	0.6156	3.9651
Extremadura	0.1844	0.6803	0.9016	0.5041	0.8607	0.1619	0.6475	3.9406
Galicia	0.1069	0.4701	0.8524	0.3442	0.7853	0.2681	0.4855	3.3125
Madrid	0.2777	0.8249	0.8868	0.3298	0.7917	0.5087	0.4958	4.1155
Murcia	0.2755	0.5313	0.7728	0.2460	0.8032	0.2746	0.3927	3.2961
Navarra	0.1187	0.6629	0.8333	0.3801	0.7437	0.2184	0.3056	3.2626
País Vasco	0.1360	0.6180	0.8727	0.3886	0.8362	0.2866	0.3249	3.4630
Rioja (La)	0.1479	0.6559	0.8617	0.3826	0.8746	0.2026	0.3521	3.4775
Ceuta y Melilla	0.0682	0.4481	0.9675	0.3247	0.7792	0.2403	0.8279	3.6558
Spanish average	0.2123	0.6226	0.8639	0.3828	0.8149	0.2856	0.5169	3.6991

Source: own elaboration from INE (2008)

Table 4.   Water conservation investments by autonomous community.

Autonomous community	invest_1	invest_2	invest_3	invest_4	sco_inves
Andalucía	0.7474	0.1226	0.4286	0.5253	1.8238
Aragón	0.6654	0.2480	0.4055	0.6892	2.0081
Asturias	0.5939	0.0265	0.1490	0.6329	1.4023
Baleares (Islas)	0.7483	0.1350	0.2540	0.6701	1.8074
Canarias	0.2152	0.1270	0.2945	0.5645	1.2012
Cantabria	0.3603	0.2820	0.2402	0.4545	1.3371
Castilla y León	0.6104	0.0611	0.2549	0.4988	1.4252
Castilla-La Mancha	0.6812	0.4650	0.3577	0.5855	2.0894
Cataluña	0.7112	0.1907	0.2941	0.6244	1.8203
Comunidad Valenciana	0.7421	0.2323	0.4375	0.8220	2.2339
Extremadura	0.6373	0.0307	0.1537	0.4191	1.2408
Galicia	0.4484	0.0661	0.1658	0.6452	1.3254
Madrid	0.6355	0.1638	0.3298	0.6989	1.8279
Murcia	0.6422	0.1771	0.2800	0.6863	1.7856
Navarra	0.6364	0.0985	0.2588	0.5966	1.5903
País Vasco	0.7153	0.1148	0.2857	0.5480	1.6637
Rioja (La)	0.6961	0.1479	0.4051	0.6437	1.8929
Ceuta y Melilla	0.5260	0.0455	0.1006	0.8889	1.5610
Spanish average	0.6743	0.1456	0.3220	0.5898	1.7317

Source: own elaboration from INE (2008)

help determine the individual choices of a given household by shaping a set of cost-benefit conditions. Second, we consider respondents' opinions and knowledge about environmental problems, because we expect attitudes to also substantially affect conservation choices. Finally, we include a bundle of regional variables, to include the effects of the general geographical context where the households are located. (Unfortunately, the data did not allow us to identify the individual municipality for each household.) Both the dependent variables and the independent variables are described in Table 5.

Most variables in the first group refer to the household as a whole, but a few correspond to questions answered only by the 'reference person'. They relate to several socioeconomic features, such as the demographics of the household, education levels and economic status. Thus, we consider the total number of people in the household (*totviv*), the percentage of household members falling within certain age intervals (*age15* and *age65*), the percentage of men in the household (*permen*), the educational level of the reference person (*bac*), the employment situation of the reference person (*fulltime*), and the whole household's income (measured by the four indicator variables *income_1* to *income_4*, the first of which is kept off the model as the benchmark category). Again, all the information related to these variables is taken from the 2008 INE survey, *Households and Environment*.

The second set of variables includes indicators of opinions and knowledge about the environment, collected from the same survey (INE 2008). The information behind all of these variables was obtained from the 'selected person' in the survey. First, we built an additional variable to measure individuals' pro-environmental opinion, *sco_opi*.[1] Respondents were then asked whether they were very concerned about the environment (*preoc*), whether they knew about any environmental awareness campaigns (*scampma*), and whether they had detected any environmental problems (*sproba*).

The third group of variables is included to test whether the regional context affects households' environmental habits and behaviours. Thus, we include some climatic variables (*rain* and *25Cdays*) and some economic variables such as the average price of

Table 5. Definition of independent variables.

Variable type	Variable	Description
Individuals' socioeconomic features	*fulltime*	1 if reference person is employed full-time, 0 otherwise
	age15	Percentage of household members 15 years or younger
	age65	Percentage of household members 65 years or older
	permen	Percentage of male members in the household
	bac	1 if the reference person's education level is at most secondary, 0 otherwise
	totviv	Total number of people in the household
	income	Monthly net income for all the members in the household: 1 = less than €1.100; 2 = €1.101 to €1.800; 3 = €1.801 to €2.700; 4 = more than €2.700; transformed into four indicator variables *income_i* (i = 1, 2, 3, 4)
Individuals' opinion and knowledge	*sco_opi*	Index of pro-environmental opinion (values 0 to 8)
	preoc	1 if the selected person is "very concerned" about the environment, 0 otherwise
	scampma	1 if the selected person has knowledge of any environmental protection campaign, 0 otherwise
	sprobma	1 if the selected person has knowledge of any environmental problem, 0 otherwise
Regional features	*rain*	Total annual rainfall (average for the period 1997–2007, in 1000 mm)
	25Cdays	Total number of days with temperatures higher or equal than 25 °C (average for the period 1997–2007, in 100 days)
	avgprice	Unitary urban water value (average for the period 1997–2007, in €/m^3)
	GDPpc	Regional GDP per capita (average for the period 2000–2007, in €)

water in the region (*avgprice*) and the gross domestic product per capita (*GDPpc*). All these variables are taken from several INE environmental statistics (available at http://www.ine.es/inebmenu/mnu_medioambiente.htm). The information about the ecological deficit is taken from MMA (2007).

Table 6 contains summary descriptions of the variables used in the analysis.

Methods

We constructed two index variables, one indicating the number of water conservation habits adopted by a given household and the other indicating the number of water-saving devices the household has installed – summarizing several of the responses to the original survey questions. Table 7 shows the frequency distribution of the index that refers to technology investments, while Table 8 shows the frequency distribution of the habits index.

Since the index variables are categorical and ordinal, we applied two ordered probit models to first separately model each index as a function of a set of independent variables related to individual household characteristics, regional environmental conditions, and attitudes towards the environment and conservation. Then, to account for the likely correlation across responses for a given household, we estimated a bivariate ordered probit (Greene & Hensher 2008, p. 147), which takes into account the potential for substitutability and complementarity between these two types of choice.

Table 6. Summary descriptives. $N = 18,953$.

Variable	Mean	Std. Dev.	Min	Max
age15	0.107	0.187	0.000	0.750
age65	0.266	0.403	0	1
bac	0.775	0.418	0	1
displav	1.558	1.105	0	4
fromcamcal	0.018	0.134	0	1
fulltime	0.492	0.500	0	1
gasto_pc	0.237	0.060	0.092	0.426
globalhap 00	3.410	2.383	− 3.254	6.034
green_08	0.461	0.131	0.270	0.770
income	1.967	0.970	1	4
income1	0.3914	0.4881	0	1
income2	0.3457	0.4756	0	1
income3	0.1668	0.3728	0	1
income4	0.0961	0.2947	0	1
25Cdays	4.696	3.969	0.112	12.546
permen	0.471	0.282	0	4
GDPpc	19.178	4.042	12.236	29.948
avgprice	0.892	0.214	0.569	1.627
preoc	0.776	0.417	0	1
rain	2.394	1.451	0.276	6.430
scampma	0.615	0.487	0	1
sco_habit	3.705	1.492	0.000	7.000
sco_inves	1.558	1.105	0	4
sco_opi	4.525	2.061	0.000	8.000
selwaste_pc	0.117	0.027	0.081	0.185
sprobma	0.265	0.441	0	1
totviv	2.587	1.186	1	11

Results

The results of our ordered probit estimations are shown in Table 9. Model bioprobit is a bivariate ordered probit, while the corresponding independent univariate ordered probits are oprobit1, whose dependent variable is *sco_inves*, and oprobit2, whose dependent variable is *sco-habits*. All three models include the same set of covariates. A statistically significant positive correlation was found between adoption (of water-saving technology) and adaptation (towards water-saving habits).[2]

When it comes to describing the size and direction of the effects of independent variables on the two water conservation indices, the choice between the univariate ordered probit models and their bivariate counterpart makes little difference in qualitative terms.

Table 7. Distribution of index of water-saving devices adopted (*sco_inves*).

sco_inves	Freq.	Percent	Cum.
0	3,579	18.88	18.88
1	5,986	31.58	50.47
2	5,504	29.04	79.51
3	2,997	15.81	95.32
4	887	4.68	100
Total	18,953	100	

Table 8.   Distribution of index of water-saving habits (*sco habit*).

sco_habit	Freq.	Percent	Cum.
0	544	2.87	2.87
1	826	4.36	7.23
2	2,282	12.04	19.27
3	4,499	23.74	43.01
4	5,210	27.49	70.5
5	3,502	18.48	88.97
6	1,645	8.68	97.65
7	445	2.35	100
Total	18,953	100	

Therefore, we will comment below on the general effects of independent variables based on the results of model bioprobit.

The index of pro-environmental opinions *sco_opi* has, not surprisingly, a positive effect on both types of choices. That is, those households where the respondent declared more positive attitudes towards environmental conservation tend to also be those with a

Table 9.   Estimation results. Univariate Ordered Probits versus Seemingly Unrelated Ordered Probit. N = 18,953.

Model Dependent variable	oprobit1 sco_inves	oprobit2 sco_habits	bioprobit sco_inves	sco_habits
fulltime	0.1350**	−0.0154	0.1354**	−0.0153
age_15	0.1680**	−0.2358**	0.1672**	−0.2357**
age_65	−0.3129**	−0.0782**	−0.3135**	−0.0782**
permen	−0.0200	−0.2202**	−0.0208	−0.2204**
bac	−0.2105**	−0.0328+	−0.2106**	−0.0330+
totviv	0.0259**	0.1016**	0.0261**	0.1016**
income2	0.1593**	−0.0442*	0.1592**	−0.0441*
income3	0.3020**	−0.1142**	0.3020**	−0.1139**
income4	0.2998**	−0.1389**	0.2993**	−0.1385**
sco_opi	0.0371**	0.0863**	0.0374**	0.0864**
preoc	0.1737**	0.1167**	0.1746**	0.1168**
scampma	0.2360**	0.1829**	0.2365**	0.1833**
sprobma	0.0950**	0.0590**	0.0952**	0.0590**
rain	−0.0519**	−0.0652**	−0.0519**	−0.0652**
25Cdays	0.0297**	0.0318**	0.0298**	0.0318**
avgprice	−0.1716**	0.0976*	−0.1716**	0.0969*
GDPpc	0.0149**	−0.0000	0.0150**	−0.0000
ρ			0.1614***	
cut1	−0.3093**	−1.2785**	−0.3029**	−1.2849**
cut2	0.6693**	−0.8106**	0.6748**	−0.8138**
cut3	1.5506**	−0.1843*	1.5563**	−0.1839*
cut4	2.4580**	0.5421**	2.4641**	0.5443**
cut5		1.2871**		1.2882**
cut6		1.9986**		1.9972**
cut7		2.7812**		2.7751**
Statistics				
χ^2	2,797**	1,583**	2,753**	
N	18,953	18,953	18,953	
Likelihood-ratio test (H_0: independent equations): $\chi^2 = 423.95**$				

Significance levels: + = 10%, * = 5%, ** = 1%

higher number of water-efficient technological devices and those that choose to use water more thriftily.

The effect of *fulltime* suggests that having a full-time job has opposite effects on the two indices of conservation. The negative effect on the habits index, *sco_habit*, follows the *a priori* intuition that those who have a job have less time available (and their time is in general more expensive) for water conservation habits (such as waiting to fill up the washing machine or the dishwasher before running them) than those who do not hold full-time employment. However, after controlling for income and other variables, this negative effect is not statistically significant. Nevertheless, also as expected, it seems to be easier for those who are fully employed to install water-efficient devices or buy/rent houses where those devices are already installed, as shown by the significantly positive effect of *fulltime* on *sco-inves*.

It seems to be more costly to adapt the water conservation of the household when there are more members under the age of fifteen. This is reflected by the negative sign of the coefficient on *age15*. However, households with a higher proportion of children seem to find it more worthwhile to own water-saving equipment. Evidently, if one expects children and young teenagers to require a lot of water and to put little effort into water conservation habits, owning efficient water-using appliances becomes a rational choice for young families.

The other variable that describes the age structure of the household (*age65*) shows that the proportion of household members over 65 is correlated with a lower value of both indices. This is probably because households with an older average age composition tend to live in older houses, thus lowering their incentive to adopt new technologies (since the cost would be recouped during a lower expected number of years). Therefore, *sco_inves* will tend to be lower. Additionally, the value of *sco_habits* is also lower for older people.

The more men in a household, the lower the value of the habits index, as shown by the negative sign of *permen*. There is no significant effect of this variable on the technology index.

The variable *bac* indicates that the reference person's education level is at most secondary (that is high-school or less), suggesting that the average level of education in the household is also comparatively low. The effect of a low education is negative on both indices. This is probably because people with less education find it more difficult to learn about water conservation practices and about water-saving technology.

Often it is not only more profitable (because of the larger level of overall water-using activity) but also easier (e.g. it is easier to wait for a fully loaded washer or dishwasher) to undertake water conservation behaviours when more people live together. Additionally, it will be more worthwhile to install more expensive water-saving technology (again because additional household members yield more scope for savings). Therefore, we find that *totviv* takes the expected positive sign in both equations.

Variable *income* has a negative impact on the index *sco-habit*. This is probably because the substitution effect of the cost of time for those who earn more makes it more costly at the margin for them to adapt their behaviour. Additionally, the income effect makes richer households better able to afford more profligate water-using practices.

Variable *rain* measures the 10-year average of total annual rainfall in the region where the household is located. As expected, water users in rainy areas worry less about adapting their behaviour or adopting water-efficient technology. For similar reasons, the variable *25Cdays* presents a positive sign in both equations. Also, in warmer areas, drought problems tend to be more pressing, so, even after controlling for the price of water in the region, we see that water users tend to be more conservative when the climate is dry and warm.

A somewhat surprising result is the negative sign on *avgprice* in the *sco_inves* equation. We would expect, as suggested by economic intuition, that price would be a key determinant behind the decision to install water-saving technology. One would expect that the higher the price of water, the higher the number of water-saving devices in a household. Thus, the negative sign goes against expectations. It must be noted, however, that the only measure of water price we had available was a regional average price. Using a more disaggregated price indicator might result in the correct sign. It is also likely that the price of water is secondary compared to energy prices when it comes to adopting water-saving technologies, and most of all when it comes to appliances that use hot water. We did not have a variable measuring energy prices, which, if the latter are correlated with water prices, could have introduced a bias in our estimation.

The level of GDP per capita in the region averaged through the years 2000 to 2007 (*GDPpc*) has no significant effect on the adaptation of water-use habits, but richer regions display higher values of the investments index, perhaps because richer autonomous communities will be able to afford more generous public programs subsidizing the purchase of efficient household equipment, which are often implemented at the regional level. Those concerned about the environment appear motivated to both adapt their behaviour further and to install more water-saving devices (as shown by the significant positive signs of variable *preoc*).

The estimated coefficients of the variables *scampma* and *sprobma* have positive signs, suggesting that those individuals who are better informed about environmental issues and environmental campaigns tend to both adapt their water use habits more and to adopt more water-efficient technology.

Conclusions, limitations, and suggestions for further research

Since water is considered a scarce natural resource and a basic good necessary for life, public policies are effected worldwide to manage it efficiently. To a great extent, both water suppliers and public authorities have recently focused their attention on demand-side water policies as a preferred alternative to supply-side initiatives. Among other measures, these policies include subsidizing low-water-consumption technologies and/or encouraging the change of users' behaviour. Those initiatives have been proposed in isolation or jointly with pricing-based polices. In the latter case, the complementarities can be especially effective in achieving significant reductions in water consumption.

In Spain, water resources are non-uniformly distributed among the regions and one can find stark regional differences in terms of both water quantity and water quality. Although residential users are not the main water consumers in terms of volume, their water consumption has increased significantly during the last decades. This increase has prompted us to analyze the main factors that influence the adoption of behaviours and habits aimed at reducing water consumption in the domestic sector. Micro-level data from a sample of Spanish households has allowed us to find some interesting results in this field.

Regarding investments in water-efficient technologies, we find that those households with higher levels of education and income tend to adopt a larger number of water-saving devices. Full-time workers and large families are also more likely to make this type of pro-environmental choice. On the other hand, the presence of a high percentage of elderly people in the house reduces the likelihood of adopting these technologies.

The analysis of the factors that drive the index of water-saving habit adoption also reveals several identifiable patterns. Perhaps the most important among these would be the negative relationship between the average number of adopted habits and the level of income: low-income families appear to have stronger water conservation habits.

Additionally, it is worthwhile to mention the positive effect that educational campaigns appear to have had on decisions both to undertake investments and to adapt habits. Therefore, it is strongly recommended to develop this kind of initiative to make households conscious about environmental problems and how to manage them, in particular in the water sector. Moreover, we have also observed that those households with pro-environmental attitudes or who are aware of water scarcity problems in their region have a higher probability of adopting efficient appliances and of adapting their behaviours.

In general terms, after controlling for the independent variables in the model, a positive correlation has been found between the indices measuring the number of habits adopted and the investments made to conserve water. This finding could indicate that, in general, those households that adopt efficient devices are also adapting their behaviour. However, our simple econometric analysis does not allow us to identify the direction of causality. This issue could be investigated in a future research project that is more focused on econometric analysis.

Our findings suggest that public policies aimed at promoting the adoption of pro-environmental habits and investments associated with water use might be particularly effective if focused on older males with low educational levels. Such orientation could lead to significant efficiency improvements in residential water consumption.

In any event, it should be noted that our results reveal substantial differences in terms of the patterns of adoption of habits and investments associated with water conservation among the different Spanish regions. Those differences lead us to recommend flexibility in the application of water conservation policies. Depending on the region where the household is located, not only the need for a conservation policy but also its effect will be different. Therefore, the use of heterogeneous policies designed and implemented at the regional level seems to be the best approach. Our findings also identify in which regions it would be advisable to concentrate this type of conservation effort, and which socio-economic groups should be the target of educational campaigns and other kinds of public policies.

Acknowledgements

We would like to thank the financial support of the Ministry of Science and Innovation (through the project with reference MICINN-09-ECO2009-08824) and the comments and suggestions we received after presenting a previous draft at the May 2011 *Workshop on Water Pricing and Roles of Public and Private Sectors in Efficient Urban Water Management*, organized by the Third World Centre for Water Management, the International Water Resources Association, Global Water Intelligence and the University of Granada.

Notes

1. We built a score of pro-environmental opinion based on several issues asked on the survey. Individuals were asked if they agreed with the following proposals: (1) to oblige people to separate waste (being fined if they do not do it); (2) to restrict water overuse; (3) to set a green tax on the most polluting combustibles; (4) to constrain private transportation use; (5) to establish a green tax on tourist activities; (6) to install renewable energy plants in their city/village; (7) to pay more for alternative energies; and (8) to reduce noise on the main roads. All of these are dummy variables which take the value 1 if the answer is yes, and 0 if the answer is no. To build the pro-environmental opinion score, we sum up all these variables. The higher the score, the more 'pro-environmental' the individual is, according to this criterion.
2. A likelihood-ratio test of independence of equations yields a statistic distributed $\chi^2(1)$ equal to 422.55, which clearly leads us to reject the null hypothesis of no correlation.

References

Arbués, F., García-Valiñas, M. Á., & Martínez-Espiñeira, R. (2003). Estimation of residential water demand: A state-of-the-art review. *Journal of Socio-Economics*, *32*, 81–102, doi:10.1016/S1053-5357(03)00005-2.

Clark, W. A., & Finley, J. C. (2008). Household water conservation challenges in Blagoevgrad, Bulgaria: A descriptive study. *Water International*, *33*, 175–188. doi:10.1080/02508060802023264.

Clarke, J., & Brown, R. (2006). Understanding the factors that influence domestic water consumption within Melbourne. *Australian Journal of Water Resources*, *10*, 261–268.

Dalhuisen, J. M., Florax, R., de Groot, H. L. F., & Nijkamp, P. (2003). Price and income elasticities of residential water demand: Why empirical estimates differ. *Land Economics*, *79*(2), 292–308.

De Oliver, M. (1999). Attitudes and inaction: A case study of the manifest demographics of urban water conservation. *Environment and Behavior*, *31*(3), 372–394.

Dietz, T., Stern, P. C., & Guagnano, G. A. (1998). Social structural and social psychological bases of environmental concern. *Environment and Behavior*, *30*(4), 450–471.

Dolnicar, S., & Hurlimann, A. (2010). Australians' water conservation behaviours and attitudes. *Australian Journal of Water Resources*, *14*(1), 43–53.

Domene, E., & Saurí, D. (2006). Urbanisation and water consumption: Influencing factors in the Barcelona Metropolitan Region. *Geoforum*, *38*, 287–298.

Doron, U., Teh, T., Haklay, M., & Bell, S. (2011). Public engagement with water conservation in London. *Water and Environment Journal*, *25*, 555–562. doi:10.1111/j.1747-6593.2011.00256.x.

Elizondo, G. M., & Lofthouse, V. (2010). Towards a sustainable use of water at home: Understanding how much, where and why? *Journal of Sustainable Development*, *35*, 3–10.

Gaudin, S., Griffin, R. C., & Sickles, R. C. (2001). Demand specification for municipal water management: Evaluation of the Stone-Geary form. *Land Economics*. *77*, 399–422, doi:10.3368/le.77.3.399.

Gilg, A., & Barr, S. (2006). Behavioural attitudes towards water saving? Evidence from a study of environmental actions. *Ecological Economics*, *57*, 400–414. doi:10.1016/j.ecolecon.2005.04.010.

Greene, W. H., & Hensher, D. A. (2008). Modeling ordered choices: A primer and recent developments (Working Paper No. 08–26). New York: Leonard N. Stern School of Business, Department of Economics, New York University.

INE (2008). *Encuesta de hogares y medio ambiente 2008* [Households and the environment survey 2008]. Retrieved from http://www.ine.es/jaxi/menu.do?L=0&type=pcaxis&path=%2Ft25%2Fp500&file=inebase

INE (2009). *Encuesta de Hogares y Medio Ambiente 2008: Nota metodológica (Versión abril de 2009)*. Retrieved from http://www.ine.es/metodologia/t25/t2530500.pdf

Jensen, J. (2008). Measuring consumption in households: Interpretations and strategies. *Ecological Economics*, *68*, 353–361. doi:10.1016/j.ecolecon.2008.03.016.

Krantz, H. (2006). Household routines – a time-space issue: A theoretical approach applied on the case of water and sanitation. *Applied Geography*, *26*, 227–241. doi:10.1016/j.apgeog.2006.09.005.

Lam, S.-P. (2006). Predicting intention to save water: Theory of planned behavior, response efficacy, vulnerability, and perceived efficiency of alternative solutions. *Journal of Applied Social Psychology*, *36*, 2803–2824. doi:10.1111/j.0021-9029.2006.00129.x.

Martínez-Espiñeira, R. (2007). Residential water demand: An empirical analysis using co-integration and error correction techniques. *Journal of Applied Economics*, *10*, 161–184. Retrieved from http://www.ucema.edu.ar/publicaciones/download/volume10/martinez_espineira.pdf.

Martínez-Espiñeira, R., & Nauges, C. (2004). Is all domestic water consumption sensitive to price control? *Applied Economics*, *36*, 1697–1703. doi:10.1080/0003684042000218570.

Millock, K., & Nauges, C. (2010). Household adoption of water-efficient equipment: The role of socio-economic factors, environmental attitudes and policy. *Environmental and Resource Economics*, *46*(4), 539–565. doi:10.1007/s10640-010-9360-y.

MMA (2007). Análisis preliminar de la huella ecológica en España [Preliminary analysis of the ecological footprint in Spain] (Technical report). Madrid: Ministerio de Medio Ambiente.

Retrieved from http://www.uam.es/personal_pdi/ciencias/jonate/Eco_Rec/Intro/HuellaEspa%
Fla.pdf

Musolesi, A., & Nosvelli, M. (2007). Dynamics of residential water consumption in a panel of Italian municipalities. *Applied Economics Letters*, *14*, 441–444. doi:10.1080/13504850500425642.

OECD (2008). *Households' behavior and the environment: Reviewing the evidence*. Paris: Organization for Economic Cooperation and Development.

Olli, E., Grendstad, G., & Wollebaek, D. (2001). Correlates of environmental behaviors bringing back social context. *Environment and Behavior*, *33*, 181–208. doi:10.1177/0013916501332002.

Renwick, M. E., & Archibald, S. O. (1998). Demand side management policies for residential water use: Who bears the conservation burden? *Land Economics*, *74*(3), 343–359. Retrieved from http://www.jstor.org/stable/3147117.

Renwick, M. E., & Green, R. D. (2000). Do residential water demand side management policies measure up? An analysis of eight California water agencies. *Journal of Environmental Economics and Management*, *40*, 37–55. doi:10.1006/jeem.1999.1102.

Sauri, D. (2003). Lights and shadows of urban water demand management: The case of the metropolitan region of Barcelona. *European Planning Studies*, *11*(3), 229–243. doi:10.1080/09654310303639.

Syme, G. J., Nancarrow, B. E., & Seligman, C. (2000). The evaluation of information campaigns to promote voluntary household water conservation. *Evaluation Review*, *24*, 539–578. doi:10.1177/0193841X0002400601.

Torgler, B., García-Valiñas, M. Á., & Macintyre, A. (2010). *Participation in environmental organizations*. Abingdon: Routledge.

Trumbo, C. W., & O'Keefe, G. J. (2001). Intention to conserve water: Environmental values, planned behavior, and information effects. A comparison of three communities sharing a watershed. *Society & Natural Resources*, *14*, 889–899, doi:10.1080/089419201753242797.

WHO/UNICEF (2008). *Progress on drinking water and sanitation. Special focus on sanitation*. New York and Geneva: UNICEF/WHO. Retrieved from http://www.who.int/water_sanitation_health/monitoring/jmp2008/en/.

Worthington, A., & Hoffman, M. (2008). An empirical survey of residential water demand modelling. *Journal of Economic Surveys*, *22*(5), 842–871. doi:10.1111/j.1467-6419.2008.00551.x.

Assessing the impact of price and non-price policies on residential water demand: a case study in Wisconsin

Arnaud Reynaud

Toulouse School of Economics (LERNA-INRA), France

This paper reports an investigation of the impact of price policies (PP) and non-price policies (NPP) on residential water demand. Using a sample of US water utilities located in Wisconsin, residential water demand was estimated by taking into account the fact that some of the characteristics of local communities that determine PP and NPP choices may also influence residential water consumption levels. It is first shown that neglecting endogeneity of PP or NPP may lead to biased parameter estimates. Second, it is demonstrated that the policy mix (PP or NPP) may be as important as the level of prices for determining water consumption. Lastly, evidence is provided that dissemination efforts made by local communities to promote NPP drive the effectiveness of those policies.

Introduction

A large body of the empirical economic literature on residential water demand has been devoted to measuring the impact of price policies (PP); see Worthington and Hoffman (2008) for a recent survey. The consensus among researchers is that residential water demand is inelastic with respect to water price, but not perfectly. This is a puzzling result, given that increasing the water price is still viewed by public authorities as the most direct economic tool for inducing water-conservation behaviours.

It has also been argued that residential consumers may react to non-price policies (NPP) such as water conservation programmes and education campaigns (Kenney, Goemans, Klein, Lowrey, & Reidy, 2008). As a consequence, there is now a growing interest in regulating water demand through NPP, especially since they are supposed to modify long-established habits and to have long-lasting results. Moreover, NPP often appear more politically or socially acceptable than high price increases. Although intuition suggests that NPP may have a significant impact on residential water demand, the exact nature of the relationship between such policies and household water demand has not been yet addressed adequately.

This paper reports an investigation of the impact of PP and NPP on residential water demand. The empirical analysis is based on a database on Wisconsin water utilities. The results demonstrate that the policy mix (PP and NPP) may be as important as water price levels for determining water consumption. Some evidence is also provided that the dissemination efforts made by local communities to promote NPP drive the effectiveness of those policies. The study therefore calls for joint implementation of NPP and PP to regulate residential water use.

The paper is organized as follows. The empirical literature on PP and NPP is surveyed; then some information is provided on residential water use in Wisconsin. The following section presents the econometric modelling and the results of the estimates. Finally, some policy implications are derived.

Relevant literature

PP include all market-based regulations that encourage behaviour through market signals rather than through explicit directives to individual households and firms regarding conservation levels. The effectiveness of PP relies on the assumption motivated by the law of demand which stipulates that residential water consumption is inversely related to water price.

NPP correspond to all non-market-based programmes designed to increase the efficiency of water use or water conservation. Although NPP are by nature very heterogeneous, they may be classified into three categories: public education, technological improvements and water restrictions (Kenney et al., 2008).

A review of demand-side management policies

A substantial number of papers have analyzed the impact of PP on residential water consumption. However, use of PP by policy makers is limited by the fact that residential water demand is relatively inelastic at current prices. For example, in their survey of the literature Worthington and Hoffman (2008) indicate a price elasticity of residential water demand varying between -0.25 and -0.75. With an elasticity of -0.4, a water utility wishing to reduce the demand by 20% (not an uncommon goal during a drought), must implement approximately a 50% increase in the water price. This may raise equity or redistribution concerns.

In addition to the measure of the demand price elasticity, assessing whether the pricing structure per se plays a significant role in influencing price responsiveness has recently emerged as an important topic in the literature on residential water demand. Conducting a meta-analysis of the literature on residential water demand estimates, Dalhuisen, Florax, de Groot, and Nijkamp (2003) concluded that the presence of increasing block rate pricing leads to residential water demands being more elastic. A similar result is reported by Reynaud, Renzetti, and Villeneuve (2005) for Canadian residential water users. In a more recent work, Olmstead, Hanemann, and Stavins (2007) analyzed the price sensitivity of residential water consumption in 11 urban areas in the United States and Canada. They concluded that households facing block prices are more sensitive to price changes than households facing uniform prices.

A number of papers have considered the impact of NPP on residential water use. Public education programmes have been shown to have a limited impact, especially in the short term (Campbell, Johnson, & Larson, 2004; Michelsen, McGuckin, & Stumpf, 1999; Syme, Nancarrow, & Seligman, 2000). The literature suggests that a certain critical mass of educational programmes is necessary to generate significant benefits (Michelsen et al., 1999).

Somewhat more attention has been given to understanding the effectiveness of technological changes, especially indoor retrofitting of water-using devices such as toilets, showerheads and washing machines. Studies with this focus are frequently based on engineering assumptions of expected reductions (Michelsen et al., 1999). One notable exception is provided by Renwick and Archibald (1998), who found that, in California, installing low-flow toilets had reduced the residential water consumption by 10% (per toilet). They also reported that adoption of water-efficient irrigation technologies had allowed an 11% reduction in water needs. Using survey data on 10 OECD countries, Millock and Nauges (2010) showed that the adoption of water-efficient equipment is strongly affected by housing ownership status, by being water-metered and charged according to a volumetric price on water consumption, and by behavioural factors. Environmental attitudes have been shown to be strong predictors of adoption of water-efficient equipment, with a marginal effect that exceeds ownership status in some cases. Gilg and Barr (2006) also focused on attitudinal factors that determine water-consumption behaviours (in particular on environmental preferences, intrinsic motivations and social norms). Their study revealed that it is possible to classify households into relatively homogeneous groups based on their water-consumption behaviour. These attitudinal differences should then be taken into account when designing NPP. Yushiou, Cohen, and Vogel (2011) assessed the impact on residential water use resulting from various water-conservation strategies (weather-sensitive irrigation controller, monthly water billing, etc.) in the Ipswich watershed in Massachusetts (US). They showed in particular that water savings attributed to weather-sensitive irrigation controllers can be large.

Lastly, some authors have specifically focused their attention on the effectiveness of restrictions in water use. For Spain, Garcia-Valiñas (2006) measured the impact on consumers of rationing policies implemented during water shortages. She demonstrated that the restrictions implemented during the drought in Seville had an important impact on water demands. Some papers have analyzed the effectiveness of outdoor watering restrictions. Those articles generally focus on the comparison of voluntary versus mandatory programmes. The literature is consistent in showing significant savings from mandatory restrictions (sometimes 30% or more). Findings regarding voluntary restrictions are much more variable (Renwick & Green, 2000).

Finally, some works have demonstrated that a valid assessment of NPP effectiveness requires carefully taking into account the wide heterogeneity of policies implemented by water utilities or public authorities. Halich and Stephenson (2009) focused on the enforcement and informational efforts of NPP. They showed on a sample of US services that voluntary restriction programmes with low-to-moderate levels of information dissemination seem to have no appreciable effect on water use. For voluntary restrictions, only the most intense informational efforts have succeeded in achieving a moderate level of success (7%) in reducing water use. Mandatory restrictions have had greater success (15% to 22%), especially programmes associated with a high effort of dissemination and a high level of enforcement. These findings help in understanding why NPP have often been shown to have a limited impact on residential water use when such policies are simply modelled as dummy variables in a demand function (Taylor, McKean, & Young, 2004).

PP versus NPP: the debate

NPP and PP have been largely debated in the economic literature. While economists generally advocate PP as a means for reducing demand, others argue that NPP, which do not affect the price of water but either place a direct control on water use (rationing) or rely on habit changes (education campaign for instance), constitute the only viable way to reduce residential water demand. This conclusion relies, in part, on empirical research indicating that residential water demand is price inelastic, making price a relatively ineffective demand-side management tool.

Some papers have directly compared PP and NPP with respect to their effectiveness in achieving a reduction in residential water consumption. Martinez-Espiñeira and Nauges (2004) compared the effectiveness of PP versus NPP (conservation measures) using aggregate data from Seville, Spain. Price elasticity was found to be -0.10 and the impact on consumption of a one-hour restriction of supply per day was found to be similar to that of a 9% increase in price. Kenney et al., (2008) analyzed the factors influencing residential water demand in Aurora (US) during the period 2000–2005. They demonstrated that residential water demand is largely a function of price, NPP and weather. They showed that pricing and outdoor water restriction policies interacted with each other in a non-additive way and that the impact of pricing and restriction policies varied among water users and between pre-drought and drought periods. Olmstead and Stavins (2009) investigated the relative cost-effectiveness of PP and NPP. They concluded that price policies are more cost-effective than non-price demand management.

However, the comparison of PP and NPP in terms of their effectiveness in achieving a reduction in residential water consumption is difficult to undertake, for two main reasons. First, PP and NPP are often jointly implemented by water utilities. Given the possible interactions between NPP and PP, it is difficult to evaluate their individual effectiveness (see Syme et al., 2000). Second, interpretation is also a problem, given possible unobserved exogenous variables. For example, a public education campaign may heighten the motivation to respond to pricing schemes. If the public campaign characteristics are not observed, any changes in residential water consumption will be incorrectly attributed to the implementation of the PP.

Taking the above into consideration, an empirical strategy was developed allowing identification of the impact of PP and NPP on residential water use on a sample of US utilities in Wisconsin.

Residential water use in Wisconsin

Background

Wisconsin is considered a water-rich state with respect to both surface and groundwater. In 2010, 263 billion gallons were withdrawn by water users (excluding power generation): 137 billion gallons from groundwater and the rest from surface water (Wisconsin Department of Natural Resources, 2011). Despite the state-wide abundance of water, there is concern about the long-term availability of water because of increases in withdrawals and pollution.

In Wisconsin, water is delivered to final customers through privately or municipally owned water utilities, classified into three categories according to their size. Class AB utilities serve 4000 or more customers, Class C utilities serve between 1000 and 4000 customers, and Class D utilities serve fewer than 1000 customers. The average number of metered customers per utility is 2338, varying from 21 to 161,945. Residential customers represent 85.7% of the customers and 58.7% of the metered volume of water sold to final users. Table 1 describes the evolution of residential water consumption and average water price in Wisconsin over the period 1997–2008. In 2008, average metered residential water consumption was 44,400 gallons per year per customer. Water consumption varies significantly with the size of the utilities, from 41,400 gallons per year per customer in the smallest utilities (class D) to 53,200 in the largest services (class AB).

Table 1. Evolution of metered residential water consumption and price in Wisconsin.

	Water consumption				Water price			
		Utility class					Utility class	
Year	ALL	AB	C	D	ALL	AB	C	D
1997	51.53	62.5	54.5	48.3	3.03	2.23	2.71	3.30
1998	53.14	65.8	56.1	49.6	3.14	2.29	2.82	3.43
1999	51.61	62.8	54.8	48.1	3.29	2.52	2.98	3.56
2000	50.81	59.8	53.9	47.8	3.40	2.70	3.02	3.68
2001	50.85	60.7	53.8	47.5	3.52	2.76	3.19	3.81
2002	50.02	60.6	52.7	46.5	3.71	2.93	3.29	4.05
2003	50.48	60.4	53.4	46.9	3.82	3.03	3.40	4.18
2004	47.44	57.0	49.9	44.1	4.10	3.19	3.59	4.52
2005	49.39	59.2	53.0	45.5	4.14	3.29	3.67	4.53
2006	46.47	55.2	48.9	43.4	4.33	3.58	3.90	4.70
2007	46.91	55.5	50.1	43.5	4.52	3.77	3.99	4.92
2008	44.44	53.2	46.1	41.4	4.81	4.09	4.58	5.10

Water consumption: annual residential water consumption in 1000 gallons per customer.
Water price: average metered residential water price in US$ per 1000 gallons.
Source: Author's calculation from PSC annual reports filed by Wisconsin water utilities. Reports are available at http://psc.wi.gov/apps40/WEGS/default.aspx

As can be seen, metered water consumption has fallen by 15% over the period 1997–2008 for the three utility classes. At the same time, the average price of water has increased, by 83%, 69% and 54% in utility classes AB, C and D, respectively. This might constitute a first evidence of the effectiveness of PP in achieving reductions in residential water use.

PP and NPP implemented in Wisconsin

In 2008, the Public Service Commission (PSC) of Wisconsin conducted a survey aimed at evaluating the water conservation and efficiency efforts of Wisconsin water utilities (Den Boer & Ripp, 2008). The survey was distributed to 535 Wisconsin water utilities and the PSC received 237 responses, a 44.3% response rate. Due to missing data the final sample used here is made up of a cross-section of 235 utilities observed in 2008. This sample cannot be considered perfectly representative of Wisconsin because responding to the survey was not mandatory. However, non-response bias appears to be limited. For example, for utilities that responded to the survey, the average residential metered water consumption is 45,110 gallons per year per customer (compared to 44,440 for Wisconsin) and the average unit residential price is $4.59 per 1000 gallons (compared to $4.81 for Wisconsin). Large utilities are however slightly over-represented: class AB utilities represent 22% of the services that responded to the survey (compared to 15% for Wisconsin).

The survey includes several types of information concerning PP and NPP implemented by Wisconsin utilities for residential water use. Table 2 gives the number and percentage of services that, as of 2008, had implemented some specific policies.

Concerning PP, information was collected on the pricing structure implemented by each utility and on the frequency of the water bill. In Wisconsin there has been a tradition of using decreasing block rates (DBR) for water pricing. However, among the 235 utilities in our sample, a few municipalities have already implemented increasing block rates

Table 2.   PP and NPP implemented in Wisconsin in 2008.

Policy	Type of policy	Municipalities Number	%
Increasing block rate (IBR)	PP	7	3.0
PSC conservation-oriented water rates	PP	7	3.0
Monthly water bill	PP	88	37.9
Develop a public information and education program	NPP - educ	27	11.5
Create a citizen water conservation advisory group	NPP - educ	4	1.7
Conduct water audits of residential customers	NPP - techno	30	12.8
Rebates to residential customers	NPP - techno	7	3.0
Promote projects that reuse or recycle water	NPP - techno	8	3.4
Promote the use of rain barrels or rain gardens	NPP - techno	27	11.5
Join the EPA's WaterSense program	NPP - techno	8	3.4
Ordinances for outdoor water use	NPP - restrict	34	14.5
Ordinances for new building	NPP - restrict	13	5.5

Source: Author's calculation from Den Boer and Ripp (2008).

(IBR) or similarly have applied for PSC conservation-oriented water rates. One may then expect an impact from IBR on residential water consumption. In Wisconsin, water bills have typically been distributed quarterly. However, 89 utilities have switched to monthly bills. Monthly bills are expected to have an impact on residential water consumption because they reduce the risk of unexpected increases in water use due to leaks and they reduce the cost of information acquisition by households. This is related to the literature on information-acquisition cost for consumers. A higher frequency of the water bill is viewed as a way to reduce the cost of information acquisition. Stevens, Miller, and Willis (1992) did one of the few studies modelling billing frequency. They found no significant influence on water consumption; nor did Griffin and Chang (1990). However, Fenrick and Getachew (2012) reported a significant impact of monthly water bill in a sample of US water utilities.

The survey also includes some information on municipalities that have implemented specific NPP targeted toward water conservation by residential users. Following Kenney et al., (2008), three types of NPP are considered here. The first type corresponds to public education programmes. Twenty-seven water utilities have implemented information and education programmes; four have created a citizen water conservation advisory group. The second type of NPP corresponds to technological improvement policies. Six different NPP have been identified by the PSC: providing water audits of residential customers; offering rebates or other financial incentives to residential customers; supporting projects that reuse or recycle water; promoting the use of rain barrels or rain gardens; and joining the WaterSense programme. WaterSense is a programme developed by the US Environmental Protection Agency to decrease indoor and outdoor non-agricultural water use through more efficient products, equipment and programmes. The last type of NPP corresponds to water restrictions. Historically, Wisconsin water utilities have relied on quantitative restrictions to manage water-scarcity episodes. Two variables capture the presence of quantitative restrictions. One represents whether a utility has enacted ordinances to regulate outdoor water use (34 utilities). The second represents whether a utility has enacted ordinances that require new developments to meet landscaping requirements that promote efficient outdoor water use (13 utilities).

It has been shown that the success of NPP in achieving significant reduction in water use depends largely upon the information-dissemination efforts made by a municipality and upon the type of media used to inform customers (Halich & Stephenson, 2009). The idea is that NPP content may do little to reduce water use if households do not know about it or do not understand the provisions of the policy. However, only a few papers have systematically evaluated how information efforts influence consumer behaviour. Given that the PSC *Survey of Water Conservation and Efficiency Efforts* includes some information on the methods used by utilities to inform customers about NPP (TV, water bill inserts, commercials, etc.), we have the opportunity to address this issue by analyzing, for each type of NPP, whether information dissemination efforts matter for achieving significant reductions in residential water use. Table 3 shows the different methods used by water utilities to inform customers about NPP. The methods which are used the most often by water utilities include water bill inserts (46.4%) and special mailings to customers (26.4%).

Information dissemination efforts were measured by the number of different methods used to inform customers. One can expect that the probability that a residential water customer will be informed about conservation policies implemented in a given municipality increases with the number of information dissemination methods. It is interesting to notice that water utilities differ widely with respect to the number of methods used to inform customers. Though 67 municipalities rely on only one method, 18 utilities have implemented at least four different methods. One may expect that household awareness might differ in such cases.

A first assessment of PP and NPP on residential water use

We consider four types of residential water-regulation regimes, depending on whether the water utility has implemented PP and/or NPP. Regime I corresponds to utilities that have implemented neither PP nor NPP. Regime II$_{NPP}$ corresponds to utilities that have implemented NPP (at least one) without any PP. Regime II$_{PP}$ corresponds to utilities that have implemented PP (at least one) without any NPP. Finally, a utility belongs to regime III if both PP and NPP (at least one of each) have been implemented.

We provide some descriptive statistics for the main variables of interest, especially focusing on differences across regimes (see Table A1 in Appendix A). The lowest average residential water consumption (43,650 gallons) is found for utilities that have implemented neither PP nor NPP (Regime I). On the other end, the highest residential

Table 3. Methods used by utilities to inform customers about NPP.

Method	Municipalities Number	%
Use of local TV or radio commercials	19	8.1
Newspaper advertisements or letters to the editor	54	23.0
Water bill inserts	109	46.4
K–12 school programs	34	14.5
Special events	14	6.0
Water conservation web pages	31	13.2
Special mailings to customers	62	26.4
None	63	26.8

Source: Author's calculation from Den Boer and Ripp (2008).

water consumption (51,300 gallons) corresponds to utilities relying exclusively on NPP (Regime II_{NPP}).

However, one should be careful not to draw from these numbers any direct causal relationship between regulatory regimes and residential water use because it is likely that NPP or PP have been implemented in areas characterized by pre-existing water-scarcity conditions and/or high levels of residential water use. As could have been expected, residential water prices (both marginal and average prices) are higher where utilities have jointly implemented PP and NPP (Regime III). It is interesting to observe that the socio-demographic characteristics of households vary significantly from one regime to another. Implementation of NPP (Regime II_{NPP}) is associated with high household income, high level of population education and high share of recent housing units (built after 1980). On the other hand, PP (Regime II_{PP}) are associated with low household income and low level of population education. Political orientation of households also differs across regimes: PP are associated with a higher proportion of votes for the Democratic Party candidates in the 2008 presidential election.

Estimating residential water demand with endogenous regulation

Data

The cross-section data-set represents 235 local communities in Wisconsin, observed for the year 2008. All data are defined at the municipality level. As discussed previously, information related to the PP and NPP implemented in each local community comes from the 2008 *Survey of Water Conservation and Efficiency Efforts* conducted by the PSC of Wisconsin (Den Boer & Ripp, 2008). Water-related information (water consumption per household, utility size, peak demand, etc.) comes from a report that must be submitted every year to the PSC by all Wisconsin water utilities. Climatic data come from the US National Weather Service Forecast Office. Other sources of information include the 2000 US Census for socio-demographic characteristics of households and the results of the 2008 presidential election (at the county level) for assessing the political orientations of the representative household in each local community. The definition of all variables used in the empirical analysis can be found in Table A2 in Appendix A.

Econometric modelling

The main objective here is to estimate the impact of PP and NPP on residential water use in Wisconsin. The conventional way would be to estimate the following residential water-demand equation:

$$Q_i = \alpha_i + \beta*(P_i) + \eta*(POL_i) + \gamma_j*(X_{ij}) + \varepsilon_i \tag{1}$$

where i indexes the municipality, Q_i is the residential water consumption per household, P_i is the water price, POL_i represents a price or non-price policy, X_{ij} includes all characteristics of households assumed to have an impact on residential water consumption α, β, η, γ are a vector of parameters to be estimated, and ε is the usual error term. One may think to estimate this equation by ordinary least squares (OLS); however, this estimation would suffer from self-selection bias. The intuition is quite simple. Suppose for instance that households in a city are worried about future water scarcity. They may vote for a "conservation-minded" city council, which may adopt PP or NPP. Over time, this city may have a per capita water consumption lower than comparable cities. We should then not simply estimate η by regressing the water consumption on the *POL* variable because the implementation of the NPP and the observed water use are determined simultaneously. Thus, we need a model that explains why the NPP or PP have been implemented and, conditionally, what is the influence of the PP or the NPP on water use.

The econometric strategy used here is therefore a two-step approach as initially proposed by Heckman (1979). In the first stage, a model is developed to explain why a local municipality is in one of the four regulation regimes defined previously (I, II_{NPP}, II_{PP} or III). The assumption is that the regulation-regime choice carried out by public authorities maximizes the surplus of the representative consumers (this could be for example the consequence of necessity of political re-election of the majority in power). Based on the random utility model, this regulation choice is estimated using a multinomial logit model.

The second stage of the procedure consists in estimating the residential water demand, taking into account the self-selection of local communities in regulation regimes. To correct for the potential problem of self-selection, applied researchers have traditionally employed the bias correction method embedded in Lee's (1983) extension of the Heckman (1979) two-stage selection model. This method consists in introducing into each water-demand equation (one for each regulation regime) the Heckman inverse Mills ratio, which measures the correlation between the disturbance term of each residential water-demand equation and the cumulative distribution of the error term in the multinomial logit model.[1] The sign of the Heckman inverse Mills ratio indicates the direction of the selection bias resulting from the selection of local communities into the regulation regime for which a water-demand function is estimated, as opposed to all other regulation regimes taken together.

Bourguignon, Fournier, and Gurgand (2007), hereafter BFG, argue that clubbing together all information based on the multinomial logit model makes the selectivity-correction mechanism unnecessarily restrictive. They offer an alternative, which takes into account the correlation between the disturbance terms from each water-demand equation and the disturbance terms from each multinomial logit equation. The resulting residential water-demand equation including the BFG selectivity-correction mechanism is written:[2]

$$Q_{ik} = \alpha_k + \beta_k P_{ik} + \sum_j \gamma_{jk} X_{ijk} + \sum_k \mu_{jk} m(P_k) + \varepsilon_{ik} \tag{2}$$

where the number of bias-correction terms, $m(P_k)$, is equal to the number of multinomial logit choices. The BFG methodology thus allows identification of not only the direction of the bias related to the allocation of local municipalities in a specific regulation regime, but also which choice among any two regulation regimes this bias stems from.

Empirical results

Multinomial logit for regulation regime adoption

The empirical specification of the multinomial logit model is the following. First, it is assumed that regulation-regime choice depends upon some situational factors (number of days without rainfall from June to August, average temperature from June to August, and share of land area with surface water) and upon some household characteristics (percentage of population 25 years and over with graduate or professional degree, median family income, percentage of the population with age between 0 and 14 years, and population density). The choice of regulation regime can also be driven by specific characteristics of the water utility. Three variables are included characterizing the water utility: two dummy variables for whether the utility belongs to Class D (small size) or Class C (medium size), and a variable representing the share of the water volume sold on the peak day to the annual volume of water. Since the decision to implement a specific regulation regime might result from some political motivations, the share of Democratic Party vote in the 2008 presidential election is included as a potential explanatory variable.

Instead of reporting the multinomial logit estimates, Figure B1 in Appendix B identifies for each regulation regime the significant determinants.[3] The main empirical results are the following. First, the probability of implementing either PP or NPP increases with the size of the municipality. One possible explanation could be that large municipalities are less budget constrained than small ones. Second, PP are more likely to be implemented in municipalities where household income is low. This may be related to the fact that lower-income households are usually found to be more price responsive than higher-income households.[4] Hence, price policy will achieve a larger reduction in residential demand in a lower-income community than in a higher-income community, all other factors held constant. This finding raises some equity concerns because, in such a case, lower-income households will bear a larger share of the conservation burden. Third, the socio-economic status of households seems to be a key determinant of NPP implementation. Municipalities with highly educated households are more likely to implement NPP. This may be related to the fact that the socio-economic characteristics of households influence the outcome of NPP. For example, Renwick and Archibald (1998) have shown that a landscape irrigation technology change more effectively reduces the water demand of households with large landscaped areas and that these households also tend to have high incomes.

Residential water demand equations

The empirical specification of the residential water demand defined by Equation (2) is the following. First, the price of water is introduced as a potential driver of residential water use. The price considered is the marginal water price in US dollars per thousand gallons. Similarly to the regulation-regime choice, it is assumed that the residential water demand depends upon some situational factors (number of days without rainfall, average temperature, and share of land area with surface water of total area) and upon some household characteristics (median family income, percentage of the population with age between 0 and 14 years, percentage of population 25 years and over with graduate or professional degree, percentage of housing built before 1980, share of detached house in 2000, population density, and share of Democratic Party vote in the 2008 presidential election).

PP are described through three variables: use of increasing block rate by the local municipality, use of conservation-oriented PSC pricing scheme, and use of monthly water bill.

NPP are characterized through the type of policy implemented and the type of method used by the local community to inform households about the NPP in place. Nine NPP are considered: use of a public information and education programme; creation of a citizen water-conservation advisory group; water audits of residential customers; rebates on water-efficient equipment offered to residential customers; promotion of projects that reuse or recycle water; promotion of the use of rain barrels or rain gardens; the EPA's WaterSense programme; ordinances for outdoor water use; and ordinances for new building. If one of these NPP is implemented in a given local community, the associated dummy variable is equal to one, and zero otherwise. Seven different methods used by the local community to inform households about the NPP in place have been included: use of TV or radio commercials; newspaper advertisement; water bill inserts; K–12 school programme; special events; water conservation web pages; and special mailing to customers. As discussed previously, the intensity of information-transmission efforts by the local community may matter. A dummy variable for local municipalities using at least four different information methods has been introduced in the demand equation.

Finally, residential water use can be influenced by some characteristics of the water utility (dummy for Classes C and D, and share of the water volume sold on the peak day to the annual volume).

Globally, the BFG estimates perform relatively well: the adjusted R^2 varies from 0.40 to 0.55. Some BFG correction terms are significant, which means that the choice of regulation regimes is endogenous. Interpreting directly the OLS estimates would have resulted in erroneous conclusions.

Table A3 in Appendix A reports the price elasticities for Wisconsin residential water demand according to the regulation regime and the econometric method used (OLS, Lee's 1983 method and BFG's 2007 method). First, whatever method was used, the price elasticity varies significantly according to the type of regulation regime implemented by the local communities. Households appear to be more price reactive when the local community has implemented only NPP. Second, even if the price elasticities differ according the econometric method implemented, they are globally convergent. Finally, one should notice that the price elasticities reported here are within the range of values of previous studies (Dalhuisen et al., 2003). Residential water demand in Wisconsin is found to be inelastic. To achieve a 10% reduction in residential water use, local communities in Wisconsin must increase the water price by 50% to 100%.

Most of the income elasticities reported in Table A3 are significant and positive. Water is viewed as a normal good. Significant differences in income elasticities across regulation regimes should be emphasized. In particular, income elasticities appear to be non-significant where local municipalities rely exclusively on PP for modifying household water consumption behaviours. The highest income elasticity is found in local communities that have implemented neither PP nor NPP.

Figure B2 in Appendix B graphically represents the estimate of the residential water demand for local municipalities that have implemented only PP, only NPP, and jointly PP and NPP.[5] For local communities that have implemented NPP (at least one), we do find a significant impact for the increasing block rate variable. Residential water consumption is significantly lower if the local community has implemented IBR. This result is consistent with the previous literature showing that households are more price reactive when they face incentive price mechanisms such as IBR.[6] Small water utilities have significantly lower residential water consumption per household. One explanation could be that small services are often located in rural areas, where alternative sources of water (wells, for instance) are more easily available.

Next, we consider local communities that have implemented NPP (at least one) but no PP. First we find that only NPP corresponding to technological improvements (rebates offered to residential water users for technological improvement, encouragement to use rain barrels or rain gardens) appear effective in reducing residential water use. Second, taken individually, information-dissemination methods do not have a significant impact on residential water use. However, if in a given local community at least four different methods have been implemented, then the residential water use appears to be significantly lower. This is consistent with previous results showing that NPP have appreciable effects on water use only in case of intense information-dissemination efforts.[7] One policy implication of this result is that the implementation of NPP must be combined with a careful design of dissemination efforts to achieve a reasonable reduction in residential water use.

Lastly, we consider local communities that have jointly implemented PP and NPP (at least one of each). No specific price policy appears to be significant in explaining residential water use. Concerning NPP, once again we find that NPP corresponding to technological improvements (rebates offered to residential water users for technological improvement, promotion of projects that reuse or recycle water) appear effective in reducing residential water use. Interestingly, some methods used to inform the population about the NPP in place are significant. In particular, K−12 school programmes and the use of water-conservation web pages significantly reduce residential water demand. Thus, it seems that the water-consumption behaviour of households is affected much more by dissemination efforts about the NPP in place when NPP and PP are jointly implemented than when the local community relies exclusively on NPP. It therefore appears that PP and NPP should be viewed more as complementary tools than as substitutes. Once again, we find that residential water use appears to be significantly lower in communities that have implemented at least four different information-dissemination methods.

Conclusion

We have analyzed the issue of PP and NPP choice by local municipalities in the US and its implications for residential water-demand estimation. The empirical analysis was based on an original sample of Wisconsin utilities, observed in 2008. We have estimated residential water demand by taking into account the fact that some of the characteristics of local communities that determine PP and NPP choices may also influence residential water consumption levels. It was first shown that neglecting endogeneity of PP or NPP implemented by municipalities may lead to biased parameter estimates. Second, it was shown that the type of PP and NPP mix may be as important as the level of water prices in determining water consumption. Lastly, some evidence was provided that dissemination efforts made by local communities with respect to the NPP in place matter.

Some policy recommendations can be derived from this work. First, we have shown that a model explaining the choice of regulation regime can be constructed. This choice reflects some efficiency considerations and some equity and political concerns. Since regulation choice is the result of local community social-welfare maximization, inducing regulation-regime changes (for example a move toward a joint use of PP and NPP) will require providing to water services some forms of incentives (for instance subsidies for implementing universal metering). Second, residential water demand in Wisconsin appears to be inelastic but not perfectly (depending on the price-regulation regime, price elasticity varies from −0.02 to −0.19). This means that a price increase will have only a limited impact on water consumption. Price increases should be combined with NPP measures by a public authority wishing to induce more water conservation. In fact, we believe that the main difference between PP and NPP is the time horizon considered. NPP may have a more effective impact in the long run than PP. Modifying household equipment, for example through fiscal subsidies, is clearly a long-term process. At the opposite end, if a regulator wishes to transmit a clear water-scarcity signal, PP should be favoured. But in fact, PP and NPP should be viewed more as complementary regulation tools than as substitutes. Third, after having corrected for regulation-regime endogeneity, the price elasticity of residential water demand still significantly differs according to the regime implemented. NPP and PP per se play a significant (but moderate) role in influencing the price responsiveness of residential water consumers in Wisconsin.

Acknowledgements

The author would like to thank the Public Service Commission of Wisconsin for making the data on water use in Wisconsin available. Special thanks to Jeffrey Ripp who kindly transmitted the original PSC database on conservation and efficiency efforts by water utilities in Wisconsin. All remaining errors or approximations are of course imputable only to the author of this article.

Notes

1. See Reynaud et al., (2005) for an application of this method in the context of choice of pricing schemes by Canadian municipalities.
2. This is a simplified form of the water-demand function with BFG selectivity correction. The interested reader may refer to Bourguignon et al., (2007) for detailed expression of the correction terms.
3. All estimates are available from the authors upon request. To save space, we present the results only for regimes II_{NPP}, II_{PP} and III.
4. In California, Renwick and Archibald (1998) found that low-income households are more than five times as price responsive as relatively wealthy households.
5. To save space, we do not present the estimate of the residential water demand for local municipalities with neither PP nor NPP. However, detailed results are available from the authors upon request.
6. Reynaud et al., (2005) reported that Canadian residential water users are twice as sensitive to water price changes when they face increasing block rates, compared to unit water price or decreasing block rates.
7. See for instance Halich and Stephenson (2009), who have shown in a sample of US municipalities that only the most intense NPP in terms of informational efforts have succeeded in achieving even a moderate reduction in water use.

References

Bourguignon, F., Fournier, M., & Gurgand, M. (2007). Selection bias correction based on the multinomial logit model: Monte Carlo comparisons. *Journal of Economic Surveys, 21*, 174–205.

Campbell, H. E., Johnson, R. M., & Larson, E. H. (2004). Prices, devices, people, or rules: The relative effectiveness of policy instruments in water conservation. *Review of Policy Research, 21*, 637–662.

Dalhuisen, J. M., Florax, R. J. G. M., de Groot, H. L. F., & Nijkamp, P. (2003). Price and income elasticities of residential water demand: A meta-analysis. *Land Economics, 79*(2), 292–308.

Fenrick, S. A., & Getachew, L. (2012). Estimation of the effects of price and billing frequency on household water demand using a panel of Wisconsin municipalities. *Applied Economics Letters, 19*, 1373–1380. doi:10.1080/13504851.2011.629977.

Garcia-Valiñas, M. A. (2006). Analysing rationing policies: Drought and its effects on urban users' welfare (Analysing rationing policies during drought). *Applied Economics, 38*, 955–965.

Gilg, A., & Barr, S. (2006). Behavioural attitudes towards water saving? Evidence from a study of environmental actions. *Ecological Economics, 57*(3), 400–414.

Griffin, R., & Chang, R. (1990). Pre-test analyses of water demand in thirty communities. *Water Resources Research, 26*, 2251–2255.

Halich, G., & Stephenson, K. (2009). Effectiveness of residential water-use restrictions under varying levels of municipal effort. *Land Economics, 85*(4), 614–626.

Heckman, J. J. (1979). Sample selection bias as a specification error. *Econometrica, 47*, 153–161.

Kenney, D. S., Goemans, C., Klein, R., Lowrey, J., & Reidy, K. (2008). Residential water demand management: Lessons from Aurora, Colorado. *Journal of the American Water Resources Association, 44*, 192–207.

Lee, L. F. (1983). Generalized econometric models with selectivity. *Econometrica, 51*(2), 507–512.

Martinez-Espiñeira, R., & Nauges, C. (2004). Is all domestic water consumption sensitive to price control? *Applied Economics, 36,* 1697–1703.

Michelsen, A., McGuckin, J., & Stumpf, D. (1999). Nonprice water conservation programs as a demand management tool. *Journal of the American Water Resources Association, 35*(3), 593–602.

Millock, K., & Nauges, C. (2010). Household adoption of water-efficient equipment: The role of socio-economic factors, environmental attitudes and policy. *Environmental and Resource Economics, 46,* 539–565.

Olmstead, S. M., Hanemann, W. M., & Stavins, R. N. (2007). Water demand under alternative price structures. *Journal of Environmental Economics and Management, 54*(2), 181–198.

Olmstead, S. M., & Stavins, R. N. (2009). Comparing price and nonprice approaches to urban water conservation. *Water Resources Research, 45.* doi:10.1029/2008WR007227.

Den Boer, K., & Ripp, J. (2008). *Survey of water conservation and efficiency efforts: An analysis of Wisconsin water utilities.* Madison, WI: Public Service Commission of Wisconsin.

Renwick, M. E., & Archibald, S. O. (1998). Demand side management policies for residential water use: Who bears the conservation burden? *Land Economics, 74*(3), 343–359.

Renwick, M. E., & Green, R. D. (2000). Do residential water demand side management policies measure up? An analysis of eight California water agencies. *Journal of Environmental Economics and Management, 40,* 37–55.

Reynaud, A., Renzetti, S., & Villeneuve, M. (2005). Estimating domestic water demand under complex pricing: The Canadian case. *Water Resources Research, 41,* doi:10.1029/2005WR004195.

Stevens, T., Miller, J., & Willis, C. (1992). Effect of price structure on residential water demand. *Water Resources Bulletin, 28,* 681–685.

Syme, G. J., Nancarrow, B. E., & Seligman, C. (2000). The evaluation of information campaigns to promote voluntary household water conservation. *Evaluation Review, 24*(6), 539–578.

Taylor, R. G., McKean, J. R., & Young, R. A. (2004). Alternate price specifications for estimating residential water demand with fixed fees. *Land Economics, 80*(3), 465–475.

Yushiou, T., Cohen, S., & Vogel, R. M. (2011). The impacts of water conservation strategies on water use. *Journal of the American Water Resources Association, 47*(4), 687–701.

Wisconsin Department of Natural Resources (2011). *Wisconsin water use 2010 report,* Retrieved from http://dnr.wi.gov/topic/WaterUse/documents/WaterUseReport2010TwoPage.pdf

Worthington, A., & Hoffman, M. (2008). An empirical survey of residential water demand modeling. *Journal of Economic Surveys, 22,* 842–871.

Appendix A: Additional tables

Table A1. Descriptive statistics by residential water regulation regimes.

Variables	I		II$_{PP}$		II$_{NPP}$		III		Total	
	Mean	SD	Mean	SD	Mean	SD	Mean	SD	Mean	SD
Water consumption	43.65	11.58	43.74	8.39	51.30	13.49	45.86	9.20	45.65	11.28
Marginal price	2.85	1.32	2.79	1.03	2.86	1.15	3.10	1.00	2.88	1.16
Average price	4.66	2.03	4.64	1.88	4.33	1.97	4.72	1.41	4.60	1.88
Income	48.54	12.97	47.81	8.98	53.76	13.24	49.89	9.96	49.67	11.80
Housing age	74.36	13.17	72.63	11.18	69.29	13.39	70.18	14.03	72.15	12.99
High education	4.77	4.73	4.37	2.71	6.97	5.09	5.67	3.23	5.28	4.25
Democrat	55.11	7.79	57.33	8.52	52.47	9.84	54.78	8.09	55.18	8.82

Water consumption: average water consumption in 1000 gallons per residential customer per year.
Marginal price: marginal residential water price in US$ per 1000 gallons.
Average price: average water price is US$ per 1000 gallons.
Income: median 1999 household income in US$1000.
Housing age: percentage of housing units built before 1980.
High education: percentage of the population having achieved a graduate or professional degree.
Democrat: percentage voting for the Democratic Party candidates in the 2008 presidential election.

Table A2.   Definitions, descriptions and sources of data.

Variable	Description	Source
Situational variables		
Temperature	Summer average cumulative temperature (°F)	NWSFO
No rain	Number of days in summer without any precipitation	NWSFO
Surface water	Share of area with surface water of total area	US census 2000
Household Characteristics		
Income	Median family income	US census 2000
Young	Percentage of the population between 0 and 14 years	US census 2000
High education	Percentage of population 25 years and over with graduate or professional degree	US census 2000
Housing age	Percentage of housing built before 1980	US census 2000
Detached house	Share of detached houses in 2000	US census 2000
Population density	Population density in habitants per square mile	US census 2000
Democrat	Percentage voting for the Democratic Party candidates in the 2008 presidential election	*USA Today*
Description of PP		
IBR	Dummy: if increasing block rate	PSC survey
PSC	Dummy: if PSC conservation-oriented water rates	PSC survey
Monthly	Dummy: if monthly water bill	PSC survey
Description of NPP		
Education program	Develop a public information and education program	PSC survey
Citizen group	Create a citizen water conservation advisory group	PSC survey
Audit	Conduct water audits of residential customers	PSC survey
Rebates	Rebates to residential customers	PSC survey
Reuse water	Promote projects that reuse or recycle water	PSC survey
Rain barrels	Promote the use of rain barrels or rain gardens	PSC survey
WaterSense	Join EPA's WaterSense program	PSC survey
Outdoor efficient	Ordinances for outdoor water use	PSC survey
Outdoor restriction	Ordinances for new building	PSC survey
Description of methods used to inform households about NPP		
TV	Use of local TV or radio commercials	PSC survey
Newspaper	Newspaper advertisements or letters to the editor	PSC survey
Water bill inserts	Water bill inserts	PSC survey
K-12 school	K–12 school programs	PSC survey
Special events	Special events	PSC survey
Web	Water-conservation web pages	PSC survey
Mailing	Special mailings to customers	PSC survey
Description of utility characteristics		
Small size	Utility in Class D	PSC survey
Medium size	Utility in Class C	PSC survey
Peak volume	Share of the water volume sold on the peak day to the annual volume of water	PSC survey
		PSC survey
Marginal water price	Marginal water price	PSC survey

Sources: NWSFO, http://www.aos.wisc.edu/~sco/; US Census 2000, http://quickfacts.census.gov/qfd/; PSC, http://psc.wi.gov

Table A3.   Price and income elasticities of residential water demand.

Regulation regime	OLS	Two-stage Lee (1983)	Two-stage BFG (2007)
Price elasticities			
I (no PP, no NPP)	− 0.12***	− 0.12***	− 0.10*
II$_{PP}$	− 0.12***	− 0.15***	− 0.16*
II$_{NPP}$ (NPP only)	− 0.16*	− 0.16*	− 0.19*
III (PP, NPP)	− 0.02	− 0.00	− 0.02
Income elasticities			
I (no PP, no NPP)	0.61***	0.63***	0.53***
II$_{PP}$	0.27*	0.28	0.27
II$_{NPP}$ (NPP only)	0.47	0.43**	0.43**
III (PP, NPP)	0.45**	0.43**	0.47*

Significance symbols: *** = 1%; ** = 5%; * = 10%.

Appendix B: Econometric estimation results

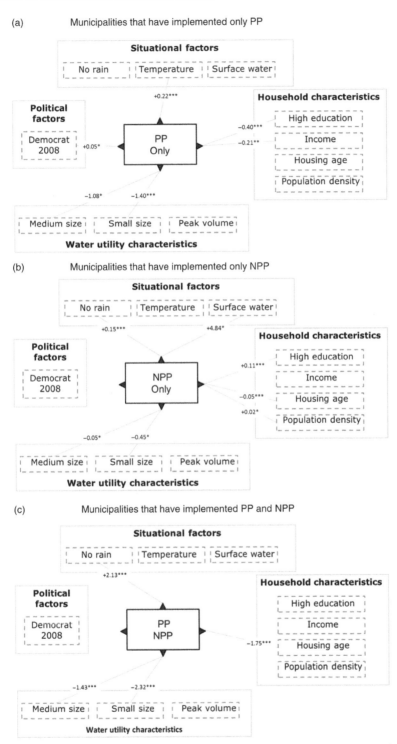

Figure B1.   Determinants of regulation regimes.

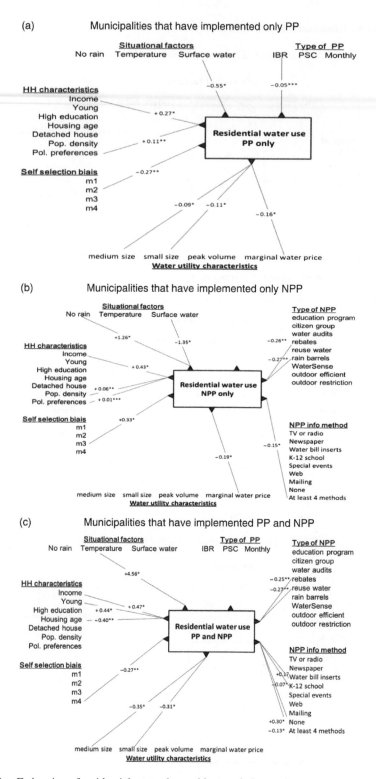

Figure B2. Estimation of residential water demand by regulation regime.

Water demand management: review of literature and comparison in South-East Asia

Eduardo Araral[a] and Yahua Wang[b]

[a]*Lee Kuan Yew School of Public Policy and Faculty Associate, Institute of Water Policy, National University of Singapore, Singapore;* [b]*School of Public Policy and Management, Tsinghua University, Beijing, China*

The present paper reviews the literature on urban water demand management and compares practices in South-East Asia. Existing literature is mostly from developed economies and is concerned mainly with elasticity studies, which are not relevant to developing countries because their main problem is non-revenue water. Cities in South-East Asia employ both price and non-price mechanisms to regulate demand. Price mechanisms include increasing block tariffs, fixed, volumetric, raw water, and conservancy charges, rebates, cross-subsidies and periodic rebasing. Non-price mechanisms such as management, engineering and regulatory mechanisms, as well as public education and community involvement, play important roles. More studies are needed to establish their efficacy and cost-effectiveness.

Introduction

Developing countries worldwide face significant challenges in managing increasing demand for urban water because of industrialization, urbanization and the potential impacts of global warming on freshwater supply. The problem of water scarcity in urban areas can be addressed through supply-side or demand-side solutions. The conventional solution to water scarcity has been to develop new sources of supply, while others advocate demand-side management in conjunction with conventional approaches (Inman & Jeffrey, 2006).

This paper reviews the literature on urban water demand management and compares practices within South-East Asia. This is important for three reasons. First, most of the literature on water demand management (WDM) comes from developed economies and has concerned mainly measurement of price and income elasticities (Nauges & Whittington, 2010). However, elasticity studies are of little relevance to developing countries, because their problems are more basic: how to ensure clean, affordable and reliable water supply; how to reduce non-revenue water; and how to ensure metering of taps, without which estimation of elasticity is of limited utility.

Furthermore, elasticity studies in developing countries can be problematic because of (1) specification problems (i.e. how to specify prices given the often complex pricing structures in developing countries); (2) the lack of data concerning households and their demands for water; and (3) typically, and most importantly, households in developing countries often rely on a variety of water sources, including piped and non-piped sources with different characteristics and levels of services (Nauges & Whittington, 2010).

Second, little is known about how countries in South-East Asia manage demand for urban water despite significant challenges due to large urban populations and rapid economic growth. For instance, in a review of 37 studies on WDM since 1980, Worthington and Hoffman (2006) found that 36 of these were from the US (e.g., Gaudin, Griffin, & Sickles, 2001; Renwick & Green, 2000; Timmins, 2002), Europe (e.g., Martinez-Espiñeira, 2002; Nauges & Thomas, 2000; Nauges & Thomas, 2003) and Australia (e.g., Higgs & Worthington, 2001; Hoffmann, Worthington, & Higgs, 2006).

In contrast, there is a limited number of WDM studies focused on South-East Asia, for instance in Indonesia (Rietveld, Rouwendal, & Zwart, 2000), Cambodia (Basani, Isham, & Reilly, 2008), the Philippines (Persson, 2002), Vietnam (Cheesman, Bennett, & Son, 2008) and Malaysia (Cherian, 2009). No comparative studies are available amongst Association of South-East Asian Nations (ASEAN) countries.

Third, the performance of water utilities in South-East Asia and India is compared in terms of water supply coverage, water availability, average tariff, public taps, metered connections, staff per 1000 connections and management salaries. We provide the comparison as a basis for lesson drawing.

Mechanisms for water demand management

In this section, we discuss the two types of mechanisms for regulating demand for water, price and non-price mechanisms and the current debates on their efficacy.

Price mechanisms

Price mechanisms – often increasing block tariffs – are the most common mechanisms for urban water demand management. However, scholars and practitioners are often divided on their efficacy. On the one hand is the conventional view that marginal-cost pricing is an effective instrument of demand management because consumers will adjust their consumption and respond to marginal prices (Olmstead & Stavins, 2009).

On the other hand, there are those who argue that residential water demand is relatively price-inelastic and therefore water tariffs are ineffective in controlling demand, for instance Garcia and Reynaud (2004) and Gaudin et al. (2001). In essence, this group argues that (1) there exist no close substitutes for water in most of its uses; (2) household spending on water is generally a relatively small share of the typical household budget; and (3) water is frequently demanded jointly with some other complementary good. For a review and critique of the literature, see Renwick and Green (2000).

A more nuanced view comes from the meta-analytic study of WDM in the US, Europe and Australia by Worthington and Hoffman (2006). They find that price-elasticity estimates are generally in the range of zero to 0.5 in the short run and 0.5 to unity in the long run. They also find that income-elasticity estimates are (usually) of a much smaller magnitude and positive. The meta-analysis by Dalhuisen, Florax, de Groot, and Nijkamp (2003) concluded that variations in price and income elasticities are due to differences in underlying tariff structures. Another meta-analysis, by Arbués, Garcia-Valiñas, and Martinez-espiñeira (2003), found that price, income and household composition are crucial determinants of residential consumption.

Table 1 provides a summary of various elasticity studies on WDM. In summary, based on the prior literature, estimates of elasticity with respect to water pricing in

Table 1.   Summary of studies on water demand management.

Author, region	Data and methods	Findings
Nieswiadomy (1992), USA	Data from 430 of the 600 largest water utilities in the US; based on marginal-price model, average-price model and price-perception model	Price elasticity is higher in the South and the West of the US; conservation programme does not appear to reduce water use, but public education appears to have reduced water usage in the West. Price-perception models indicate that consumers react more to average than to marginal prices in all regions.
Espey, Espey, and Shaw (1997), USA	Gives 124 estimated price elasticities from 24 journal articles published between 1967 and 1993	Inclusion of income, rainfall and evapotranspiration are all found to influence the estimate of price elasticity. Population density, household size and temperature do not significantly influence the estimate. Pricing structure and season significantly influence the estimate.
Renwick and Green (2000), California, USA	Econometric model comparing alternative policy instruments such as water allocations, use restrictions, public education and increasing block pricing schedules	Both price and alternative demand-side management policies were effective in reducing demand, but the magnitude of the reduction in demand varied among policy instruments.
Arbués et al. (2003), Worldwide	Meta-analysis of the state of the art in residential water demand modelling using 110 studies	Water price, income and or household composition are crucial determinants of residential consumption; most studies have shown that demand is inelastic; most water tariffs have complex structures that combine fixed and variable charges; promotion of low-consumption technologies has significant effects on water conservation.
Dalhuisen et al. (2003), USA, Europe, Australia	Gives 296 estimates from 64 studies that appeared between 1963 and 2001	Residential water demand is relatively price-elastic, but income elasticities are relatively low, under increasing block rate pricing. The absolute magnitudes of price and income elasticities are significantly greater for areas with higher incomes.
Martínez-Espiñeira and Nauges (2004), Spain	For the period 1991–1999 in Seville; the Stone-Geary utility function	Price elasticity: −0.10; income elasticity: 0.10.
Taylor, McKean, and Young (2004), USA	Data from a sample of Colorado utilities; the preferred double-log marginal price model	Price elasticity was −0.3. When the fixed fee was purged from the data, average price was not significant, but marginal price remained significant.
Coleman (2009), USA	Salt Lake City, Utah, for the years 1999–2002	Moderate price elasticities (between 0.378 and 0.665) were found for most models during the study period. However, large price elasticities were estimated during the summer months.

(Continued)

Table 1. – *continued*

Author, region	Data and methods	Findings
Nauges and Whittington (2010)	A review of literature between 1985 to 2006 in developing countries worldwide	Most estimates of own-price elasticity of water from private connections are in the range from -0.3 to -0.6.
Fenrick and Getachew (2012), Wisconsin, USA	A 1997 to 2006 panel of 200 Wisconsin water utilities; double-log functional form	The price is inelastic yet negative and statistically significant, and this elasticity response grows stronger as the marginal price level is increased.

empirical studies vary widely, depending on the different locations and different instruments – even different income groups and seasonal changes – and hence there is no consensus on the efficacy of using block tariffs as a policy instrument to regulate demand for water.

Non-price mechanisms

Non-price mechanisms for WDM include public education, community mobilization, supply restrictions such as rationing, prohibition of certain types of consumption, and use of technical and engineering solutions such as pressure-reducing valves, constant-flow meters, double-flush cisterns, leak-detection instruments, and system control and data collection (SCADA) technology, among others.

While economists generally advocate higher residential water prices as a means of reducing demand, there is increasing support in the literature for non-price mechanisms.

Based on time-series analysis of 116 municipalities in France, Nauges and Thomas (2000) indicated that price elasticity of demand is very low, while non-price policies work better to induce consumers to use less water. Martinez-Espiñeira and Nauges (2004) showed that water demand becomes insensitive to price changes below a certain level, such that non-price policies should be considered beyond this level.

However, estimating the effects of non-price mechanisms on urban water demand management is not easy. Kenney, Goemans, Klein, Lowrey, and Reidy (2008) found that pricing and outdoor water-restriction policies interact with each other, ensuring that total water savings are not the sum of each programme operating independently. Syme, Nancarrow, and Seligman (2000) argued that the possible interactions of non-price campaigns with other policy instruments make it difficult to evaluate their effectiveness; e.g. a marketing campaign may heighten the motivation to respond to the pricing schedule.

Reynaud (2012) showed that neglecting endogeneity of price or non-price policy may lead to biased parameter estimates and that the type of policy mix may be as important as the level of water prices in determining water consumption. However, Halich and Stephenson (2009) found that residential water-use reductions increased with progressively higher levels of information and enforcement efforts.

However, critics of non-price mechanisms such as supply restriction argue that these mechanisms lead to inefficiencies such as decreased consumer welfare and increased deadweight losses, are inequitable and unpopular, and place an unnecessary administrative burden on struggling public and private-sector water utilities (Arbués et al., 2003).

The case of South-East Asia

Data and analysis

Data for South-East Asia in this study are based on secondary sources and a survey of managers of water utilities in key cities, states and provinces in South-East Asia: Singapore, Thailand (Bangkok), the Philippines (Cebu and Manila), Cambodia (Phnom Penh and Sihanoukville), Indonesia (Palembang, Jakarta), Malaysia (Johor Bahru and Selangor) and Vietnam (Ho Chi Minh). These are some of the largest urban utilities in their respective countries.

Data collected from secondary sources and surveys were examined for their similarities and differences and were categorized and compared along common parameters (i.e. use of tariff, management and regulatory instruments, technical and engineering solutions and consumer education).

Challenges to urban water demand management

Before discussing urban water demand management practices in South-East Asia, we first outline some of the challenges faced by this region in managing demand for urban water. These include non-revenue water, high levels of water losses (and the related problem of ageing infrastructure), and enforcement of regulations.

Non-revenue water (NRW) is one of the major issues affecting urban water demand management in the developing world, including South-East Asia. NRW results in major financial, supply and pressure losses, as well as excessive energy consumption. It varies widely, from low levels in Singapore (4%), Phnom Penh (below 6%) and Manila East (11%) to more than 35% (national average) in the case of Thailand, Vietnam, Indonesia, Laos and Malaysia.

Within countries in the region the picture can also vary significantly. For instance, in middle-income Malaysia, average NRW is high, at 40%, but ranges from 18% to 73% among various states. In 2010, the average percentage of non-revenue water for the state of Perak in Malaysia was 29.4% (Alkasseh, Adlan, Abustan, Aziz, & Hanif, 2013). In Indonesia, of the 402 public and private water utilities, about 75% were rated in bad health operationally (high NRW) and financially (not financially viable). In Metro Jakarta, in particular, the privatization of water utilities there in 1997 did not lead to significant reductions in NRW. It remains stubbornly at around 48%, compared to around 60% in 1997 (JWSRB, 2009). In contrast, in Manila (East), NRW has been reduced significantly, from 70% to the current 11%, over the same period.

High NRM is usually the result of leakage from ageing infrastructure. In Mandalay, Myanmar, and Hanoi, Vietnam, for example, water infrastructure has not been upgraded for more than 50 years. Different countries in the region, depending on their economic status, finance their water infrastructure using internally generated funds (Singapore, Brunei), public-private partnership schemes including concession agreements in middle-income countries (Malaysia, Jakarta, Manila, Thailand), and funding from donors in low-income countries (Vietnam, Myanmar, Cambodia, Laos). In Manila and Jakarta, the private sector played key roles in rehabilitating infrastructure. More recently, the concessionaire for Manila has bought half of the shares of the concessionaire in Jakarta and has been tapped to undertake NRW reduction projects in Ho Chin Minh City in Vietnam.

Enforcement of regulations is another challenge to urban water demand management in some South-East Asian countries, especially in the case of abstraction of groundwater.

This problem is particularly acute in Manila and Jakarta, where enforcement capacity and the resources of regulatory agencies and local governments are constrained. About a quarter of Metro Jakarta's 28 million people rely on groundwater. Land subsidence in Jakarta as a result of over-abstraction varies in different areas from 28 cm to 56 cm between 1993 and 2005. A significant part of the problem is a weak regulatory framework on ground water management.

In summary, South-East Asia faces serious challenges in urban water demand management: high non-revenue water due to leakage; lack of metering; and weak regulations. These challenges have not been addressed in the conventional literature, with its emphasis on estimation of price and demand elasticities (Babel, Rivas, & Seetharam, 2010; Biswas & Tortajada, 2010; Gupta, 2001; Vo, 2007). In the next section, we examine the practices of water demand management in South-East Asia.

Urban water demand management in South-East Asia

Depending on country circumstances, cities in South-East Asia employ a wide range of solutions to manage demand for urban water. These solutions can be broadly classified into four categories: (1) tariff solutions; (2) management and regulatory solutions; (3) technical and engineering solutions; and (4) public education and community involvement. Table 2 summarizes these practices, which are then discussed in the subsequent sections.

Water tariffs

Increasing block tariffs are one of two main instruments used by South-East Asian cities for urban water demand management. There are wide variations within and among these countries on how water tariffs are applied, but the underlying principles essentially rely on economic valuation while also balancing affordability, conservation and sustainability. Among five cities in South-East Asia, Singapore had the highest average tariff at USD1.22/m^3 (PUB, 2012), with Kuala Lumpur the lowest at USD0.45/m^3 (Berg & Danilenko, 2011). Manila and Jakarta, both of which had large-scale privatization, had similar tariff levels of USD0.7/m^3 (FDC, 2009; Syaukat, 2009). Figure 1 summarizes these differences.

Most countries in South-East Asia rely on increasing block tariffs to manage demand for urban water. For instance, in Malaysia, the states of Johor Bahru and Selangor employ increasing block tariffs while ensuring the affordability of water to low-income groups based on water-demand studies and charging full cost recovery to higher-income groups. In Metro Cebu, Philippines, the price of water is about three times the national average, reflecting its scarcity. In Metro Manila (East), the price of water has increased 169% since privatization in 1996.

In Vietnam, water is now valued as an economic good – through the use of a water resource tax – and priced to reflect scarcity. In Cambodia, both in Phnom Penh and Sihanoukville, water tariff affordability studies have been undertaken as a basis for formulating tariff reform. In Singapore, increasing block tariffs with a water conservation tax have been used as one of the three key pillars of WDM – the other two pillars being mandatory reduction to cut down on excessive flow and wastage of water, and a voluntary approach to promote ownership of water conservation.

Indeed, compared with cities from South Asia (Lahore, Pakistan; Dhaka, Bangladesh; Colombo, Sri Lanka; Chennai, India), more cities in South-East Asia use increasing block tariffs to address concerns of affordability and to promote conservation (ADB, 2007).

Table 2. Summary of urban water demand management practices in selected utilities in South-East Asia (excluding supply-side solutions), based on the authors' surveys.

	Use of price mechanism to regulate demand	Management and regulatory solutions	Engineering and technical solutions	Public education and community involvement
Singapore	Yes; based on economic valuation; increasing block tariffs; water conservation tax; subsidies for poor households to use water-conserving technologies	Demand zone management; mandatory allowable flow rates; registration of water products	Leak-detection meters; pressure-reducing valves; self-closing delayed-action taps; low-capacity flushing cisterns, constant-flow regulators	Yes; education campaigns (10-litre challenge); water conservation week; learning centres for students; water efficiency labelling schemes; water efficiency funds for small and medium-size enterprises to fund feasibility studies; training for technicians; audit checklist; guidebooks
Malaysia (Selangor)	Yes; economic valuation of water; fixed, volumetric and raw water charge; increasing block tariffs; rebates for shifting to efficient toilets and washing machines	Reduction in NRW from 43% to 34% through pipe replacement; certification, licensing and labelling of water-efficient products; mandatory efficiency plans for high-volume users; instituting a WDM agency	Dual-flush toilets; pressure-reducing valves; constant-flow regulators; thimbles	Yes; communicating to consumers their marginal price information and block rate structure in the water bill
Philippines (Manila East)	Yes; increasing block tariffs; regular rate rebasing based on weighted average cost of capital; tariff adjustments for inflation and foreign currency; free water for public schools, jails, orphanages, hospitals	NRW reduction from 63% to 11% in 15 years through metering and pipe replacement; decentralized management units; process and performance benchmarking tied to rewards; water regulatory agency to monitor performance	Metering; single bulk meters in slum areas; leak-detection instruments; pressure-reducing valves; SCADA technology	Yes; educating consumers about marginal price information and block rate structure in water bill; also through community-based approaches and NGOs in slum areas

(Continued)

Table 2. – *continued*

	Use of price mechanism to regulate demand	Management and regulatory solutions	Engineering and technical solutions	Public education and community involvement
Thailand (Bangkok)	Yes	NRW reduction from 43% to 29% through pipe replacement; water transmission and distribution control centre; district metering areas	Integrated leakage-management system; leak-detection meters; metering; pressure-reducing valves	Yes; telling consumers their marginal price information and block rate structure in the water bill
Indonesia (Jakarta)	Seven types of tariff (customers in highest category pay 14 times those in lowest); cross-subsidies (top 6% of consumers subsidize bottom 60%); regular rate rebasing exercise; tariff increased three times since 1997	Public–private partnerships; technical and administrative audits of public water utilities pipe-replacement programmes; regulatory agency to monitor performance	Water meters; SCADA; single bulk meters in slum areas; computerization of database	Yes; telling consumers their marginal price information and block rate structure in the water bill; community-based approaches and NGOs in slum areas
Vietnam (Ho Chi Minh)	Yes; increasing block tariffs; fixed, volumetric, raw water and conservancy charges; subsidies for poor households	SCADA; demand-zone management; training of technicians in leak management	Metering; computerization of database; leak-detection instruments; SCADA; dual-flush toilets; pressure-reducing valves; constant-flow regulators	Yes; telling consumers their marginal price information and block rate structure in the water bill
Cambodia (Phnom Penh)	Yes; using economic valuation; increasing block tariffs; graduated subsidies for connection fees to the poor; subsidies for water service to absolute poor	NRW reduction from 72% to 6% in 20 years though pipe replacement; leak management; community involvement; demand-zone management	Metering; computerization of database; leak-detection instruments	Yes; telling consumers their marginal price information and block rate structure in the water bill; community-based approaches in slum areas

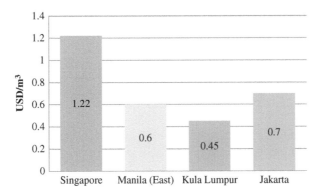

Figure 1.   Average water tariffs in selected cities in South-East Asia. Sources: Public Utilities Board (2012) for Singapore; FDC (2009) for Manila; Berg and Danilenko (2011) for Kuala Lumpur; Syaukat (2009) for Jakarta.

As a result of a progressive tariff structure and autonomous operations, the performance of urban water utilities in South-East Asia is significantly better than most of their counterparts in India. For instance, water is available on average for 20 hours in South-East Asia, compared to less than 5 hours in India, and households have significantly more piped connections in South-East Asia than in India (although standard deviations in South-East Asia are also significant). Noticeably, average water tariffs in South-East Asia are about three times those of India (but also with large standard deviations) (Figure 2).

Metering

Increasing block tariffs are only useful as an instrument of urban water demand management if accompanied by metering. Millock and Nauges (2010) found that households that were both metered and charged for their water individually had a much higher probability of investing in water-efficient equipment, compared to households that paid a flat fee. In fact, most of the literature on water management advocates the introduction of household metering (Bartoszczuk & Nakamori, 2004; Dalhuisen & Nijkamp, 2001). Yepes and Dianderas (1996) have suggested that the introduction of metering results in reduced water consumption, regardless of the pricing structure used.

In South-East Asia, metering is a common mechanism for WDM. In fact, countries in the region fare much better than their Indian counterparts in terms of metered connections, operating ratio, number of staff per 1000 connections and management salaries. On average, 80% of urban households in South-East Asia have metered connections. In contrast, of the urban households in India only about 30% have metered connections. Operating ratios in South-East Asia – an indicator of operating efficiency – are about half those in India (although there is a large standard deviation in India) (Figure 3).

Management and regulatory solutions

South-East Asian countries share a common approach in employing various management and regulatory solutions to urban water demand management. For example, in Indonesia, the Philippines, Cambodia and Malaysia, performance targets are commonly employed to reduce NRW. In Indonesia, the target is for public water utilities to bring NRW down to 15% from a high of 40%. In Malaysia, the target is to reduce it from 37% to 30% by 2015.

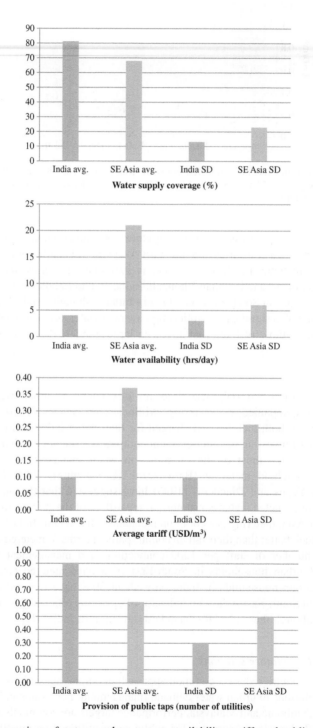

Figure 2.   Comparison of water supply coverage, availability, tariffs and public taps in South-East Asia and India (2005). Calculations based on ADB (2007) and SEAWUN and ADB (2007).

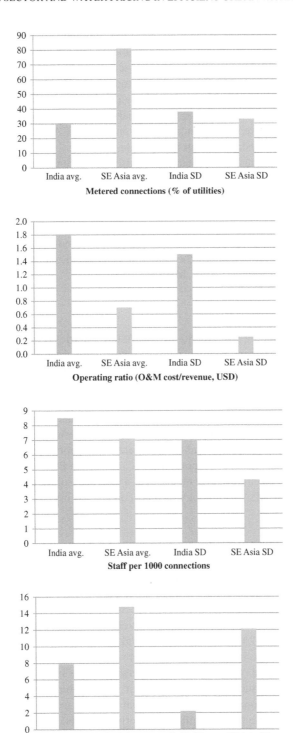

Figure 3. Comparison of metering, operating ratio, staff per 1000 connections and management salaries among utilities in India and South-East Asia (2005). Calculations based on ADB (2007) and SEAWUN and ADB (2007).

Decentralized management is another common approach to urban water demand management. In Malaysia (Johor Bahru), Singapore, Phnom Penh in Cambodia and Manila (East) in the Philippines, demand-management zones or territory-management approaches have been effectively employed as strategic approaches to managing NRW. Manila (East) was particularly successful in using demand-management zones to reduce NRW from 64% to 11% in a period of 15 years. Likewise, the use of information technology such as geographic information systems and SCADA technology are also extensively used in Malaysia, Vietnam and Manila.

Performance and process benchmarking is also widely employed in Indonesia, the Philippines, Malaysia and Vietnam, where urban water utilities are rated in terms of their health. In Indonesia, benchmarking studies show that close to 75% of the 400 urban utilities are not in good health (Perpamsi, 2008). Performance-based contracts for NRW reduction have been employed in Sihanoukville, Cambodia, in Kuala Lumpur, and in Bangkok, Thailand. Capacity building, including employee empowerment and twinning arrangements, is crucial to improving the ability of water utilities to improve WDM, as has been the experience in Cambodia and Manila.

Technical and engineering solutions

A key challenge to reducing NRW in South-East Asian countries is the problem of old and leaking pipes. Cities such as Manila, Cebu, Phnom Penh, Mandalay and Hanoi have embarked on programmes to replace their ageing and leaking pipes. Singapore has substantially replaced its pipes over the years and has introduced 100% metering.

Along with pipe-replacement programmes, these countries have also introduced engineering solutions such as pressure-reducing valves to manage water pressure. Phnom Penh, Singapore and Manila (East) are several examples of how programmes on holistic pipe replacement and management can be an effective solution to demand management, particularly in reducing NRW. Singapore, Manila and Phnom Penh are some examples of water utilities that put an emphasis on metering as a technical solution. Most utilities in the region also employ SCADA technology as their control and operating system.

Institutional and regulatory reforms

Several ASEAN member countries have adopted institutional and regulatory reforms to promote accountability in urban water utilities. In Indonesia, public water utilities are undergoing a process of debt restructuring to make them more viable. Responsibility and accountability for these utilities have also been transferred to local governments. Definitions of the responsibilities of different levels of government – federal and state governments in the case of Malaysia, provinces and districts in the case of the Philippines and Indonesia – were also important institutional reforms to promote accountability.

In Manila and Jakarta, public-private partnerships were instrumental in improving water service delivery. Successful private-sector participation requires, among other things, the alignment of corporate goals with social goals, as well as effective regulation. In Malaysia and the Philippines, regulatory reforms have been introduced to separate service providers from regulators. Permitting and licensing system for groundwater extraction are used in Thailand, the Philippines, Indonesia, Myanmar, Laos and Vietnam, but enforcement is challenging. Regulations for engineering and service standards are also important in managing urban water demand, as shown in the case of Singapore (Luan, 2010).

Leadership, public education and community involvement

The experience in South-East Asia strongly suggests that leadership plays an important role in improving the performance of urban water utilities, including with respect to demand management. A stable, competent and committed leadership can make a substantial difference in performance, as has been documented in the cases of Singapore (Tortajada, 2006), Phnom Penh (Araral, 2008) and Palembang (Syaiful, 2011). The top leadership of these water utilities stayed with their jobs for no less than 10 years, overseeing the protracted processes of replacing ageing and leaking pipes, upgrading management and technology (including metering), and introducing tariff reforms, among others.

In all these cases, NRW was substantially reduced over time, and most of these utilities received national and international recognition. For instance, the Manila Water Company was recognized by the International Finance Corporation as an example of successful water-utility privatization. Wu and Malaluan (2008) attribute their success to corporate governance, financial management and operations management. Singapore's Public Utilities Board received the Stockholm Industry Water Award. The Ramon Magsaysay Award recognized Phnom Penh's Water Supply Authority for its remarkable turn around story, while Palembang's Water Supply Authority is regarded as Indonesia's top-performing utility. In all these cases, stable, competent and committed leadership played a key role.

Moral suasion or public education on water conservation is commonly used by utilities in South-East Asia to manage water demand, but with varying degrees of efficacy relative to other instruments. The most commonly used methods of moral suasion are communicating to consumers their marginal cost information, benchmarking their consumption with respect to national averages and highlighting block-tariff information.

However, rigorous empirical studies on the effect of moral suasion are rare because of inherent difficulties such as problems of simultaneity and multi-collinearity; i.e. it is difficult to disentangle the effects of moral suasion from the effects of other instruments such as increasing block tariffs and the application of technical and management solutions.

The available empirical study estimating the effects of moral suasion, along with price mechanisms and alternative mechanisms such as water rationing and use restrictions, is that of Renwick and Green (2000) in California. They found that both price and alternative demand-side management policies (rationing, moral suasion, water restrictions) were effective in reducing demand, but the magnitude of the reduction varied among these policy instruments.

In developing countries, which have to deal with large informal settlements, water utilities that have effectively reduced demand often have community-based water-conservation programmes. Manila Water is an example. The large informal settlements in Metro Manila, which for years have been a major source of NRW due to leakage, theft, non-metering and non-billing, have been effectively organized into self-managed water districts, with each district connected to a bulk meter and provided with public taps. The officers of these water user associations are responsible for collecting water bills and paying the water concessionaire. The water user associations are also responsible for monitoring and reporting theft and leakage. These community-based schemes played an important role – along with a pipe-replacement programme – in reducing Manila water's NRW from a high of 63% to its current low level of 11%. The story of community involvement in Manila is the same as that of Phnom Penh, which helped reduce its NRW to 6%.

Conclusions

Several conclusions can be drawn from this study. First, the literature on water demand management – mostly from developed economies – is mainly concerned with estimating income and price elasticities using a variety of techniques. However, elasticity studies are of little relevance to developing countries, because their problems are more basic: for example, how to reduce non-revenue water and how to ensure metering of taps.

Second, countries in South-East Asia employ both price and non-price mechanisms to regulate water demand. Price mechanisms rely mainly on increasing block tariffs but also include, to varying degrees, fixed, volumetric, raw water and conservancy charges, rebates, cross-subsidies and periodic tariff rebasing. Non-price mechanisms also play important roles in demand management in South-East Asia, perhaps more so than price mechanisms, although systematic comparison among countries is impractical.

The paper has shown that cities from South-East Asia employ a wide variety of non-price mechanisms, which can be classified into four categories: (1) management solutions such as demand-zone management, performance management and process benchmarking, twinning and public private partnership; (2) technical and engineering solutions such as metering, including single bulk meters in slum areas, pressure-reducing valves, constant-flow meters, geographic information systems, leak-detection technology, and system control and data acquisition technology; (3) institutional and regulatory solutions such as rationing and prohibition of certain types of consumption, and product certification, labelling and licensing (although regulatory enforcement varies significantly among countries); and (4) public education and community and NGO involvement, especially in developing countries where there are significant slum areas.

Of the cities compared in this study, Singapore arguably has the most progressive set of practices in terms of urban water demand management; it also relies significantly on regulatory and technology measures (Sharma & Vairavamoorthy, 2009). For instance, Singapore employs mandatory allowable-flow rates and registration of water products. It also employs water-efficiency funds for small and medium enterprises to fund feasibility studies, training for technicians, and audit checklists and guidebooks, among other things. Other cities in South-East Asia have none of these practices. In terms of managing water demand in slum areas, the practices in Manila (East), Phnom Penh and Jakarta using single bulk meters and relying on community-based solutions with the help of NGOs has arguably had significant impacts on demand, particularly in reducing NRW.

Finally, while there are differences in practices, there are also many similarities and convergences of practices among the utilities compared in this study in terms of the use of tariffs, moral suasion, technology, management and community-based solutions. However, no judgment or inference can be made in terms of their efficacy, owing to the lack of comparable data. At best, this paper is able only to compare their practices. More rigorous studies are needed to establish the efficacy and cost-effectiveness of these instruments in managing water demand.

Acknowledgements

We are grateful to the anonymous reviewers and editors for their valuable comments and suggestions. We also thank the National Science Foundation of China (Grant No. 70973064) for its support of this work.

References

ADB (Asian Development Bank). (2007). *Benchmarking and data book of water utilities in India*. New Delhi, India: Asian Development Bank and the Ministry of Urban Development, Government of India.

Alkasseh, J. M. A., Adlan, M. N., Abustan, I., Aziz, H. A., & Hanif, A. B. M. (2013). Applying minimum night flow to estimate water loss using statistical modeling: A case study in Kinta Valley, Malaysia. *Water Resources Management, 27*, 1439–1455. doi:10.1007/s11269-012-0247-2.

Araral, E. Jr (2008). Public provision for urban water: Getting prices and governance right. *Governance: An International Journal of Policy, Administration, and Institutions, 21*, 527–549. doi:10.1111/j.1468-0491.2008.00412.x.

Arbués, F., Garcia-Valiñas, M. Á., & Martınez-Espiñeira, R. (2003). Estimation of residential water demand: A state-of-the-art review. *The Journal of Socio-Economics, 32*, 81–102. doi:10.1016/S1053-5357(03)00005-2.

Babel, M. S., Rivas, A. A., & Kallidaikurichi, S. (2010). Municipal water supply management in Bangkok: Achievements and lessons. *International Journal of Water Resources Development, 26*, 193–217. doi:10.1080/07900621003710661.

Basani, M., Isham, J., & Reilly, B. (2008). The determinants of water connection and water consumption: Empirical evidence from a Cambodian household survey. *World Development, 36*, 953–968. doi:10.1016/j.worlddev.2007.04.021.

Bartoszczuk, P., & Nakamori, Y. (2004). Modelling sustainable water prices. In M. Quaddus & M. Siddique (Eds.), *Handbook of sustainable development planning: Studies in modelling and decision support* (pp. 1–26). Cheltenham: Edward Elgar.

Berg, C., & Danilenko, A. (2011). *The IBNET water supply and sanitation performance blue book: The international benchmarking network for water and sanitation utilities databook*. Washington, DC: The World Bank.

Biswas, A. K., & Tortajada, C. (2010). Water supply of Phnom Penh: An example of good governance. *International Journal of Water Resources Development, 26*, 157–172. doi:10.1080/07900621003768859.

Cheesman, J., Bennett, J., & Son, T. V. H. (2008). Estimating household water demand using revealed and contingent behaviors: Evidence from Vietnam. *Water Resources Research, 44*(11), 1–11. doi:10.1029/2007WR006265.

Cherian, J. (2009). *Water demand management in Selangor, Malaysia - Why and how?* CRBOM Small Publications Series No. 7. Indonesia: Center for River Basin Organizations and Management (CRBOM).

Coleman, E. A. (2009). A comparison of demand-side water management strategies using disaggregate data. *Public Works Management & Policy, 13*, 215–223. doi:10.1177/1087724X08327648.

Dalhuisen, J., & Nijkamp, P. (2001). *The economics of H_2O*. In Economic instruments and water policies in Central and Eastern Europe: Issues and options. Paper presented at the meeting of Synthesis report of REC, Szetendre, Hungary.

Dalhuisen, J. M., Florax, R. J. G. M., de Groot, H. L. F., & Nijkamp, P. (2003). Price and income elasticities of residential water demand: A meta-analysis. *Land Economics, 79*, 292–308. doi:10.3368/le.79.2.292.

Espey, M., Espey, J., & Shaw, W. D. (1997). Price elasticity of residential demand for water: A meta-analysis. *Water Resources Research, 33*, 1369–1374. doi:10.1029/97WR00571.

FDC (Freedom from Debt Coalition). (2009). *Recalibrating the meter*. Manila, Philippines: Freedom from Debt Coalition.

Fenrick, S. A., & Getachew, L. (2012). Estimation of the effects of price and billing frequency on household water demand using a panel of Wisconsin municipalities. *Applied Economics Letters, 19*, 1373–1380. doi:10.1080/13504851.2011.629977.

Garcia, S., & Reynaud, A. (2004). Estimating the benefits of efficient water pricing in France. *Journal of Resource and Energy Economics, 26*(1), 1–25. doi:10.1016/j.reseneeco.2003.05.001.

Gaudin, S., Griffin, R. C., & Sickles, R. (2001). Demand specification for municipal water management: Evaluation of the Stone-Geary form. *Land Economics, 77*, 399–422. doi:10.3368/le.77.3.399.

Gupta, A. D. (2001). Challenges and opportunities for water resources management in South-East Asia. *Hydrological Sciences Journal, 46*, 923–935. doi:10.1080/02626660109492886.

Halich, G., & Stephenson, K. (2009). Effectiveness of residential water-use restrictions under varying levels of municipal effort. *Land Economics, 85*, 614–626.

Higgs, H., & Worthington, A. (2001). Consumer preferences and water charging options in a large urban municipality: A case study. *Public Works Management and Policy, 5*, 209–217. doi:10.1177/1087724X0153003.

Hoffmann, M., Worthington, A. C., & Higgs, H. (2006). Urban water demand with fixed volumetric charging in a large municipality: The case of Brisbane, Australia. *The Australian Journal of Agricultural Resource Economics, 50*, 347–359. doi:10.1111/j.1467-8489.2006.00339.x.

Inman, D., & Jeffrey, P. (2006). A review of residential water conservation tool performance and influences on implementation effectiveness. *Urban Water Journal, 3*, 127–143. doi:10.1080/15730620600961288.

JWSRB (Jakarta Water Supply Regulatory Body). (2009). *The first 10 years of implementation of the Jakarta water supply 25-year concession agreement*. Jakarta, Indonesia. Retrieved from: http://www.jakartawater.org/images/stories/unduh/10tahunbrEng.pdf.

Kenney, D. S., Goemans, C., Klein, R., Lowrey, J., & Reidy, K. (2008). Residential water demand management: Lessons from Aurora, Colorado. *JAWRA Journal of the American Water Resources Association, 44*, 192–207. doi:10.1111/j.1752-1688.2007.00147.x.

Luan, I. O. B. (2010). Singapore water management policies and practices. *International Journal of Water Resources Development, 26*, 65–80. doi:10.1080/07900620903392190.

Martinez-Espiñeira, R. (2002). Residential water demand in the northwest of Spain. *Environmental and Resource Economics, 21*, 161–187. doi:10.1023/A:1014547616408.

Martínez-Espiñeira, R., & Nauges, C. (2004). Is all domestic water consumption sensitive to price control? *Applied Economics, 36*, 1697–1703. doi:10.1080/0003684042000218570.

Millock, K., & Nauges, C. (2010). Household adoption of water-efficient equipment: The role of socio-economic factors, environmental attitudes and policy. *Environmental and Resource Economics, 46*, 539–565. doi:10.1007/s10640-010-9360-y.

Nauges, C., & Thomas, A. (2000). Privately operated water utilities, municipal price negotiation, and estimation of residential water demand: The case of France. *Land Economics, 76*, 68–85.

Nauges, C., & Thomas, A. (2003). Long-run study of residential water consumption. *Environmental and Resource Economics, 26*, 25–43. doi:10.1023/A:1025673318692.

Nauges, C., & Whittington, D. (2010). Estimation of water demand in developing countries: An overview. *The World Bank Research Observer, 25*, 263–294. doi:10.1093/wbro/lkp016.

Nieswiadomy, M. L. (1992). Estimating urban residential water demand: Effects of price structure, conservation, and education. *Water Resources Research, 28*, 609–615. doi:10.1029/91WR02852.

Olmstead, S. M., & Stavins, R. N. (2009). Comparing price and nonprice approaches to urban water conservation. *Water Resources Research, 45*. doi:10.1029/2008WR007227.

Perpamsi. (2008). *Indonesian association of drinking water companies benchmarking report for 2008*. Jakarta, Indonesia. Retrieved from: http://perpamsi.or.id/technical_database_detail.php?id=35

Persson, T. H. (2002). Household choice of drinking-water source in the Philippines. *Asian Economic Journal, 16*, 303–316. doi:10.1111/1467-8381.t01-1-00154.

Public Utilities Board. (2012). Annual Report, Singapore.

Renwick, M. E., & Green, R. D. (2000). Do residential water demand side management policies measure up? An analysis of eight California water agencies. *Journal of Environmental Economics and Management, 40*, 37–55. doi:10.1006/jeem.1999.1102.

Reynaud, A. (2012). Assessing the impact of price and non-price policies on residential water demand: A case study in Wisconsin. *International Journal of Water Resources Development.* doi:10.1080/07900627.2012.721670.

Rietveld, P., Rouwendal, J., & Zwart, B. (2000). Block rate pricing of water in Indonesia: An analysis of welfare effects. *Bulletin of Indonesian Economic Studies, 36*, 73–92. doi:10.1080/00074910012331338983.

SEAWUN (South-East Asian Water Utilities Network), & ADB (Asian Development Bank). (2007). *Data book of South-East Asian water utilities 2005*. Manila: ADB.

Sharma, S. K., & Vairavamoorthy, K. (2009). Urban water demand management: Prospects and challenges for the developing countries. *Water and Environment Journal, 23*, 210–218. doi:10.1111/j.1747-6593.2008.00134.x.

Syaiful, H. Ir (2011). *The Palembang water utility*. Paper presented at the Temasek Water Leaders Forum, Lee Kuan Yew School of Public Policy, National University of Singapore.

Syaukat, Y. (2009). *Development of piped water supply in Indonesia: Problems and solution*. Paper Presented at Indonesia-Australia Business Conference and Regional Business Forum, Bali, Indonesia.

Syme, G. J., Nancarrow, B. E., & Seligman, C. (2000). The evaluation of information campaigns to promote voluntary household water conservation. *Evaluation Review, 24*, 539–578. doi:10.1177/0193841X0002400601.

Taylor, R. G., McKean, J. R., & Young, R. A. (2004). Alternate price specifications for estimating residential water demand with fixed fees. *Land Economics, 80*, 463–475. doi:10.3368/le.80.3.463.

Timmins, C. (2002). Measuring the dynamic efficiency costs of regulators preferences: Municipal water utilities in the arid west. *Econometrica, 70*, 603–629. doi:10.1111/1468-0262.00297.

Tortajada, C. (2006). Water management in Singapore. *International Journal of Water Resources Development, 22*, 227–240. doi:10.1080/07900620600691944.

Vo, P. L. (2007). Urbanization and water management in Ho Chi Minh City, Vietnam-issues, challenges and perspectives. *GeoJournal, 70*, 75–89. doi:10.1007/s10708-008-9115-2.

Worthington, A. C., & Hoffman, M. (2006). *A state of the art review of residential water demand modelling* (Report No. 06/27). Australia: School of Accounting and Finance, University of Wollongong.

Wu, X., & Malaluan, N. A. (2008). A tale of two concessionaires: A natural experiment of water privatisation in Metro Manila. *Urban Studies, 45*, 207–229. doi:10.1177/0042098007085108.

Yepes, G., & Dianderas, A. (1996). *Water and wastewater utilities: Indicators*. Washington, DC: The World Bank.

Water service quality in Tanzania: access and management

María Á. García-Valiñas[a] and Josepa Miquel-Florensa[b]

[a]Efficiency Group, University of Oviedo, Spain, and LERNA, Toulouse, France; [b]Toulouse School of Economics, France, and ARQADE, Toulouse, France

Problems related to water access and quality are significant in several countries around the world. Thus water management becomes a key issue, especially in developing countries, where the institutional and regulatory context is not always properly designed. The aim of this research is to analyze the residential water service in Tanzania, using data taken from several government reports and the survey "Views of the People 2007". This survey includes information on perceived problems and improvements on water services, allowing identification of the key drivers of Tanzanian households' perceptions of water services. The best-performance framework is also identified, and some policy recommendations are provided.

Introduction

The Committee on Economic, Social and Cultural Rights of the United Nations has formally recognized access to water as a basic human right (UN, 2002). This right is deemed indispensable for leading a life of human dignity and a prerequisite for the fulfilment of other human rights. Water is essential for life and health, so access to a sufficient supply of quality drinking water is basic to guaranteeing people's well-being.

According to UNICEF and WHO (2012), more than 780 million people do not have access to reliable sources of drinking water, and 2.5 billion lack decent sanitation. Additionally, 1.6 million child deaths per year can be attributed to unsafe water, poor sanitation and lack of hygiene (UNICEF & WHO, 2008). In developing countries, households have access to and may use more than one of several types of water sources, such as in-house tap connections, public or private wells/boreholes, public or private taps, water vendors, tank trucks, water provided by neighbours, rainwater collection, or water collected from rivers, streams, or lakes (Nauges and Whittington, 2009). The lack of access to safe and good-quality water contributes to ongoing poverty, through the economic costs of poor health and through the high proportion of household expenditure necessary for water supply in many poor communities, arising from the need to purchase water and/or the time and energy expended in water collection (Howard & Bartram, 2003).

Some investments are required to improve the situation, leading to higher capital and variable costs, and, as a consequence, to higher prices and lower affordability. Gaining better physical access by expanding the network coverage, the rehabilitation of aged water systems, and the maintenance of the new infrastructure could easily lead to higher water charges. Recent estimates of the cost of reducing the number of people without access to water and sanitation at the global level at the half range are from $57 to $63 billion for clean water and $29 to $42 billion for sanitation, or a total of $86 to $105 billion (Lenton, Wright, & Lewis, 2005). In light of the importance of water in regard to development and health issues, the main aim of this paper is to analyze the residential water sector in Tanzania, from both an objective and a subjective point of view. The water sector's institutional framework is described, and an analysis of household perceptions related to water services is carried out. This exercise is in line with previous studies that have analyzed the subjective well-being and/or satisfaction related to particular aspects of people's life in Sub-Saharan Africa (Bookmarter & Dalenberg, 2002). This paper also focuses on several dimensions of water services, identifying the main problems and weak points that households perceive related to water services and offering a broad view of the water sector in Tanzania.

First, this paper briefly describes the Tanzanian water sector from an institutional and an economic point of view. It focuses in particular on the differences between the urban and rural environments and also on the distribution and allocation of resources (both by the Tanzanian government and by aid donors). The second part describes the *Views of the People 2007* database, the result of a survey in which Tanzanian households gave their opinions about the provision of several basic services. Among others, households answered questions related to several dimensions of water services, such as the continuity of the supply, water quality, and implicit and explicit costs of access (prices, distance, queuing, etc.). A simple empirical exercise is then presented which identifies the main factors that influence the perceptions of problems and improvements among Tanzanian households. From these findings, some interesting policy implications can be gathered.

The water sector in Tanzania

Tanzania is one of the poorest countries in Africa, with 89% of the population living under the $1.25-a-day poverty line, the highest rate in Sub-Saharan Africa (UNDP, 2010). When other poverty measures are considered (e.g. the Multidimensional Poverty Index), Tanzania still ranks 25th among the 104 developing countries evaluated. Though gross domestic product (GDP) growth rates are positive for the country (7.4% in 2008, 5.5% in 2009 and 7% in 2010), the country still has a long way to go, and micro-level indicators are still far from meeting the UN's Millennium Development Goals.[1]

Tanzania is a country in which access to water is recognized as a human right by law, but no further details on facilitation of this are found in any laws or regulations. The organization of the Tanzanian water sector is such that it has decentralized competences, and it takes a fully demand-responsive approach to service delivery.[2] The central government acts as a coordinator in the water sector, and the district-level administration holds the main competencies for implementation. Communities manage their water services and participate in the design of related-water projects; full operation and maintenance costs are also their responsibility. In 2009, 54% of Tanzanian people had access to improved drinking water sources and 24% to improved sanitation (WHO, 2010). In practice, there are serious problems related to pollution and seasonality (Jiménez & Pérez-Foguet, 2010).

In urban areas, the increase of population, due mainly to rural-to-urban migration, is placing increasing pressure on the existing water supply infrastructure. In rural areas, where access is complex in many cases due to physical and climatologic constraints, less than half of the population has access to clean and safe water, as shown in Table 1.

The government of Tanzania, specifically the Ministry of Water and Irrigation,[3] has reshaped its structure to make possible the decentralization, reform policies and inter-sector

Table 1. Access to clean and safe water (% of population).

	2002	2004–05	2007
Urban	85.3	78.6	79.5
Rural	42.0	45.3	40.5

Sources: Census (2002), Demographic and Health Survey (2004–05), Household Budget Survey (2007), all available from Tanzania Bureau of Statistics, http://www.nbs.go.tz/.

coordination strategies proposed in the National Water Policy (2002) and the National Water Sector Development Strategy (2006). To facilitate the implementation of the National Water Policy, Water Resources Management Act No. 11 and Water Supply and Sanitation Act No. 12 were approved in 2009 (United Republic of Tanzania Ministry of Water, n.d.).

Decentralization has implied a new framework of roles and responsibilities, in both urban and rural areas. Among other changes, the Water Resources Management Act of 2009 established the National Water Board as an advisory board to the Ministry of Water and Irrigation on the coordination of all sectors involved in the service delivery process. This act also established the basin water boards as corporate bodies to increase their legal responsibilities and decentralized the registration procedures for water user associations. The Water Supply and Sanitation Act of 2009 establishes a series of efficiency measures with which the service provision authorities should comply. For example, the possibility for existing water supply and sanitation authorities to become commercial urban water supply and sanitation authorities, depending on their commercial viability, enables the clustering of the previous small entities to ensure their efficiency and commercial viability once attaining a more efficient size. The Water Supply and Sanitation Act of 2009 also establishes the regulation of water supply and sanitation services and establishes the legal setting for the registration of community-owned water supply organizations.

As presented in detail in the next subsection and as discussed in the empirical analysis of the *Views of the People 2007* data-set, these legal changes have had an important impact on people's perception of the service and on the financial sustainability of the water network.

Urban areas: urban water and sanitation authorities

In urban areas, the development and maintenance of water and sewerage infrastructure is carried out by the urban water and sanitation authorities. These are autonomous legal entities that operate on the basis of commercial principles. Urban and district water utilities are not responsible for on-site sanitation, an area that remains in the hands of the relevant local council. Urban water and sanitation authorities are classified into three categories in relation to their financial viability:

- Category A authorities cover all of the operation and maintenance (O&M) costs of water supply and sewerage, including cost of power, staff wages, and some investment contributions.
- Category B authorities meet their O&M costs, including sharing the cost of power and full salaries of the permanent employees.
- Category C authorities meet their O&M costs but require government support to pay for power supply and salaries of the permanent employees.

Table 2 shows the trends of some indicators for urban areas: piped connections have increased, there has been an increase in the number of metered households, and we also see a positive trend in the construction of new water points.[4] However, the situation of the urban areas is far from homogeneous. For example, while in 2006–07 the average

Table 2.   Urban water supply and sewerage.

	2006	2007	2008
Coverage with potable reliable water (%)	78	80	83
Household connection to piped water service (%)	78	80	83
New water points	1197	1656	1844
Metered household water connections	162,611	169,252	331,163
Average hours of water supply per day	17	17	18
Operating cost coverage ratio in utilities (%)	0.95	1.07	0.92
Non-revenue water (%)	36.1	37.5	37.4
Sewer connections	14,046	16,060	35,645

Source: EWURA *Water Utilities Performance Report 2008/09.*

metering ratio was 82.8% for Category A authorities, it was 44.1% for B and C authorities, marking a difference from 86.2% to 67.5% in 2008–09. The difference is also significant when looking at the proportion of the population served with water (73.2% for Category A authorities to 63.6% for Category B authorities in 2006–07 and 66% to 72% in 2008–09) or the percentage of the population served with water but without any hourly supply interruption (74% for Category A authorities to 34% for Category B authorities in 2006–07 and 70% to 30% in 2008–09) (EWURA, 2009).

These numbers reflect the diversity in financial stability of the authorities, their capacity to collect payments for metered premises, and their ability to offer reliable service to the population. The best results are those related to water quality compliance, which highlights the effort of all authorities to provide good-quality service.

Rural areas: community-owned water supply organizations

In rural areas, water supply and sanitation services are provided by community-owned water supply organizations (COWSOs). They are expected to meet all of the costs of operating and maintaining the water supply systems through charges levied to water consumers and to contribute to the capital cost of their systems. There are two types of COWSO:

- water consumer associations (*vikundi vya huduma ya maji* in Swahili), which are responsible for drinking-water supply
- water user associations (*vikundi vya watumiaji maji* in Swahili), which are responsible for water resources and for solving conflicts among water users.

With just the data available, it is not possible to evaluate the impact of the implementation of the Water Resources Management Act of 2009, which as described above aims to create an easily implementable legal framework for water user associations and other institutions involved in the rural water system. However, we can observe a relevant increase in the number of water committees legally established according to the Water Supply and Sanitation Act of 2009, especially during the 2008–2009 period. We can also observe in Table 3 that the number of community water distribution points saw an increasing trend, both from new points constructed and from the rehabilitation of existing points. The increase in rehabilitated points is very relevant, especially in a rural setting in which maintenance is always challenging.

As described in terms of both resource allocation and estimation results, it is in the rural areas where allocation of resources is specially complicated, due in part to the difficulty of accurately assessing the current situation of the sector in rural areas and the unsatisfied demand. Moreover, rural water associations face an important challenge in terms of financial sustainability and of enforceability of the pricing schemes. As shown in the empirical analysis, a person's involvement in a community association has a

Table 3.   Water supply in rural areas.

	2006	2007	2008	2009	2012 (target)
New community water points constructed	2427	2949	3751	n.d.	34,700
Rehabilitated community water points	670	711	1123	n.d.	4500
Water committees legally registered	11	14	42	65	n.d.

Note: n.d., no data available. Source: Tanzanian Ministry of Water and Irrigation (2009).

significant effect on his or her perception of the problems, highlighting the importance of information problems in this setting.

Resources: origin, distribution and effectiveness

To help it toward the Millennium Development Goals, Tanzania has received important aid flows, with net official development assistance (ODA) representing an average of 15.5% of gross national income for the 2000–2008 period. In 2008, Tanzania had 34 donors (21 Development Assistance Committee and Korea Partner Countries, and 13 multilateral agencies), which makes Tanzania the country with the greatest number of donors among the group of Less Developed Countries.[5]

This fragmented scenario is especially challenging in the water sector, where the allocation of resources to new infrastructure and to maintenance is essential to ensure equity in access and quality and sustainability of the service provided. The distribution of resources among urban and rural areas and between new infrastructure and maintenance involves a complex analysis.

Aid flows represent an important source of funds for the Tanzanian government; the ODA allocated to the water sector represents a small but increasing share of these funds. Table 4 shows an increasing share of ODA to the sector, from approximately 2% in 2002 to almost 6% in 2009. A significant part of these funds, over 60%, comes from multilateral donors, which frequently use country systems for transferring funds and are important coordination poles in a fragmented setting like that of Tanzania.

Table 4.   Official development assistance (ODA) to the water and sanitation sector (USD millions).

	2002	2003	2004	2005	2006	2007	2008	2009
Water supply & sanitation ODA	22.32	57.65	34.13	54.45	89.20	127.99	148.92	173.18
Percentage of water ODA bilateral (DAC)	*61.19*	*32.92*	*46.62*	*47.81*	*37.04*	*28.57*	*36.19*	*35.53*
Water sector % of total ODA	*1.92*	*3.82*	*1.91*	*3.49*	*1.50*	*4.65*	*6.45*	*5.99*
Water resources policy and administrative management	6.10	9.33	6.32	6.07	17.27	14.29	18.77	22.94
Water resources protection	0.03	0.03	0.08	0.04	n.d.	0.01	5.21	0.02
Water supply and sanitation, large systems	7.23	33.66	15.48	21.14	40.07	52.21	63.59	116.92
Basic drinking water supply and basic sanitation	8.84	14.53	11.31	24.19	27.69	59.52	59.26	31.58
River development	n.d.	n.d.	0.95	2.68	4.06	1.64	1.36	1.16
Waste management/disposal	0.01	0.02	n.d.	0.25	n.d.	0.03	0.03	0.06
Education and training in water supply and sanitation	0.11	0.09	n.d.	0.09	0.10	0.30	0.77	0.51

Note: n.d., no data available. Source: OECD Development Assistance Committee and Creditor Reporting System, available at http://www.oecd.org/dac/.

With respect to the purpose distribution of ODA, large systems, basic drinking-water supply and basic sanitation have been the biggest beneficiaries of funds, followed by water resource policy and administrative management. These funds aim to increase coverage of basic service and to build, maintain and manage infrastructure, which is the main target for improving the present situation in terms of access and quality of water services.

In addition to allocating funds to different tasks, the ministry faces the challenge of assigning funds to rural and urban areas, each with different deficiencies and challenges. As the 2008 Afrobarometer Survey reflects, 44% of the citizens in rural areas cite water supply among the top three issues for the government to address, versus 25% in urban areas. In the same survey, 51% of the citizens in urban areas express satisfaction with the government's efforts to deliver water and sanitation services, versus 39% in rural areas (Afrobarometer, 2008). Moreover, as discussed in the preceding section, rural and urban areas present different provision structures. The evolution of the distribution of the water sector development budget between rural and urban areas after 2007 must be highlighted, moving from a 20/80 share for rural/urban areas in 2005 to a 50/50 split in 2007 and maintaining this trend (TAWASANET, 2009).

However, increasing the share of government-managed resources allocated to the rural areas does not ensure an increase in access equity. A great challenge in rural areas is the distribution of these funds to target the areas and populations that need them the most. According to the Tanzania Water and Sanitation Network's *Water and Sanitation Equity Report 2009*, the top priority in selecting communities for water projects was to ensure that projects were equally divided between the constituencies of the district's members of Parliament. TAWASANET's 2008 report on *Monitoring Equity in Water and Sanitation* reported that the majority of new funding for rural water supply was being targeted at wards that already had relatively good access to clean and safe water. The 2009 report, using data from waterpoint mapping surveys and project data provided by the ministry, shows that the distribution also has a large variance between districts: while 83% of the new projects in Kondoa were targeted to wards in the bottom half of the district league table, the proportion was only 10% for the Nzega district. Less than half of the projects identified in the districts of Mpwapwa, Kongwa, Iramba and Nzega were targeted at wards in the bottom half of the district league, compared to 75% of the NGO-funded projects (Taylor, 2009). This highlights the important coordination problems due to aid fragmentation, affecting the effectiveness of the scarce funds.

Data from the *Views of the People 2007* survey

This section presents the data-set used in the empirical exercise. The data are taken from the survey *Views of the People 2007*, conducted by Research on Poverty Alleviation (REPOA).[6] This is the largest and most representative perception survey conducted in Tanzania to date. Tanzanian households were asked to express their opinion on several issues. The survey included modules on household characteristics, basic services (health, roads and road safety, domestic water supply, and sanitation), rural livelihoods, interests, participation, knowledge of government policies and views on performance, and two modules on special concerns of the elderly and the youth.

This analysis used a final sample of 4,986 Tanzanian households.[7] The questionnaire included a broad set of items related to water. It contained both objective questions, like those regarding the kind of water access, source, and payment mode, and subjective questions with the aim of revealing the views and opinions of the users on different water service characteristics. Households expressed their opinions regarding which issues were perceived as the main problems and the improvements related to several dimensions of water services, like shortages and price.

Tanzanian households shared their opinions about the three most important problems in their daily lives. Summary information on these problems is shown in Appendix A (Table A1). It is interesting to see that, in all cases, the shortage of water for drinking and personal use is always in the first two positions in the ranking. This gives us an idea of the importance of residential water supply deficiencies in this country. In the first ranking, water issues are considered the second most frequent problem for Tanzanian households, just behind health considerations. The cost of medical treatments is located in the third position, registering a percentage close to that of water problems. Corroborating those results in the second ranking, water shortage is considered to be the most important problem for households, above other important issues like the condition of the roads they use most frequently (second position) or the price they pay for food (third position). Finally, water shortage presents the second-greatest percentage in the third rank of problems, just behind the price that households are paying for food.

Figures 1 and 2 present the distribution of the sample by the main source of drinking water and by the management of that source. Figure 1 shows that about 40% of Tanzanian households in the sample declare that their main source of drinking water is piped. However, the percentage is similar if we consider both unprotected wells and surface water. As the quality of the latter types of sources is more difficult to control and regulate, water problems are probably more significant for their users. Protected wells also have a non-negligible weight. Finally, there is a very low percentage of households that buy bottled water, probably because it is neither affordable nor a widely available source of drinking water.

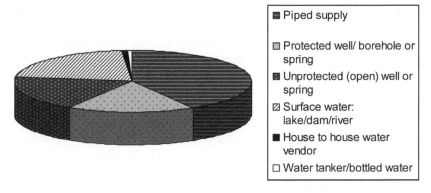

Figure 1.   Drinking water: main source. Source: own elaboration from REPOA (2007).

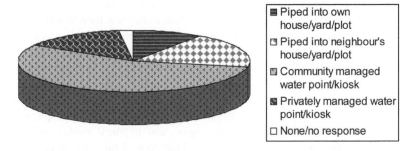

Figure 2.   Drinking water: who manages. Source: own elaboration from REPOA (2007).

Figure 2 shows the different alternatives within the management of water services. Some 56% of the households declare that drinking water is managed by a community-owned water supply organization, and for only 10% of the sample is water properly piped to their own house by an urban water and sanitation authority.

Finally, Table 5 shows some household perceptions on several features of water services. They were asked, indicated on one side, whether they had certain problems (denoted by p_) with their main water source, and as indicated on the other side, if they had noticed changes in those features (denoted by i_) during the past year. The higher the values are, the more significant the problem is for this household. Households answered based on a scale from 1 to 3 (1 = not a problem; 2 = minor problem; 3 = major problem). For perceived improvements, higher values are interpreted positively, because they mean greater improvements for each dimension (1 = worse; 2 = about the same; 3 = improvement). Thus, households were asked about their perception on water shortages on average (i_shortage), distinguishing between dry and rainy seasons (p_shortagd, p_shortagr), the distance they have to cover to get water (p_distance, i_distance), water dirtiness and treatment (p_dirtywat, i_cleanness), the cost of water (p_expensive, i_cost), and the time spent queuing to get water (p_queuing, i_queuing).

Among the identified problems in water service provision, shortages during the dry season seem to be the most important deficiency for Tanzanian households. In the second place, problems with water quality are a significant issue. Finally, the distance that households cover when they need to get water is in the third position. On the other side, shortages during the rainy season appear to be the least important problem in this context. Looking at perceived improvements, water seems to have become slightly more affordable for Tanzanian's households. In addition, problems related to queuing and also to the distance covered by households to get water are other dimensions of the service that have slightly improved during the last year. On the other hand, shortages during the dry season and low water resource quality are problems that remain unimproved from the year before the survey.

Explanatory factors for household perceptions

The main household perceptions related to water services having been observed, several groups of variables are now presented that can explain these perceptions. Some of them are typical variables used in previous perception studies. Further description and statistics are shown in Appendix B.

Table 5. Water service problems and perceived improvements.

	Variable	Mean	Std. Dev.
Problems	p_shortagd	2.41	0.81
	p_shortagr	1.42	0.65
	p_distance	1.78	0.85
	p_dirtywat	2.10	0.89
	p_expensiv	1.60	0.85
	p_queuing	1.69	0.85
Perceived improvements	i_shortage	1.92	0.71
	i_distance	1.99	0.51
	i_cleaness	1.91	0.54
	i_cost	1.95	0.52
	i_queuing	1.96	0.54

Source: own elaboration from REPOA (2007).

With respect to socio-demographic characteristics, variables are considered related to the respondent's gender, age, educational level and marital status; household size is also included. Regarding the dwelling's characteristics, some characteristics of the household's living premises are considered, such as the number of rooms, the household's ownership, and the presence of flushing toilets.

The next group of variables is linked with social capital and perceptions. Stiglitz (2000) defines social capital as knowledge, networks and reputation, thus enabling communities and individuals to address the problems of moral hazard and incentives. Paldam (2000) describes three social capital concepts: trust (cognitive social capital), cooperation and networks. Here the focus is on participation (collective actions) in three different measures: (1) membership in a water management committee, (2) participation in the preparation of a ward plan, and (3) membership in a community-based development organization. On the one hand, collaboration in public institutions can generate attention, and people can increase awareness of the problems linked to public services management, decreasing the asymmetry of information on real problems. On the other hand, sometimes socially active people have optimistic attitudes towards problems, and hence their perceptions could be more positive than that of the rest of the population. Involvement could also make individuals more aware of the little progress attained. The set of variables related to social capital also includes a general attitudinal variable related to the individual participation in public decision making concerning basic services.

Finally, households were asked about their perceptions on the improvement of basic services. This variable in included because it is possible that there is a connection between the perception of improvements related to other basic services (health, education) and water services. This variable will be included only in the improvement equations.

Regarding the block of variables related to water payment methods, four variables can be included depending on the procedure under which the household is paying for water services. The alternative methods of payment considered in the survey are (1) billing by a water company, (2) paying cash at a water pump, kiosk or neighbour's house, (3) paying cash to a water vendor, and (4) getting water for free. Some of these variables could have an impact on affordability perceptions.[8]

Additionally, the source of drinking water and the management of that source are significant factors to consider; for example, whether water is taken from a protected well, borehole or spring, unprotected well or spring, or surface water. We also consider whether water is piped into residents' houses or into neighbours' houses or if it is community managed.

Finally, location variables could be important, like the rural or urban character of the municipality or the region in which the household is located. Consideration of these variables enables controlling for the differences among regions with respect to wealth, climate and other features. Moreover, it also controls for the regional heterogeneity with respect to distribution and allocation of government and aid funds.

According to the descriptive statistics included in Table B2 in Appendix B, the representative respondent is a married person around 40 years old, having completed 6 years of education. It is also interesting to observe that almost 80% of households in the sample own their house or apartment. The average household size is around 5, which is in line with the expectation in developing countries, in which fertility rates are higher and it is common to find several generations living in the same household (bigger families than in developed countries). Only 6% of the Tanzanian households in the sample have flushing toilets installed in the dwelling.[9]

Active participation in different public tasks is not very high, with the exception of participation in the preparation of a ward plan (the percentage is around 20%). However, the majority of people think that it would be necessary for ordinary people to be more involved in decision making concerning basic economic and social development issues that affect their lives.

Regarding water payment and management, nearly 50% of Tanzanian households in the sample do not pay anything for drinking water, while 33% pay cash at a water pump, kiosk, or neighbour's house. Only 9% of households are billed by a water company, with a huge difference between rural (2.7%) and urban (19%) areas. In terms of the water source, percentages are close to one each other, and it is not possible to observe big differences among them. It is also worth notice that more than 50% of the Tanzanian households in the sample get water services from a water community provider.[10] Finally, the average distance to regional headquarters is representative of the mainly rural character of Tanzanian households. Households in the sample are also shared among regions in a uniform way, with the exception of the Dar Es Salaam area, in which almost 30% of the people are living.

Findings and policy implications

Results

The empirical methods and estimation results of the analysis are broadly described in Appendix B. In general, socio-demographic and dwelling characteristics are not very significant in explaining perceived problems related to water supply and sanitation. We only find some intuitive results. For instance, the higher the household size, the bigger the perceived problems are related to distance (it is necessary to provide water for more people, so it could be more difficult to get water) and cost (this is a problem especially when big families are charged by an increasing block tariff).[11] Married people perceive shortages during the rainy season, and queuing, as less significant problems than non-married people. Dwelling/apartment owners have fewer problems with queuing, and perceptions of shortages are worse among people who have bigger dwellings (higher number of sleeping rooms) with flushing toilets on the living premises.

In terms of social capital and perception variables, we find that individuals who have been members of a community-based organization have a more realistic view of water problems, especially in terms of distance and quality of water (both features have a strong link to water infrastructures). In the same direction, we find that individuals who are more fond of increasing people's participation in public life are also more critical about perception of shortages and quality issues.

Related to water pricing, it is worth noting that billed households have better perceptions linked to shortages during the dry season, water quality, and queuing. In addition, when water is obtained for free, fewer problems related to price and queuing are perceived. On the opposite side, the perception of the majority of Tanzanian households is negative in relation to shortages of service to supply water during the rainy season. When it comes to water management and source, households who take water from a surface source or an unprotected well have identified the most serious problems. When water is piped or community managed, fewer problems are perceived. With respect to location variables, the greater the distance to the regional headquarters (and hence the more rural the character of the village in which the household is located), the more significant the perceived problems linked to distance and water quality are.[12]

In terms of management, it seems that all options related to piped water are linked to higher probabilities of perception of "no problem" in the majority of the dimensions considered (shortage, water quality, distance, queuing and price). For instance, when water is piped into a neighbour's house, the probability that the household perceives that there are no quality problems increases by approximately 12%. Additionally, the probability of not perceiving any problem related to shortages during the dry and rainy seasons, distance, price and queuing increase to around 13%, 10%, 25%, 14% and 19%, respectively. Something similar happens with community-managed services. In this case, it is especially significant that this kind of management leads to an increase of 27% in the probability of not considering water an expensive service.

Regarding those variables that increase the probability of perceiving water problems, we find that social-capital variables lead to a reduction in the probability of being satisfied with water services. However, marginal effects are not significant in the majority of cases (between 1% and 7%). On the other hand, we find that the probability of being satisfied with water quality decreases between 23% and 29% when the main water sources are unprotected wells or surface water. Something similar happens in the case of distance that households have to cover to get water, with reductions in the probability of being satisfied with water services between 16% and 23%. These results, as we discuss in the following section, support the reforms carried out by the government of Tanzania with respect to strengthening community management and water authorities to increase the population covered by piped water.

When it comes to analyzing perceived improvements, we observe that older and more educated people are more likely to perceive improvements in problems related to water shortage. Additionally, households living in larger dwellings have perceived improvements in the case of shortage, distance and water quality. As expected, people who have perceived improvements in other public services have also noticed some improvement in water service. Again, households with piped and community-managed water are more optimistic, perceiving some improvements in all water service dimensions.

Regarding the probability of perceiving improvements related to shortages, this probability increases between 4% and 7% when the household is connected to the network. Moreover, it is between 7% and 16% more probable that connected households perceive improvements in distance and queuing dimensions, respectively. That strong impact could be partially explained by the fact that some Tanzanian households could obtain connection to a water network near the year of the survey, so they could notice a drastic improvement related to those dimensions (shortages, distance and queuing). Regarding water quality, the probability of perceiving improvements rises by 5% when water is piped into a neighbour's house and 2% when the service is community managed. In the latter situation, we also observe that the probability of water being considered more affordable increases by approximately 4%. A similar effect is observed when households get tap water into their own houses.

Policy recommendations

These findings are helpful in the design of the best policies to minimize perceived problems and maximize perceived improvements. We have been able to identify some socio-demographic groups and areas which are in a worse situation or have a worse perception of the water services they are provided with, and we also obtained some information about the best organizational forms and sources to provide water services. We strongly recommend further application of this kind of survey in the future; these surveys are especially useful in evaluating institutional reforms and public policies.

In general, Tanzanian households are not satisfied with the water services provided. There are important perceived faults affecting all dimensions of water service. These problems are confirmed by the organizations that have collaborated on water management boards or in other community organizations. The important institutional efforts of the government of Tanzania after the 2006 changes in regulations must be highlighted. However, the survey shows that water services had not shown significant improvements during the year prior to the survey. Thus, it is necessary to propose some initiatives to improve the situation.

Water shortages during both dry and rainy seasons are viewed as a significant issue to solve. Additionally, quality issues are especially worrying, given their link with hygiene and health. Quality problems, for example bacteriological pollution, need to be addressed by public authorities in Tanzania. That action would lead to the design of public policies oriented toward gaining better control of some water sources that present low quality levels and are more sensitive to droughts. As we observe in the estimation results, the situation is particularly serious in the case of unprotected wells and surface water. Public policies should be guided toward improvement of these sources' conditions.

We have also observed that community-owned water supply organizations have developed strategies to provide better-quality water and to solve other problems related to water services. Those organizations become essential, especially in rural areas where problems are more severe. In fact, households managed by COWSOs, along with piped-water households, have not perceived significant problems, and they have also noticed some improvement in all dimensions of water services.

The findings show that it is important to extend piped water to a greater percentage of the Tanzanian population through the implementation of progressive investment planning which should be developed with both public and private institutions' financial support. Hence, the efforts of the government to strengthen urban and rural water services to increase the coverage of piped water and ensure the economic viability of community-managed sources seems to be going in the right direction.

Concluding remarks

Water access and quality problems emerge as significant issues for Tanzanian households. In many cases, people have to walk long distances to access water, and the quality of such water is usually not optimal. Shortages in water for drinking and personal use are considered among the main worries, even more important than the cost of several basic services and goods, like food, medical treatment, and education. Additionally, there are strong differences in water supply conditions depending on the region. In this respect, rural areas present the worse scenario.

The Tanzanian government and several NGOs have made great efforts in past years to improve the quality and coverage of water services, yet these have not been sufficient. It seems that funds have not been allocated in a fair and efficient way. The data from the *Views of the People 2007* survey (REPOA 2007) show that no significant improvements were perceived by Tanzanian households between the years 2006 and 2007.

However, this empirical exercise has identified some positive issues. The findings show that piped water and community-managed services are the best alternatives for the provision of drinking water. Additionally, the most important improvements have been perceived when water supply services have been managed by community-owned water supply organizations. These results indicate that public policies that are oriented to extend these forms of management could improve the quality of water service in Tanzania.

Acknowledgements

We would like to thank the financial support of the Ministry of Science and Innovation (through the project with reference MICINN-09-ECO2009-08824) and the comments and suggestions we received after presenting a previous draft at the *Workshop on Water Pricing and Roles of Public and Private Sectors in Efficient Urban Water Management,* organized by the Third World Centre for

Water Management, the International Water Resources Association, Global Water Intelligence and the University of Granada in May 2011. All errors remain our own.

Notes

1. For further information about the UN's Millennium Development Goals in Tanzania, see http://www.mdgmonitor.org/country_progress.cfm?c=TZA&cd=834.
2. In a demand-responsive approach, the allocation of resources is not supply driven but responds to the demand expressed by communities and service providers.
3. Detailed description of the legal structure of the water sector can be found in the Tanzanian Ministry of Water and Irrigation's *Water Sector Status Report* (2009).
4. According to the Water Supply and Sanitation Act of 2009, a water point is a single source of water, which may be a well, borehole, a tap or a public tap.
5. Number of donors corresponds to the information compiled by the OECD Creditor Reporting System (OECD, n.d.).
6. See REPOA (2007) and Openmicrodata (2010) for further information about the data-set. For more information on this and other Tanzanian Household surveys and links to the sources of information, see the Twaweza website (http://twaweza.org/go/householdsurveys).
7. The sample used corresponds to the respondents on the modules, including the questions related to water.
8. In this setting, some issues related to the enforceability of the tariff need to be clarified. For example, examination of the tariff schemes and metered customers shows great variance among urban authorities. So, being billed may or may not imply being metered and forced to pay, while enforcement is more likely when there is face-to-face contact with the vendor.
9. Only half of the rural population has access to a water source, a status that is considered 'improved' by the WHO, and only 9% use improved toilet facilities that are not shared with other households (Tanzanian National Bureau of Statistics, 2010).
10. In our sample, 80% of rural households get water from a community-managed source, while the percentage is 45% for rural areas and 11% for Dar es Salaam.
11. For a survey of equity and social issues in water pricing, check OECD (2003, 2010).
12. Regarding regional effects, we find that shortages during the dry season are perceived as a more significant problem in the regions of Singida and Shinyanga. However, shortages during the rainy season seem to be more problematic in Tanga, Dar es Salaam, and Lindi. Affordability problems emerge in Dar es Salaam and Lindi, and queuing is a significant issue in Dar es Salaam and Singida.

References

Afrobarometer (2008). *Round three. Afrobarometer Survey in Tanzania*. Retrieved from http://www.afrobarometer.org/results/results-by-country-n-z/tanzania

Bookmarter, J., & Dalenberg, D. (2002). Subjective well-being and household factors in South Africa. *Social Indicators Research, 65*, 333–353.

EWURA (Energy and Water Utilities Regulatory Authority), *Water utilities performance report 2008/09*. Retrieved from http://www.ewura.com/annualreports.html

Howard, G., & Bartram, J. (2003). *Domestic water quantity, service level and health* (Working Paper No. 03.02). World Health Organization. Retrieved from http://www.who.int/water_sanitation_health/diseases/WSH0302.pdf

Jiménez, A., & Pérez-Foguet, A. (2010). Challenges for water governance in rural water supply: Lessons learned from Tanzania. *International Journal of Water Resources Development, 26*(2), 235–248.

Lenton, R., Wright, A. M., & Lewis, K. (2005). *Health, dignity, and development: What will it take?* London: UN Millennium Project Task Force on Water and Sanitation.

Nauges, C., & Whittington, D. (2009). Estimation of water demand in developing countries: an overview. *World Bank Research Observer, 25*(2), 263–294.

OECD (Organisation for Economic Co-operation and Development) (N.d.). *Development Assistance Committee and Creditor Reporting System datasets*. Retrieved from http://www.oecd.org/dac/

OECD (2003). *Social issues in the provision and pricing of water services*. Paris: Author.

OECD (2010). *Pricing water resources and water sanitation services*. Paris: Author.

Openmicrodata (2010, 26 February). Tanzania: Views of People Survey 2007. Retrieved from http://openmicrodata.wordpress.com/2010/02/26/tanzania-views-of-people-survey/

Paldam, M. (2000). Social capital: one or many? Definition and measurement. *Journal of Economic Surveys*, *14*, 629–653.

REPOA (Research on Poverty Alleviation). (2007). *Views of the people survey 2007*. Retrieved from http://www.repoa.or.tz/index.php/publications/views_of_the_people_2007/

Stiglitz, J. (2000). *Economics of the public sector*. New York: W.W. Norton.

Tanzanian Bureau of Statistics (2010). *Demographic and health survey 2010*. Retrieved from http://www.nbs.go.tz/tnada/index.php/ddibrowser/12

Tanzanian Ministry of Water and Irrigation (2009). *Water sector status report*. Dar es Salaam: Author.

TAWASANET (Tanzania Water and Sanitation Network) (2008). *Water: More for some . . . or some for more? Monitoring equity in water and sanitation*. Dar es Salaam: Author.

TAWASANET (2009). *Water and sanitation equity report 2009*. Dar es Salaam: Author.

Taylor, B. (2009). *Water point mapping, planning and obstacles to equity in rural water supply. A review in Mpwapwa, Kongwa, Iramba and Nzega*. Dar Es Salaam: Water Aid Tanzania.

UN (2002). *Substantive issues arising in the implementation of the International Covenant on Economic, Social and Cultural Rights*, General Comment number 15. Geneva: Committee on Economic, Social and Cultural Rights, United Nations. Retrieved from http://www.unhchr.ch/tbs/doc.nsf/0/a5458d1d1bbd713fc1256cc400389e94/$FILE/G0340229.pdf

UNDP (2010). *Human development report, 2010*. New York, NY: Author.

UNICEF & WHO (2008). *Progress on drinking water and sanitation. Special focus on sanitation*. New York and Geneva: Author.

UNICEF & WHO (2012). *Progress on drinking water and sanitation: 2012 update*. New York and Geneva: Author.

United Republic of Tanzania Ministry of Water (n.d.). Website of the Ministry of Water. Retrieved from http://www.maji.go.tz/

WHO (2010). *World health statistics*. Geneva: Author.

Appendix A

Table A1. Tanzanian households' main problems (% of respondents).

	Major problem	Second problem	Third problem
Sickness (self)	16.78	2.87	2.46
Sickness/death (others)	4.81	3.33	1.39
Cost of medical treatment	11.21	12.54	7.20
Availability of medicines	2.07	4.70	4.78
Finding work	7.00	4.88	4.68
Cost of schooling	5.86	6.32	5.38
Domestic violence, rape	0.50	0.53	0.39
Robbery with violence	0.95	1.26	1.03
Theft of crops, livestock	0.70	0.87	0.81
Availability of electricity	3.82	4.72	4.65
Distance/time taken to reach markets & services	3.20	4.61	3.79
Disputes over land ownership/use	1.17	1.55	1.22
Disputes over inheritance	0.20	0.53	0.39
Witchcraft	0.76	0.98	1.06
The condition of the roads you use most frequently	9.36	11.55	9.56
Difficulty obtaining firewood/charcoal	2.39	5.04	6.19
Shortage of water for drinking and personal use	**11.43**	**12.56**	**13.28**
Shortage of water for crops/livestock	0.32	1.18	1.32
Price you pay for food	9.90	11.28	14.77
Price you pay for other basic goods	1.27	3.88	8.17
Owing people money	0.58	0.37	1.03
Owed money by people	0.42	0.45	0.68
Smoke fumes from cooking	0.54	0.55	1.49
Pollution from solid waste/sanitation/bad smells	1.51	1.59	2.01
Noise (traffic, music, neighbours)	0.48	0.67	1.18
Other	2.76	1.20	1.10

Source: own elaboration from REPOA (2007)

Appendix B

Our empirical model is based on two sets of equations, with the aim of explaining (1) water problems perceived by the household i ($p_{i\_}$) and (2) the improvements perceived by the household i during the last year ($i_{i\_}$):

$$p_{i\_} = f\left(SD_i, SCP_i, WP_i, SM_i, LOC_i\right) \tag{1}$$

$$i_{i\_} = f\left(SD_i, SCP_i, WP_i, SM_i, LOC_i\right) \tag{2}$$

Together with the source of drinking water and the management of that source, we include a rich set of explanatory variables. We consider a bundle of socio-demographic and dwelling features (SD_i), a group of variables linked to households' social capital and perceptions (SCP_i), a set of variables linked to the kind of water payment of the household (WP_i) and a set of variables linked to source and management issues (SM_i). We also include several 'location' variables (LOC_i): one representing the urban or rural character of the municipality where the household is located, and finally, dummy variables linked to the region where the household is located. Table B1 gives descriptions of the variables included in each set, while Table B2 shows some basic statistics.

To estimate Equations (1) and (2), we used an ordered probit methodology. Given that the scale for both questions of interest is from 1 to 3 (1 = not a problem, 2 = minor problem, 3 = major problem for perceived problems; 1 = worse, 2 = about the same, 3 = improvement for perceived improvements), this is a suitable econometric method. Tables B3 and B5 show the ordered-probit estimates for perceived problems and improvements, respectively. In all the cases, regional variables have been introduced as control variables in all the estimations, but are omitted from the tables for clarity. To expand on the policy implications of this analysis, we show a marginal effects analysis on the probability of not perceiving any problem (Table B4) and of perceiving some improvement (Table B6) in water services. Marginal effects analysis allows a clearer interpretation of the coefficients and their significance. This provides a guideline for the policy changes to be implemented to minimize perceived problems and maximize perceived improvements related to the water services.

Table B1. Variable descriptions.

Group of variables	Name	Description
Socio-demographic and dwelling features	gender	Dummy variable which takes value 1 if the respondent is female, 0 otherwise
	age	Age of respondent
	educ	Number of years of formal education completed by the respondent
	married	Dummy variable which takes value 1 if the respondent is married, 0 otherwise
	hhsize	Number of people living in the house
	owner	Dummy variable which takes value 1 if the household owns the dwelling, 0 otherwise
	nrooms	Number of rooms in the dwelling
	toiletf	Dummy variable which takes value 1 if there is a flush toilet in the dwelling, 0 otherwise
Social capital and perceptions	partic1	Dummy variable which takes value 1 if the respondent is or has beenq a water management committee member
	partic2	Dummy variable which takes value 1 if the respondent participates or has participated in the preparation of a village/ward plan
	partic3	Dummy variable which takes value 1 if the respondent is or has been a member of a community-based development organization (CBO)
	indpart	Dummy variable which takes value 1 if the respondent agrees that ordinary people should be more involved in decision making concerning basic economic and social development issues that affect their lives
	pquality	Dummy variable which takes value 1 if the respondent has recently observed a big improvement in basic public services
Water payment	billed	Dummy variable which takes value 1 if the household is billed by a water company
	cashp	Dummy variable which takes value 1 if the household pays cash at the water pump/kiosk/neighbour's house
	cashv	Dummy variable which takes value 1 if the household pays cash to the water vendor
	free	Dummy variable which takes value 1 if the household does not pay at all (water is free)
Source and management	pwell	Dummy variable which takes value 1 if main source of drinking water for the household is a protected well, borehole or spring
	upwell	Dummy variable which takes value 1 if main source of drinking water for the household is an unprotected (open) well or spring
	surface	Dummy variable which takes value 1 if main source of drinking water for the household is surface water: lake, dam, river, stream or pond
	opiped	Dummy variable which takes value 1 if water is piped into own house/yard/plot
	npiped	Dummy variable which takes value 1 if water is piped into neighbour's house/yard/plot
	commun	Dummy variable which takes value 1 if water is community managed
Location	distance	Distance from household's village/town/city to the regional headquarter (in km)
	reg_	Regional dummy variables: Arusha; Tanga; Dar Es Salaam; Lindi; Mtwara; Mwanza (reference group); Iringa; Singida; Rukwa; Shinyanga

Source: own elaboration from REPOA (2007).

Table B2. Descriptive statistics for independent variables.

Variable	Mean	Std. Dev.	Min	Max
gender	0.51	0.50	0	1
age	41.26	13.34	24	99
educ	6.02	3.45	0	20
married	0.71	0.46	0	1
hhsize	5.27	2.57	1	25
owner	0.77	0.42	0	1
rooms	2.81	1.70	0	20
toiletf	0.06	0.24	0	1
partic1	0.05	0.22	0	1
partic2	0.18	0.38	0	1
partic3	0.08	0.28	0	1
indpart	0.65	0.48	0	1
pquality	0.15	0.35	0	1
billed	0.09	0.28	0	1
cashp	0.33	0.47	0	1
cashv	0.06	0.25	0	1
free	0.49	0.50	0	1
pwell	0.17	0.38	0	1
upwell	0.18	0.39	0	1
surface	0.21	0.41	0	1
opiped	0.10	0.30	0	1
npiped	0.18	0.39	0	1
commun	0.56	0.50	0	1
distance	73.32	82.11	0	408
reg_Arusha	0.09	0.29	0	1
reg_Tanga	0.08	0.27	0	1
reg_Dar Es Salaam	0.27	0.44	0	1
reg_Lindi	0.05	0.21	0	1
reg_Mtwara	0.07	0.26	0	1
reg_Iringa	0.09	0.28	0	1
reg_Singida	0.07	0.25	0	1
reg_Rukwa	0.07	0.25	0	1
reg_Shinyanga	0.11	0.31	0	1

Source: own elaboration from REPOA (2007).

Table B3. Perceived problems: ordered probit.

	p_shortagd	p_shortagr	p_distance	p_dirtywat	p_expensiv	p_queuing
gender	−0.0231	−0.0651*	−0.0065	−0.0630*	0.0417	0.0359
age	−0.0031**	−0.0012	−0.0035**	−0.0000	0.0011	−0.0017
educ	−0.0111*	−0.0087	−0.0108*	0.0051	−0.0074	−0.0045
married	−0.0041	−0.1292***	−0.0734*	−0.0627	−0.0575	−0.0993**
hhsize	0.0112	0.0016	0.0195***	0.0070	0.0183**	0.0066
owner	0.0004	−0.0306	0.0382	−0.0600	−0.0341	−0.1795***
rooms	−0.0061	0.0446***	−0.0197*	−0.0156	−0.0129	0.0178
toiletf	0.2208***	−0.0764	−0.0824	−0.0349	0.0767	−0.0650
partic1	−0.0544	−0.0214	0.1198	0.0637	0.0814	0.1509*
partic2	−0.0472	−0.0405	−0.0013	0.0292	0.0104	0.0500
partic3	−0.0224	0.1200*	0.1235*	0.2164***	0.0573	−0.0181
indpart	0.0583	0.1304***	0.0300	0.1564***	−0.0473	0.0279
billed	−0.3978**	0.7683***	0.0269	−0.4005***	0.1701	−0.8680***
cashp	0.1145	0.6165***	0.0316	−0.0269	0.1951	0.1267
cashv	−0.1490	0.3945**	−0.2024	−0.0887	0.1397	−0.1518
free	0.0520	0.3923***	−0.0831	0.1328	−1.3902***	−0.4494***
pwell	−0.0161	−0.0140	0.1363***	0.0926*	−0.0534	−0.1087**
upwell	0.4139***	0.1105	0.4302***	0.7555***	−0.3195***	−0.1009
surface	0.2506***	0.1933***	0.5989***	0.9696***	−0.4149***	−0.5283***
opiped	−0.1954*	−0.5001***	−1.3337***	−0.1193	−0.6107***	−1.1210***
npiped	−0.4580***	−0.3006***	−0.6552***	−0.3225***	−0.5141***	−0.5259***
commun	−0.2168***	−0.2958***	−0.1937***	0.0165	−0.8297***	−0.1593***
distance	0.0004	−0.0004	0.0012***	0.0007**	−0.0005	0.0005*
N	4,986	4,986	4,986	4,986	4,986	4,986
r2_p	0.0735	0.0592	0.0989	0.1206	0.3354	0.1331

District-region controls were included in the regression.

Legend: * $p < .1$; ** $p < .05$; *** $p < .01$; r2_p = pseudo R^2

Table B4.   Marginal effects: perceived problems (1 = no problem).

	pshortagd	pshortagr	Pdistance	pdirtywat	pexpensiv	pqueuing
gender	0.0061	0.0235*	0.0026	0.0225*	− 0.0133	− 0.0140
age	0.0008**	0.0004	0.0014**	0.0000	− 0.0003	0.0007
educ	0.0030*	0.0032	0.0043*	− 0.0018	0.0023	0.0018
married	0.0011	0.0471***	0.0293*	0.0223	0.0184	0.0388**
hhsize	− 0.0030	− 0.0006	− 0.0078***	− 0.0025	− 0.0058**	− 0.0026
owner	− 0.0001	0.0111	− 0.0152	0.0213	0.0109	0.0705***
rooms	0.0016	− 0.0161***	0.0078*	0.0056	0.0041	− 0.0069
toiletf	− 0.0536***	0.0271	0.0328	0.0126	− 0.0249	0.0251
partic1	0.0148	0.0077	− 0.0477	− 0.0225	− 0.0265	− 0.0594*
partic2	0.0127	0.0145	0.0005	− 0.0104	− 0.0033	− 0.0195
partic3	0.0060	− 0.0442*	− 0.0492*	− 0.0739***	− 0.0185	0.0070
indpart	− 0.0156	− 0.0466***	− 0.0119	− 0.0566***	0.0151	− 0.0109
billed	0.1208**	− 0.2967***	− 0.0107	0.1519***	− 0.0565	0.2865***
cashp	− 0.0299	− 0.2284***	− 0.0126	0.0097	− 0.0633	− 0.0495
cashv	0.0419	− 0.1506**	0.0802	0.0323	− 0.0462	0.0581
free	− 0.0138	− 0.1409***	0.0332	− 0.0475	0.4212***	0.1734***
pwell	0.0043	0.0050	− 0.0543***	− 0.0327*	0.0168	0.0420**
upwell	− 0.0970***	− 0.0405	− 0.1689***	− 0.2324***	0.0942***	0.0390
surface	− 0.0624***	− 0.0712***	− 0.2324***	− 0.2886***	0.1206***	0.1947***
opiped	0.0556*	0.1605***	0.4356***	0.0436	0.1592***	0.3464***
npiped	0.1369***	0.1031***	0.2511***	0.1200***	0.1442***	0.1927***
commun	0.0570***	0.1071***	0.0772***	− 0.0059	0.2673***	0.0621***
distance	− 0.0001	0.0001	− 0.0005***	− 0.0003**	0.0002	− 0.0002

District-region controls were included in the regression

Legend: * p < .1; ** p < .05; *** p < .01

Table B5.   Perceived improvements: ordered probit.

	i_shortage	i_distance	I_cleanness	I_cost	I_queuing
gender	− 0.0493	− 0.0430	− 0.0123	− 0.1259***	− 0.0487
age	0.0024*	0.0013	0.0003	0.0005	0.0007
educ	0.0113**	0.0058	0.0005	0.0024	0.0088
married	0.0133	− 0.0381	0.0423	0.0527	0.0514
hhsize	0.0042	0.0016	− 0.0062	− 0.0040	0.0068
owner	0.0222	− 0.0287	− 0.0229	0.0614	0.0829*
rooms	0.0218**	0.0222*	0.0436***	0.0170	0.0030
toiletf	− 0.1760**	− 0.1826**	− 0.0794	− 0.2383***	− 0.1848**
partic1	− 0.0141	0.0215	0.0621	− 0.0531	− 0.1450*
partic2	− 0.0738	− 0.0751	− 0.1029**	− 0.0394	− 0.0496
partic3	− 0.0589	− 0.1281*	− 0.3004***	0.0393	− 0.0834
indpart	0.0338	− 0.0151	− 0.0994***	− 0.0030	− 0.0162
pquality	0.1048**	0.2750***	0.3210***	0.0286	0.0773
billed	0.1497	− 0.1729	0.0766	− 0.3920**	0.1040
cashp	0.1282	− 0.3744***	− 0.2679**	− 0.3688***	− 0.1178
cashv	0.0189	− 0.5317***	− 0.4710***	− 0.2938**	− 0.1631
free	0.0815	− 0.3381***	− 0.3297***	0.0508	0.0412
pwell	0.1225**	− 0.0850	− 0.1075**	− 0.0117	0.0775
upwell	− 0.1316**	− 0.1951***	− 0.4399***	0.0210	0.0393
surface	− 0.1096*	− 0.4042***	− 0.5897***	− 0.2165***	0.0323
opiped	0.2331**	0.5136***	0.1514	0.2012*	0.6535***
npiped	0.1445**	0.4709***	0.2665***	0.0723	0.3177***
commun	0.1094**	0.2376***	0.1258**	0.2439***	0.1109**
distance	− 0.0009***	− 0.0016***	− 0.0016***	− 0.0006*	− 0.0012***
N	4,970	4,962	4,963	4,887	4,927
R2_p	0.0437	0.0657	0.0819	0.0811	0.0647

District-region controls were included in the regression.

Legend: * $p < .1$; ** $p < .05$; *** $p < .01$

Table B6. Marginal effects: perceived improvements (3 = improvement).

	ishortage	idistance	icleaness	icost	iqueuing
gender	− 0.0139	− 0.0081	− 0.0020	− 0.0212***	− 0.0091
age	0.0007*	0.0002	0.0001	0.0001	0.0001
educ	0.0032**	0.0011	0.0001	0.0004	0.0017
married	0.0037	− 0.0072	0.0066	0.0087	0.0095
hhsize	0.0012	0.0003	− 0.001	− 0.0007	0.0013
owner	0.0062	− 0.0054	− 0.0037	0.0101	0.0151*
rooms	0.0061**	0.0042*	0.0069***	0.0029	0.0006
toiletf	− 0.0464**	− 0.0310**	− 0.012	− 0.0348***	− 0.0312**
partic1	− 0.004	0.0041	0.0102	− 0.0086	− 0.0250*
partic2	− 0.0204	− 0.0137	− 0.0156**	− 0.0065	− 0.0091
partic3	− 0.0163	− 0.0225*	− 0.0401***	0.0068	− 0.0149
indpart	0.0095	− 0.0028	− 0.0161***	− 0.0005	− 0.003
pquality	0.0304**	0.0579***	0.0592***	0.0049	0.0150
billed	0.0443	− 0.0297	0.0127	− 0.0529**	0.0205
cashp	0.0368	− 0.0652***	− 0.0401**	− 0.0575***	− 0.0215
cashv	0.0054	− 0.0741***	− 0.0562***	− 0.0416**	− 0.0279
free	0.0230	− 0.0635***	− 0.0525***	0.0085	0.0077
pwell	0.0356**	− 0.0154	− 0.0163**	− 0.0019	0.015
upwell	− 0.0358**	− 0.0339***	− 0.0578***	0.0036	0.0075
surface	− 0.0301*	− 0.0658***	− 0.0749***	− 0.0335***	0.0061
opiped	0.0707**	0.1219***	0.0261	0.0375*	0.1635***
npiped	0.0422**	0.1051***	0.0474***	0.0125	0.0670***
commun	0.0307**	0.0439***	0.0198**	0.0404***	0.0206**
distance	− 0.0002***	− 0.0003***	− 0.0002***	− 0.0001*	− 0.0002***

District-region controls were included in the regression.

Legend: * p < .1; ** p < .05; *** p < .01

State-of-the-art review: designing urban water tariffs to recover costs and promote wise use

Sonia Ferdous Hoque and Dennis Wichelns

Institute of Water Policy, Lee Kuan Yew School of Public Policy, National University of Singapore

Urban water tariffs vary substantially across cities and regions, for reasons that reflect water scarcity conditions, local or regional objectives, and political considerations. Comparisons of average water prices across regions are not generally meaningful, as the prices are not weighted or adjusted to account for variation in socio-economic or political characteristics. This study endeavours to describe the observed variation in water tariffs, with the goal of highlighting key features and the degree to which some tariff programs achieve local objectives. To this end, the domestic and non-domestic water and wastewater tariffs in 60 cities across 43 countries were examined. The non-weighted average of the per unit domestic water and wastewater bills in the cities considered was USD $2.10/m^3$. The average per unit bills in Asia and Africa were generally lower than those in Western Europe, North America and Australia. On average, households spend about 1.5% of their monthly incomes on water and wastewater bills. In Asia and Africa, the average unit bills for the non-domestic sector were higher than those for the domestic sector, suggesting cross-subsidy. The study also analyzed the components of a metered tariff schedule with regard to the goals of cost recovery, demand management and affordability. The article also discusses the effectiveness of existing tariffs in addressing local challenges in the context of water pricing examples from Singapore, Los Angeles and Manila.

Introduction

Water and wastewater tariffs differ notably across cities, as do the local costs of water extraction, purification and distribution. There are also differences in the socio-economic conditions of households, the revenue requirements of water supply utilities, political implications, and the scarcity value of water. Appropriately designed tariffs can be helpful in achieving the goals of revenue sufficiency, equity and affordability, provided that other desirable aspects of water governance and resource policies are in place. Prices are also helpful in communicating resource scarcity and promoting household practices that are consistent with the goal of managing urban water resources in sustainable fashion.

Most regional and global surveys of water and wastewater tariffs have focused exclusively on the domestic sector. The Organization for Economic Cooperation and Development (OECD) conducted surveys of residential water tariffs in 1999 and in 2007–08, using a reference consumption of $15\,m^3$ per household per month (OECD, 2009). In parallel with the OECD survey, Global Water Intelligence (GWI) launched two surveys on

---

This article was originally published with errors. This version has been corrected. Please see corrigendum (http://dx.doi.org/10.1080/07900627.2013.837596)

pricing levels and structures in 2007 and 2008. These covered more than 150 cities in OECD countries and 100 cities in non-OECD countries. GWI has repeated its survey every year from 2009 to 2012, increasing the number of cities surveyed to 310 in 2012 (GWI, 2012). Zetland and Gasson (2012) used the GWI tariff data to examine sustainability, efficiency and equity. In addition, the database of the International Benchmarking Network (IB-Net), managed by the World Bank, contains performance data for more than 2000 utilities in 85 countries (International Benchmarking Network for Water and Sanitation Utilities (IB-NET), 2011). The International Water Association (IWA) conducts a biennial study of household water and wastewater bills in 30 countries, and includes other parameters such as GDP, water consumption, water abstractions and water deliveries (IWA, 2010).

The present authors studied the water and wastewater tariffs for the domestic and non-domestic sectors in 60 cities in a total of 43 developed and developing countries. In addition to calculating the combined water and wastewater monthly bills, this study disaggregated the bills into different tariff components to gain insight regarding the proportions of fixed, variable and miscellaneous charges paid by consumers. Direct monetary comparison of the bills can be enhanced by considering the socioeconomic conditions in each city. Thus, monthly household water and sewerage bills are expressed as a proportion of household income. In addition to describing the observed variation in water and wastewater tariffs, the study highlights the effectiveness of alternative tariff structures in achieving local goals, using examples from Singapore, Los Angeles and Manila.

Overview of water and wastewater tariffs

Urban water and wastewater prices vary notably within and between regions, as do the types of tariff structures and the components included in each. For example, some cities have separate tariffs for metered and non-metered connections: metered consumers pay according to the volume of water consumed, while non-metered consumers pay a fixed charge per month. Tariffs can also be differentiated by broad consumer groups, such as domestic and non-domestic users. Domestic consumers are sometimes subcategorized by dwelling type, while non-domestic consumers are often separated by the type of activity, such as government, commercial or industrial.

Metered water and wastewater tariffs generally include a combination of fixed and variable charges (Table 1). Combinations can be chosen in conjunction with local goals regarding cost recovery, revenue generation, equity and investment. Figure 1 depicts some of the components found in the water and wastewater tariffs in the cities considered in this study.

Monthly household water consumption is determined by many factors, including the price of water, the number of household members, the dwelling type and size, weather conditions, household income, water fixture technology and the extent of outdoor landscaping. Monthly domestic water consumption varies substantially between cities and also between different dwelling types within the same city (see the example of Singapore in Case 1, below). Thus, it can be difficult to gain insight when comparing average water and wastewater bills across cities. In an attempt to gain insight from the data in the present sample, the water and wastewater bill were calculated for a household consuming an average of $20 \, m^3$ of water per month, using the metered tariff rates for each city.[1] The bill is expressed as a proportion of household income (Figure 2).

Given the observed variation in tariff components and water prices across cities, generalized conclusions at the global or regional level could be misleading. However, a snapshot of the domestic water and wastewater bills from the present sample reveals that average unit bills in Asia and Africa are generally less than USD $1.00/m^3$, which is lower

Table 1. Typical components of water and wastewater tariffs.

Tariff component	Description
Basic service charge	
Fixed charge	This is a fixed amount, paid per month or year, and does not allow any minimum amount of consumption. The charge usually depends on the meter size and accounts for the cost of infrastructure and account maintenance. There can be combined or separate basic charges for water and wastewater.
Minimum charge	This is a fixed amount, paid per month, and allows a minimum amount of free consumption of water.
Volumetric water charge	
Increasing block tariff (IBT)	This is a charge per unit volume which increases stepwise according to the level of consumption.
Decreasing block tariff (DBT)	This is a charge per unit volume which decreases stepwise according to the level of consumption.
Constant unit charges (CUC)	This is a charge per unit volume which is the same for all levels of consumption.
Seasonal charge	This is a charge per unit volume which changes with the time of the year to account for peak (summer) and off-peak (winter) demands. The tariff can be of any of the three types listed above (IBT, DBT, or CUC).
Wastewater or sewerage charge	
Volumetric charge	Volumetric charges can take the form of any of the three tariffs listed above (IBT, DBT or CUC). Generally, the volume of wastewater generated is considered to be the same as the volume of water delivered.
Flat	A flat charge is a fixed percentage (usually less than 100%) of the water bill. Mathematically, this can also be interpreted as a volumetric charge, but in this case a rate per unit volume is not specified.
Additional components	
Conservation or pollution tax	These are additional components that account for the scarcity value of water or the environmental externalities caused by discharge of wastewater. These are usually a fixed portion of the total water bill.
Stormwater or property drainage charge	This fixed charge per month or year, which varies with property size, accounts for the fact that rainwater falling on a paved surface ultimately discharges into public sewers, thus increasing the volume of wastewater requiring treatment.
Water resource development fee or capital contribution	Some utilities impose a temporary fixed charge on consumers to earn revenue for development of additional infrastructure to meet expanding demands.

than the average for all of the cities considered (USD $2.10/m^3$). In Europe, North America and Australia, the unit bill is generally higher than USD $3.50/m^3$. The GWI (2012) survey of domestic water and wastewater tariffs in 310 cities showed similar results. Of the 51 cities with a unit bill greater than USD $4.00/m^3$, 39 are in Western Europe, 6 in North America, 5 in Australia, and 1 in Latin America (GWI, 2012). Similarly, of the 81 cities with a unit bill less than USD $0.50/m^3$, 49 are in South, East or South-East Asia, while 13 are in the Middle East, North Africa, or Sub-Saharan Africa (GWI, 2012).

On average, households spend about 1.5% of monthly income on their water and wastewater bills. In some European, Australian and American cities, the proportions are

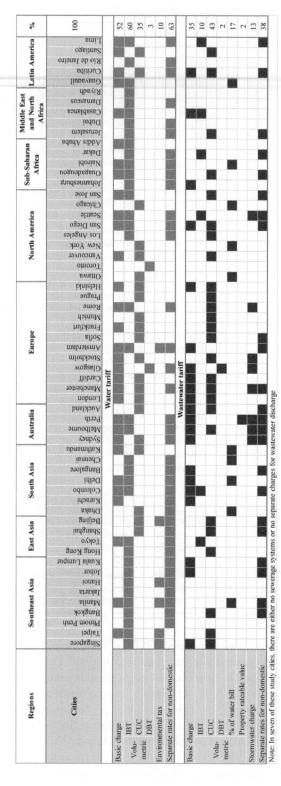

Figure 1. Components of water and wastewater tariff structures implemented in 60 selected cities.

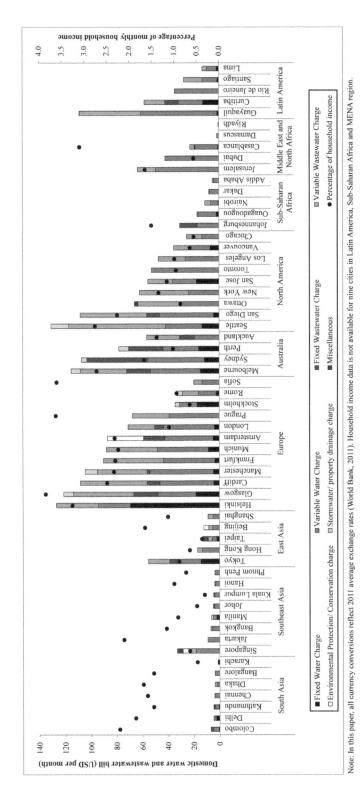

Note: In this paper, all currency conversions reflect 2011 average exchange rates (World Bank, 2011). Household income data is not available for nine cities in Latin America, Sub-Saharan Africa and MENA region.

Figure 2. Domestic water and wastewater bill for a consumption of 20 m³ per month compared with monthly household income. (Tariff rates were obtained from the website of the water supply authority in each city).

greater than 2%. In many of the Asian cities, although monthly bills are quite small, they represent notable portions of the small incomes earned in those cities. The average household income for each city was used when performing these calculations. Yet, incomes vary substantially, particularly in developing cities, so that the actual proportions for many residents are larger than the average values reported here.

The non-domestic sector comprises a wide range of consumer types, including shops, commercial buildings, hospitals, hotels, construction sites and factories. Water consumption and the volume and quality of wastewater discharged can vary substantially across non-domestic water customers. Yet, only a few cities have different tariff rates for each of these subcategories.[2] Figure 3 depicts the estimated monthly water and wastewater bill for a non-domestic facility with a monthly water consumption of $100 \, m^3$ in each of the study cities.

The non-weighted average water and wastewater bill for the non-domestic sector in the countries considered (USD $2.20/m^3$) is similar to that in the domestic sector. Interestingly, in the selected developed cities in Europe, North America and Australia, the unit bill in the non-domestic sector is smaller than that in the domestic sector. In the cities considered in Asia, Latin America and Africa, the average unit price in the non-domestic sector is higher than that in the domestic sector, suggesting cross-subsidy.

Analysis of water and wastewater tariffs

Water tariffs are often designed primarily to achieve cost recovery or to raise sufficient revenue to cover operations, maintenance and investment. Well-designed tariffs can also play important roles in promoting behavioural changes and in improving affordability and access for the poor. The choice of tariff components and rates depends on the major priorities in each city. However, local goals can conflict in some settings. For instance, while lower tariff rates are often prescribed for low-income groups, lower revenues from water sales can result in reduced investment in poor areas of the city, thus preventing the poor from obtaining access to the water delivery system. This section discusses the characteristics and general outcomes of selected water tariffs and presents examples from cities in which each of the tariff components has been implemented.

Two-part tariffs: fixed plus volumetric charges

This is one of the most common forms of water pricing, consisting of a basic service charge and a volumetric pricing component. The rationale behind the basic charge is that all connections impose a cost on the utility due to installation of permanent infrastructure (such as pipes or meters) and related administrative costs. Fixed charges can account for these costs even when there is no consumption, thus reducing revenue volatility for the utility. The volumetric component provides consumers with some degree of flexibility in controlling their water bills, based on their consumption. However, if fixed charges constitute a large portion of the water bill, consumers have limited ability to control their bills, and hence a smaller monetary incentive to conserve water. The balance between fixed and variable charges should be carefully determined, in conjunction with local priorities.

Some utilities do not have separate fixed and variable charges as such, but do have a minimum charge that consumers pay for a basic consumption allowance. Any consumption beyond the minimum allowance is charged using volumetric rates. For example, in Kathmandu, domestic connections with a meter size of 0.5 in. (20 mm) pay a

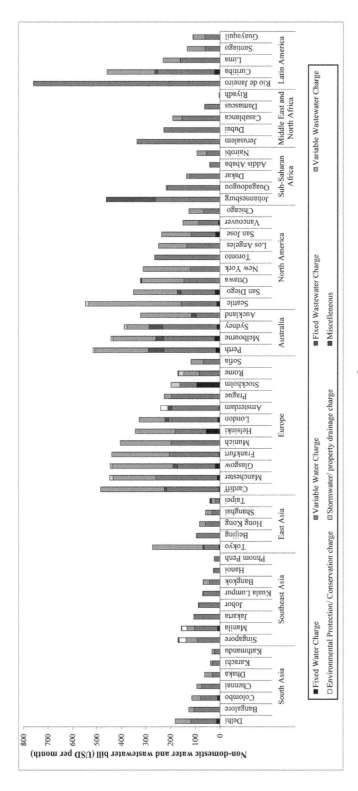

Figure 3. Non-domestic water and wastewater bill based on a consumption of 100 m³ per month. (Tariff rates were obtained from the website of the water supply authority in each city).

minimum charge of NPR 55 per month (USD 0.74) for consumption of $10\,m^3$ or less, and a uniform volumetric charge of NPR $17.5/m^3$ (USD 0.24) for exceeding the minimum allowance (Kathmandu Upatyaka Khanepani Limited, 2009).

According to the Independent Pricing and Regulatory Tribunal (IPART) of New South Wales, a two-part tariff with a fixed charge and a uniform variable charge is the most efficient pricing structure for monopoly service providers. This is because the variable charge can be based on the marginal cost of supply while the fixed cost can recover the difference between the average cost and marginal cost (Cox, 2010).[3]

Single-part tariffs: increasing block rates

Increasing block-rate tariffs (IBT) are being increasingly adopted by utilities worldwide. With an IBT, the amount of water required for essential uses can be provided at a low price per unit, while consumers using large volumes of water per month are charged higher per unit prices. The initial consumption block can be offered at a zero price, provided that the prices pertaining to higher consumption blocks are sufficient to generate the necessary revenue. In Johannesburg and Hong Kong, the first $6\,m^3$ of water consumed each month are provided at no charge.

The IBT is usually referred to as a conservation-oriented rate design, which also promotes revenue generation and cross-subsidy between high- and low-income consumers. However, to achieve the dual goals of water conservation and revenue generation, the sizes of the blocks and volumetric rates must be selected in accordance with local water-consumption patterns. Wichelns (2013) shows that a three-part objective including affordability, revenue generation and conservation can be achieved using an IBT if: (1) consumption in the initial pricing block is subsidized; (2) the volumetric rate in the second pricing block is sufficient to cover the operational costs and subsidies provided to consumers in the first pricing block; and (3) the volumetric rate in the third block is sufficient to cover both operational and investment costs.

One of the common arguments against using an IBT is that it imposes a disproportionate burden on households with many members or where several households share a common connection (Whittington, 1992). In its early years, when Singapore decided to shift from a constant unit charge (CUC) to an IBT structure to account for the increasing costs of developing new infrastructure, it designed concessional rates for households with many persons. The general domestic tariff had four tiers, in which the first block of 0 to $25\,m^3$ was charged at SGD $0.22/m^3$ (USD $0.17/m^3$), the second block of 25 to $50\,m^3$ at SGD $0.26/m^3$ (USD $0.21/m^3$), the third block of 50 to $75\,m^3$ at SGD $0.33/m^3$ (USD $0.26/m^3$) and the remainder at SGD $0.44/m^3$ (USD $0.35/m^3$). Concessional rates were designed for two or more households living in one block and for connections with 10 to 20 persons. While the rate in each block remained the same, the size of the blocks was increased for these consumers. The first block ranged from 0 to $50\,m^3$, the second from 50 to $100\,m^3$, and the third from 100 to $150\,m^3$; the fourth block was for consumption above $150\,m^3$ (Tortajada, Joshi, & Biswas, 2013).

An IBT may not be suitable for cities in which bulk meters serve high-rise buildings. One of the ways in which this issue can be solved is by using the average consumption per apartment to determine the applicable tariff rate. This approach has been adopted in Johannesburg, where the domestic water tariff consists of seven tiers. If a multi-dwelling residential connection comprising 10 households uses $100\,m^3$ per month, then, based on the normal IBT rates, the total water charge (involving all seven tiers) would be $(6 \times 0) + (4 \times 4.93) + (5 \times 7.31) + (5 \times 9.59) + (10 \times 11.98) + (10 \times 12.36) + (60 \times 14.94)$

= ZAR 1244.00 (USD 171.00) and each household would pay ZAR 124.40 (USD 17.10). However, on the average-consumption approach, the total consumption of $100\,m^3$ would be divided by 10 households, thus obtaining a consumption of $10\,m^3$ per household. The tariff for each household would then be $(6 \times 0) + (4 \times 4.93) = $ ZAR 19.72 (USD 2.72) and the total bill would be just ZAR 197.20 (USD 27.20) (Johannesburg Water, 2010).

In theory, increasing block-rate tariffs can be designed to subsidize poor consumers who use small amounts of water per month. However, this goal is not achieved in some cities in developing countries, where many poor households in informal settlements are not connected to the water delivery system. Moreover, increasing the number of connections in poorer communities with lower water consumption will result in lower revenues for utilities, compared to increasing the number of connections to high-volume users. This notion may serve as a disincentive for the utility to increase access to the poor, especially in the case of profit-seeking private operators.

Increasing block-rate tariffs also are considered to be less efficient than uniform charges. In an IBT structure, the first block is usually subsidized and is priced lower than the marginal cost of service, while the additional blocks are priced at rates higher than the marginal cost. Moreover, all consumers, irrespective of their ability to pay, enjoy the subsidized rates for some portion of their consumption (Cox, 2010; Hoehn, 2011).

Single-part tariffs: constant unit charges

This is the simplest form of volumetric tariff, which enables utilities to perform a straightforward calculation of water bills and enables consumers to easily comprehend and control their bills in relation to consumption. A uniform charge seems to be less effective in promoting water conservation compared to IBT, but can be equally efficient in generating revenues if the rate is fixed at an appropriate level. Hoehn (2011), however, suggests that if a uniform volumetric charge (without any fixed charge) aims to cover both fixed and variable costs, the rate might become too high, and consumers might attempt to forgo beneficial water uses and waste time, money and resources in inefficient water saving.

Single-part tariffs: decreasing block rates

This tariff structure is appropriate in cities where abundant raw water sources allow average costs to decline when water supply increases. For instance, large industrial customers often enable the utility to capture economies of scale in water resource development, transmission and treatment. Moreover, industrial users typically take their supplies from the larger trunk mains and thus do not require the expansion of neighbourhood distribution networks (Whittington, 2003).

Well-designed decreasing block-rate tariffs (DBTs) allow utilities to recover costs. However, they penalize consumers with low levels of consumption and provide a disincentive for improving water management. There is a trend to move away from this kind of tariff, essentially because water conservation has found a place in the political agenda of many governments and because the marginal costs of providing water are now relatively high in many countries. A review of tariff policies in OECD countries reveals a continued decline in the use of DBTs for households in favour of a two-part tariff structure with a basic charge and a volumetric charge, such as CUC and IBT, and limited application of DBT among industrial users in a few countries (OECD, 2009).

In Glasgow, domestic connections with a meter diameter up to 20 mm pay GBP 2.14/ m^3 for the first $25\,m^3$ of water consumed in a year and GBP $0.77/m^3$ for any consumption beyond that. For wastewater, the volumetric charge is GBP $2.76/m^3$ for the first $23.75\ m^3$ in a year and GBP $1.31/m^3$ for the remainder. These tariffs are charged on top of a fixed annual water charge of GBP 136.42 and a wastewater charge of GBP 140.10 (Scottish Water, 2012).

Single-part tariffs: seasonal water pricing

This pricing arrangement is primarily designed to promote water conservation during peak-demand periods and also to account for the additional costs associated with supplying water when availability is low. Seasonal pricing can also increase revenues during peak-demand periods (if consumption remains the same) or prevent shortfalls of revenue (if consumption declines due to conservation). Seasonal water pricing is implemented in cities where there is a significant difference between summer and winter water consumption, and where water shortage becomes a critical problem during summer. Moreover, regular increases and decreases in tariffs constantly remind consumers of the need for conservation, compared to constant conservation charges year round. One of the drawbacks is that changes in water prices must be communicated to consumers with some frequency, thus increasing transaction costs. *Case 2*, below, discusses the implementation of a seasonal tariff to manage water demand in Los Angeles.

Additional tariff components: conservation taxes

Additional charges such as water conservation fees, pollution charges or resource development fees are sometimes imposed by water utilities, on top of the usual water charges, to account for water shortages or the costs of developing alternative water supplies. Singapore uses an IBT along with a water conservation tax. *Case 1*, below, describes changes in water tariffs over time in Singapore.

The Taipei Water Department collects a water resource conservation and compensation fee, which is equivalent to 10% of the water charge. The collected sum is applied specifically to investments in infrastructure to support water conservation, to achieve improvements in water quality, and to compensate owners of restricted lands. This fee is charged in addition to a basic service charge, a volumetric water charge, a sewerage charge, and a pumping facility and maintenance charge (Taipei Water Department, 2011).

Income-based measures: discounts or payment assistance

Given that water is a basic necessity and a human right, low-income households should not be deprived of access to clean water, even if they cannot afford to pay. However, keeping the general level of tariffs low for all consumers can be counter-productive. Lower tariffs lead to decreased revenues, which in turn result in lower investment in water supply infrastructure, especially in poor, peripheral areas of the city. Hence, instead of having a utility with ailing financial health, it is sometimes better to charge all customers at a cost-effective rate and subsidize the low-income households with targeted programs.

In Singapore, low-income households having difficulty in paying their water bills receive assistance in the form of Utilities-Save (U-Save) rebates. This involves placing a fixed amount of cash in the household's utility account, which can be drawn from at any time to pay any utility bill, including water. Moreover, if the cash is not used in one month, it remains in the account and can be used for subsequent months (Tan, Lee, & Tan, 2009). Thus, rather than having a low unit charge for the first block under an IBT structure, which is enjoyed by all consumers irrespective of their income levels, this targeted subsidy achieves three purposes: (1) assisting the poor; (2) spreading the message that conservation is important, even at low consumption levels; and (3) collecting payments from all consumers who can afford to pay.

In London, customers defined as 'vulnerable' by the government may reduce their bills under the WaterSure scheme, by paying GBP 333 per year (GBP 199 for water and GBP 134 for wastewater) or their metered bill (if it is lower). Eligible customers are those on certain specified state benefits who either have large families or use significant additional volumes of water because someone residing in the household has a qualifying medical condition (Thames Water, 2012).

Income-based measures: subsidized network connections

Sometimes, even if the water tariff charged by a utility is much lower than alternative water supply sources, such as informal vendors, poor households prefer not to connect to the formal network due to high one-time connection fees. Excluding the poor from access to improved piped water supply can generate public health and equity concerns; it also prevents the water utility from earning additional revenues from potential consumers. Moreover, this may lead to a rise in illegal connections and increase non-revenue water (NRW) for the utility. *Case 3* discusses how Manila Water decreased its NRW and increased its revenues by expanding network coverage.

Non-metered flat tariffs

Volumetric water pricing through metering is one of the important preconditions to ensuring water conservation. When households are not metered but charged a fixed fee per month, there is no incentive to conserve water, as any reduction in consumption will not reduce the water bill. Yet, even in developed countries, water connections are largely non-metered. For instance, the proportions of metered water connections in Cardiff, London and Manchester are 33.4%, 30.5% and 30.4% respectively (OFWAT, 2011). Many of these household connections were established long ago, and installing meters in the existing old houses might not be cost-effective. This is the case in cities where the benefits accrued from conserving water through universal metering may not be sufficient to offset the costs of installing, reading and maintaining meters. However, the proportion of metered connections is gradually increasing in many of these cities.

In Glasgow, although calculations based on a monthly consumption of $20\,m^3$ yield a very high water and wastewater bill for domestic consumers (Figure 2), in practice, such high bills are rarely incurred, as very few connections are metered. According to Scottish Water, the average annual household charge in 2012–13 was GBP 324 (USD 514). Most households in Scotland are levied Scottish Water's non-metered household tariffs, and as of March 2012, about 2,440,000 households were non-metered and only 497 were metered. While a metered domestic consumer in Band A (based on council tax on property) would pay GBP 904 (USD 1435) in 2012–13 for consumption of $20\,m^3$ per month, a non-metered consumer would pay GBP 262 (USD 416) for the same consumption (personal communication with Scottish Water, January 2013).

Local challenges and water pricing

This section discusses the cases of three cities and examines the ways in which some of the tariffs discussed above have been implemented to address local challenges.

Case 1: Singapore

In Singapore, the scarcity of surface water and groundwater has led to the development of alternative water sources, such as rainwater harvesting in local catchments, the importing of water from Malaysia, the recycling of wastewater, and desalination. To reduce dependence on imported water and become self-sufficient, the Public Utilities Board (PUB) has implemented several demand management strategies, with emphasis on water pricing. Reflecting the country's pricing policy, which promotes the full cost recovery of water production and distribution and water saving to cope with water scarcity, the water tariff includes the following components: water tariff; water conservation tax; sanitary

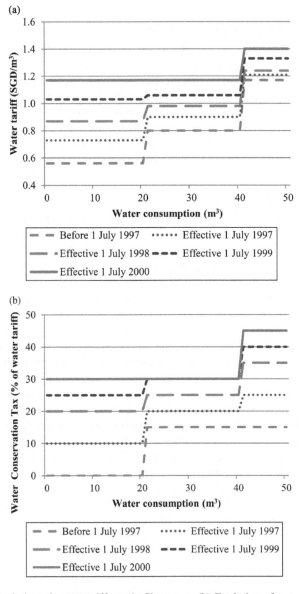

Figure 4. (a). Evolution of water tariff rate in Singapore. (b) Evolution of water conservation tax rates in Singapore. Data in both figures from Tortajada (2006).

appliance fee; and waterborne fee. From 1997 to 2000, the water tariff was revised step by step, in particular for the domestic sector (Figures 4a,b).

Together with water pricing, the Singapore government has adopted other complementary measures for water demand management, such as mandatory and voluntary labelling of water fixtures, public awareness campaigns, and programs involving public engagement in water-conservation activities (Tortajada & Joshi, 2013). As a result of these efforts, per capita domestic water consumption in Singapore has declined over the years from 165 litres per person per day (lpd) in 2002 to 153 lpcd in 2011 (Public Utilities Board, 2012b).

While tariff rates are important in shaping consumption behaviour, it is also important to make consumers aware of their water use and corresponding bills, via detailed information on the water bill itself. In Singapore, households receive a monthly utility bill from Singapore Power (SP Services). The bill gives a breakdown of the water bill into its different components, along with graphs showing the household's water consumption in the past six months in comparison to the national average for similar dwelling types. However, the invoice also contains electricity and natural gas bills, which make up the bulk of the total – ranging from SGD 35 (USD 27) in single-room apartments to SGD 695 (USD 551) in bungalows (Singapore Power (SP Services), 2013a). Households are thus more concerned about electricity consumption, and might not be looking separately into their water bill. Many consumers will not even notice the water portion of their bill, as the charges are deducted directly from their bank accounts. Combined billing reduces administrative costs compared to sending three separate meter readers and bills; it also reduces transaction costs for households. Yet the practice is probably not effective in communicating information regarding water prices.

While Singapore has not raised its water prices since 2000, its operating expenses have more than doubled in the last decade, and the increase has been greater than the increase in operating income. For the first time in many years, the PUB incurred a net loss (before government grant) in FY 2010 and 2011 (Public Utilities Board, 2012b). This implies that if the PUB wishes to increase its operating income, a revision in tariff structure is necessary. However, in order to address the issues of affordability, the water consumption patterns and incomes of households need to be analyzed in greater detail.

In 2011, the median monthly household income from work (excluding the Central Provident Fund) among residents in employed households was SGD 6286 (USD 5110), compared to an average of SGD 8864 (USD 7206) (Department of Singapore Statistics, 2011). Based on a monthly domestic water consumption of $20 \, m^3$, the average water and wastewater bill is SGD 40.6 (USD 33.84) (excluding the Goods and Services Tax of 7%), which amounts to just 0.58% of monthly income. However, to reflect the actual scenario, data can be disaggregated by type of household, accounting for the differences in incomes and water use patterns.

Figure 5 shows that water consumption in one- and two- room Housing Development Board (HDB) flats is substantially lower ($11.2 \, m^3$) than the national average, while landed properties such as terraced houses, semi-detached properties and bungalows have substantially higher consumption ($39.7 \, m^3$). Similarly, average household incomes vary according to dwelling type. Families living in HDB one-to-four-room flats (57% of all households) have an average monthly income of SGD 2000 to SGD 5000, while those living in condominiums and landed properties (11% of all households) earn between SGD 12,000 and SGD 15,000 per month. Thus, poorer families in HDB one- and two- room flats spend as much as 2% of their incomes on water, while wealthier families living in condominiums pay as little as 0.5%.

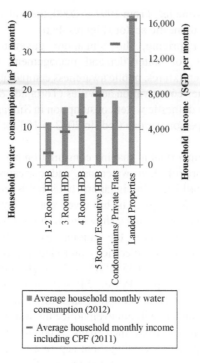

Figure 5. Monthly household income (Department of Singapore Statistics, 2011) and water consumption (Singapore Power (SP Services), 2013b).

The average monthly water consumption data indicate that very few households ever reach the second tier (in excess of 40 m³); most households, except those in condominiums and landed properties, consume less than 20 m³. Thus, lowering the consumption band of the first tier to 20 m³ could increase revenue for the utility by penalizing those who consume excessively, while not impacting the general population. This recommendation implies that the PUB might consider reverting to a three-tier structure, as was the case before 2000.

In Singapore, in contrast to the situation in many other countries, many of the PUB's connections are to the non-domestic sector. Currently, Singapore has a water demand of 1.44 million m³ per day, 55% of which comes from the non-domestic sector. This is expected to increase in the next 50 years, with about 70% of the demand coming from the non-domestic sector and domestic consumption making up the other 30% (Public Utilities Board, 2012a). Currently, the domestic and non-domestic water tariffs in Singapore are the same (except for shipping). To increase its revenue, Singapore might consider implementing a higher water price for its non-domestic customers. However, as Singapore seeks to remain a competitive business and industrial hub, it may be reluctant to charge higher rates for the commercial sector.

Case 2: Los Angeles, California

In 1993, the Los Angeles Department of Water and Power (LADWP) restructured its water rates to provide customers with a clear financial signal to use water efficiently. The LADWP introduced a two-tiered, seasonal pricing structure, in which higher volumetric rates are charged during the high season (summer) compared to the low season (winter). According to Hanemann (1993), the two-tiered structure was aimed at reducing the right-hand tail of the distribution of demand by having a substantial price differential between the two blocks and locating the switch-point at a level of use where demand might be reasonably responsive to price. For the price incentive to work, Hanemann believed, it is not necessary to make everyone pay the higher rate on some units of their consumption. Rather, the incentive will still be effective for consumers below the switch-point as long as it is sufficiently close that the higher price looms in their consciousness and influences their purchase of water-saving appliances. In contrast, tariff structures with more blocks and quite small differentials between the blocks often dilute the incentive effects.

Unlike most other utilities where the boundaries of the consumption blocks are fixed for all consumers year round, a feature of this rate structure is that the first-tier allocation considers factors that influence an individual residential customer's water use patterns. This type of arrangement not only sends an effective price signal for conservation; it also addresses equity, provides basic water needs at an affordable price, and generates adequate revenue for maintaining and upgrading the water system. Moreover, as in few other cities, the water bill in Los Angeles is based only on water consumption, and does not include any fixed costs.

For single-family residential customers, the breakpoint between the first and second usage tiers is based on lot size (five categories), temperature zone (three zones), and household size (the household adjustment involves a sliding scale of allowed extra first-tier usage for households of 7 persons or more) (Table 2). For multi-family residential customers, and for commercial, industrial and governmental customers, the Tier 1 allotment is based on a proportion of the customer's maximum daily average use during the previous December through March.

During periods of drought, shortage-year rates are implemented, during which the switch-point between the first and second tiers is reduced by 10%, 15% or 25% to encourage additional water conservation and also to offset any revenue losses resulting from lower consumption. In June 2009, shortage-year rates became effective under which first-tier allotments are reduced by 15%. In 2012, the monthly amounts of water allotted for single-dwelling residential units of land area less than 7500 square feet (696 m²) in a medium-temperature zone are 1200 ft³ (34 m³) and 1500 ft³ (44 m³) for low and high seasons, respectively. Hence, assuming household consumption of 20 m³ per month, all

Table 2. Size of the initial consumption block (in 100 ft³ per month) for single-family residential customers in the increasing block-rate tariff implemented in Los Angeles.

Lot size group (ft²)	Season	Temperature zone		
		Low	Medium	High
1–7499	High	16	18	19
	Low	13	14	14
7500–10,999	High	23	26	27
	Low	16	17	17
11,000–17,499	High	36	40	42
	Low	24	25	25
17,500–43,599	High	45	51	53
	Low	28	29	29
43,560 and above	High	55	62	65
	Low	36	38	38

Notes: 1 ft² = 0.0929 m²; 100 ft³ = 2.83 m³. High season is 1 June to 31 October; low season is 1 November to 31 May. Temperature zone is determined from property location (Zip code).
Source: Los Angeles Department of Water and Power (2012)

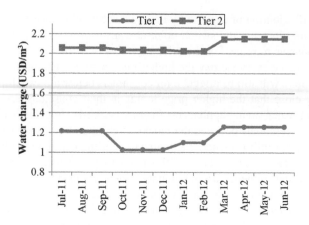

Figure 6. Water tariff for single-family residential customers (Los Angeles Department of Water and Power, 2012).

consumers fall within the allotted amount and pay Tier 1 rates (Los Angeles Department of Water and Power, 2012). Figure 6 depicts the water tariff for single-family residents.

This seasonal tiered tariff, along with other demand management strategies, has allowed Los Angeles to reduce its total water consumption since 1990, despite the increase in population. The average per capita water use (i.e. total water supplied to both domestic and non-domestic sectors, divided by total population) decreased from 654 lpd in 1989–90 to 601 lpd in 1999–2000, and finally to 442 lpd in 2009–10 (LADWP, 2010, p. 38). This is still high in comparison with other cities, as much of the water supplied is used for outdoor purposes. Based on data collected from 2004 through 2007, for single-family and multi-family dwellings respectively, 54% and 32% of domestic water goes to outdoor use (LADWP, 2010, p. 40).

Case 3: Manila

Since 1997, the responsibilities for water and wastewater services in Metro Manila have been delegated to Manila Water Company, Inc. (MWCI) for the east zone (1400 km²) and to Maynilad Water Services, Inc. (MWSI) for the west zone (540 km²) via two 25-year concessions, which were extended by another 15 years in 2009. MWCI has significantly reduced its NRW, from 63% in 1997 to 11.2% in 2011, and improved its reliability, in terms of 24-hour availability, from 26% of customers in 1997 to 99% in 2011 (Manila Water, 2011).

This success is the result of the policies adopted by MWCI with regard to improving operational efficiencies, managing human resources, decentralizing business areas and increasing service coverage (Luz & Paladio-Melosantos, 2012). In its first year of operation, MWCI launched its flagship social program, Water for the Community (*Tubig Para Sa Barangay*, or TPSB), designed to rapidly increase connections to poor households through community-based arrangements. Under this program, MWCI provides one official connection with a master meter placed just outside the community. MWCI meters the volume of water delivered to the community, which is responsible for installing the infrastructure required to deliver water to individual households. This approach essentially shifts responsibility for household delivery from MWCI to the communities, while also enabling MWCI to report smaller volumes of non-revenue water, as any water losses that occur within communities are not reflected in MWCI's water accounting program. To date, more than 700 TPSB projects have been completed, serving 1.7 million people, or 28% of the 6.1 million people served by MWCI.

This arrangement was initially highly appreciated by donor organizations, local politicians, communities and external evaluators as a successful means of increasing connections to poor households without land tenures in informal settlements. However, in recent years the program has been the subject of criticism due to several factors. First, through such arrangements MWCI shifts the responsibility of water losses, bill collection and maintenance to the community organizations, avoiding the costs of installing and maintaining individual connections yet taking credit for increasing access and significantly reducing NRW. Second, operational inefficiencies became concerns within the communities, as water was inevitably lost through pilferage (creating holes in the rubber pipes) and delinquent consumption (intentionally allowing taps to drip). Third, the entire community was initially considered as one large consumer and thus subject to higher-tier rates based on the IBT structure. After many complaints, MWCI eventually introduced a highly advertised 'social rate' for TPSB which reflected the number of households supplied in each community. However, the poor households still had to pay more than normal consumers with individual connections, as community leaders needed extra funds for equipment maintenance, administrative costs and payment delays. Finally, the emerging community leaders gradually began using their increasing influence and organizational capacity and the financial resources that they gained from control over water distribution to use the water organizations as effective platforms for community organizing, leading to legal actions against the authorities for the collective rights of the slum-dwellers (personal communication with Metropolitan Waterworks and Sewerage System (the government agency in charge of regulating the private concessionaires), March 2013).

Eventually, due to pressures from the local government and regulatory office, MWCI reformed their policies and started providing individual connections to poor households with the help of subsidies from the Philippine government and the Global Partnership for Output-Based Aid (GPOBA), which provides direct payment to MWCI for each connection installed in identified low-income areas. As surveys by MWCI revealed that the poor households can only afford to pay the meter and guarantee deposit of PHP 1620 (USD 40), the remaining connection fee of PHP 5911 (USD 144) will be paid by the subsidy upon independent verification of satisfactory service delivery for three months (Global Partnership on Output-Based Aid, 2009).

MWCI implements a complex six-component tariff structure. For residential consumers, this consists of a basic charge of PHP 101.01 (USD 2.33) per connection for the first $10\,m^3$ of water, an IBT consisting of 9 tiers, a foreign currency differential adjustment of 1.23% of the water charge, an environmental charge of 20%, a sewerage charge of zero (compared to 30% for business groups 1 and 2), and a maintenance service charge of PHP 1.50–50 per connection for a range of meter sizes (Manila Water, 2012). MWCI has been implementing a social lifeline tariff rate for low-income consumers using less than $10\,m^3$ per month, and in 2012, while tariffs for all other categories increased, this social rate was reduced further, such that low-income consumers (accounting for about 8% of all consumers) now enjoy a 40% discount.

Non-domestic connections (semi-business, and business groups 1 and 2) also have the 6-component tariff, with significantly higher rates and an IBT structure of 33 tiers. However, effective cross-subsidy may not be achieved because the proportion of business consumers is very low. In MWCI, 91% of all connections belong to the residential group, while 4.7%, 4.3% and 0.3% belong to semi-business, business group 1 and business group 2 respectively (personal communication with Regulatory Affairs Department, Manila Water Company, February 2013).

Conclusions

The monthly household water and wastewater bills in the sampled Asian cities are generally less than USD 10, while the bills in developed cities in America, Europe and Australia are generally more than USD 60. The proportion of household income paid as water and wastewater bills ranges from 0.5% to 2.5% in the cities considered here, while significant variation exists within each city, due largely to differences in household income. The average per unit bill for water and wastewater service in the selected cities in Asia and Africa is usually less than USD $1.00/m^3$, whereas in Europe, Australia and North America it is greater than USD $3.50/m^3$.

The average prices calculated here are not weighted or adjusted to account for variation in socio-economic or political characteristics. Thus, detailed comparisons beyond these general statements would not be meaningful. However, the analysis of alternative tariff structures and the case studies involving three cities support several recommendations regarding water tariffs:

1. Rather than maintaining low water prices for all consumers, targeted subsidies can be provided to the poor; the poor can be identified by household income, by the floor area of the dwelling, or as those who receive low-income benefits from the government.
2. Increasing block-rate tariffs are helpful in providing low-income consumers with essential water volumes at low prices while encouraging wealthier consumers to use water wisely. In such tariffs, the initial consumption block often ranges between $10\,m^3$ and $25\,m^3$, depending on local situations.
3. Cross-subsidy involving low water prices for low-income consumers and higher prices for wealthier consumers can be achieved using an increasing block-rate tariff or by charging non-domestic customers higher prices. The optimal prices for each category of water customer will vary with the number of customers in each category, the revenue goals of the water utility, and the importance of achieving equitable distribution of water supplies.
4. Metering is essential to promote conservation using price signals. Yet, most multi-family dwellings, such as apartment buildings, have only one water meter. This provides no financial incentive for individual households to conserve water. (In Singapore each residence in large apartment buildings has a separate water meter.)
5. Many utilities implement fixed water charges to ensure they generate a target level of revenue each year. Often, such tariffs include a relatively low volumetric price for delivered water, thus providing little financial incentive for households to use water wisely.
6. Water bills are important in conveying information regarding the link between water consumption and monthly expenditures. Water bills can be enhanced in many cities by including information describing both current and past water consumption, water prices, and the process of bill calculation. It is also helpful to report the average monthly consumption in similar dwellings, thus enabling quick comparison by consumers.

Acknowledgements

The Totalizer Board and the Public Utilities Board of Singapore provided financial support for this research. We also appreciate the helpful comments of two anonymous reviewers.

Notes

1. Applicable tariff rates as of January 2013 were used to calculate the monthly bills. In cities in which the domestic water and wastewater charges are differentiated by meter size, dwelling type, income category or household location, the tariff rate pertaining to most of the consumers was used. No taxes or income-based discounts were included in the calculations.
2. In such cases, the tariff rates for commercial facilities were generally used to calculate the monthly bills.
3. The marginal cost of supplying water is largely dependent on the capacity of large capital investments, such as dams, desalination plants and pipelines. Once this cost has been incurred, the marginal cost of supplying water is much lower than the average cost of supply. If prices are set to marginal cost, the water utility might not fully recover its costs (Cox, 2010).

References

Cox, J. (2010). IPART's approach to urban water pricing in NSW. Retrieved from https://www.google.com.sg/url?sa=t&rct=j&q=&esrc=s&source=web&cd=1&cad=rja&ved=0CDAQF-jAA&url=http%3A%2F%2Fwww.aares.org.au%2FCMDownload.aspx%3FContentKey%3Db406d79c-d009-4257-ae24-de3d23f204f2%26ContentItemKey%3D2f9f0529-a3cb-4106-8d7e-ea16a2b176ac&ei=qTpZUerFCpDJrQf5o4CADA&usg=AFQjCNF-o186edHWpPq9kzmmDolKstjUJA&sig2=UixTPo16Pu5_gRW-Pepkcw&bvm=bv.44442042,d.bmk (accessed 26 March 2013).

Department of Singapore Statistics. (2011). Key household characteristics and household income trends. Retrieved from http://www.singstat.gov.sg/pubn/papers/people/pp-s18.pdf (accessed 7 December 2012).

Global Partnership on Output-Based Aid. (2009). Improved access to water services for poor households in metro Manila. Retrieved from https://www.gpoba.org/sites/gpoba.org/files/GPOBA%20Manila%207-29-09%20screen.pdf (accessed 25 January 2013).

Global Water Intelligence. (2012). Tariff survey. Retrieved from http://www.globalwaterintel.com/tariff-survey/ (accessed 21 January 2013).

Hanemann, W. M. (1993). Designing new water rates for Los Angeles. University of California, Berkeley. Retrieved from http://opensiuc.lib.siu.edu/cgi/viewcontent.cgi?article=1421&context=jcwre (accessed 28 March 2013).

Hoehn, J. P. (2011). Economic principles of water conservation tariffs and incentives. University of Michigan. Retrieved from http://cdn.intechopen.com/pdfs/24683/InTech-Economic_principles_for_water_conservation_tariffs_and_incentives.pdf (accessed 28 March 2013).

International Benchmarking Network for Water and Sanitation Utilities (IB-NET). (2011). Database. Retrieved July 1 2013 from http://www.ib-net.org/production/

International Water Association (IWA). (2010). International statistics for water services. Retrieved from http://www.sswm.info/sites/default/files/reference_attachments/IWA%20SPECIALIST%20GROUP%202010%20International%20Statistics%20Water%20Services.pdf (accessed 7 July 2013).

Johannesburg Water. (2010). Water and sanitation tariffs 2010/11 – JW annexure A 2011 update. Retrieved from http://www.johannesburgwater.co.za/ (accessed 28 March 2013).

Kathmandu Upatyaka Khanepani Limited. (2009). Annual operating report: 1 Falgun 2064–31 Asadh 2065. Retrieved from http://www.kathmanduwater.org/reports/Annual%20Operating%20Report(FY64_65).pdf (accessed 12 February 2013).

Los Angeles Department of Water and Power. (2010). Urban water management plan. Retrieved from http://www.water.ca.gov/urbanwatermanagement/2010uwmps/Los%20Angeles%20Department%20of%20Water%20and%20Power/LADWP%20UWMP_2010_LowRes.pdf (accessed 20 February 2013).

Los Angeles Department of Water and Power. (2012). Water rates. Retrieved from https://www.ladwp.com/ladwp/faces/ladwp/aboutus/a-financesandreports/a-fr-waterrares?_adf.ctrl-state=vspn0fuvq_79&_afrLoop=348018122901000 (accessed 15 November 2012).

Luz, J. M., & Paladio-Melosantos, M. L. (2012). Manila, Philippines. In S. K. Anand Chiplunkar (Ed.), *Good practices in urban water management: Decoding good practices for a successful future.* Singapore: Asian Development Bank and National University of Singapore.

Manila Water. (2011). Annual report. Retrieved from http://www.manilawater.com/investor/Investor%20Resources/Pages/DownloadableMaterials.aspx (accessed 16 February 2013).

Manila Water. (2012). Water tariff with effect from January 2013. Retrieved from http://www.manilawater.com/investor/Corporate%20Governance/Pages/SECFillings.aspx (accessed 16 February 2013).

OECD. (2009). Managing water for all: An OECD perspective on pricing and financing. Retrieved from http://www.oecd.org/greengrowth/sustainable-agriculture/44476961.pdf (accessed 28 March 2013).

OFWAT. (2011). Household data: Metered and unmetered household numbers for water 2010–11. Retrieved from http://www.ofwat.gov.uk/regulating/reporting/rpt_tar_2010-11householddata (accessed 28 January 2013).

Public Utilities Board. (2012a). Long-term water masterplan. Retrieved from http://www.pub.gov.sg/LongTermWaterPlans/pub.pdf

Public Utilities Board. (2012b). Annual report 2011–12. Retrieved from http://www.pub.gov.sg/annualreport2012/images/PUB_AR12_web.pdf (accessed 24 January 2013).

Scottish Water. (2012). Metered household charges 2012–2013. Retrieved from http://www.scottishwater.co.uk/you-and-your-home/your-charges/2012-2013-charges/information-about-your-charges/metered-household-charges-201213-leaflet (accessed 24 January 2013).

Singapore Power (SP Services). (2013a). Electricity tariff revision for the period 1 July to 30 September 2013. Retrieved from http://www.singaporepower.com.sg/irj/go/km/docs/wpccontent/Sites/SP%20Services/Site%20Content/Tariffs/documents/latest_press_release.pdf (accessed 07 July 2013).

Singapore Power (SP Services). (2013b). Average water consumption by household type. Retrieved from http://www.singaporepower.com.sg/irj/servlet/prt/portal/prtroot/docs/guid/609ffede-040d-2f10-f5b4-de464caacd39?spstab=Our%20Services (accessed 12 March 2013).

Tan, Y. S., Lee, T. J., & Tan, K. (2009). *Clean, green and blue: Singapore's journey towards environmental and water sustainability* Ministry of Environment and Water Resources. Singapore: ISEAS Publishing.

Taipei Water Department. (2011). Water charges. Retrieved from http://english.twd.gov.tw/ct.asp?xItem=994144&CtNode=23944&mp=114012 (accessed 16 October 2012).

Thames Water. (2012). Metered charges 2012–13. Retrieved from http://www.thameswater.co.uk/tw/common/downloads/literature-water-waste-water-charges/201213-metered-charges-leaflet.pdf (accessed 16 October 2012).

Tortajada, C., & Joshi, Y. (2013). Water demand management in Singapore: Involving the public. *Water Resources Management, 27*(8), 2729–2746. doi 10.1007/s11269-013-0312-5

Tortajada, C. (2006). Water management in Singapore. *International Journal of Water Resources Development, 22,* 227–240.

Tortajada, C., Joshi, Y., & Biswas, A. K. (2013). *The Singapore water story: Sustainable development in an urban city-state.* New York, NY: Routledge.

Whittington, D. (1992). Possible adverse effects of increasing block water tariffs in developing countries. *Economic Development and Cultural Change, 41,* 75–87.

Whittington, D. (2003). Municipal water pricing and tariff design: A reform agenda for South Asia. *Water Policy, 5,* 61–76.

Wichelns, D. (2013). Enhancing the performance of water prices and tariff structures in achieving socially desirable outcomes. *International Journal of Water Resources Development, 29*(3), 310–326. doi: 10.1080/07900627.2012.721675

World Bank. (2011). Official exchange rates (LCU per USD, period average). Retrieved from http://data.worldbank.org/indicator/PA.NUS.FCRF (accessed 20 January 2013).

Zetland, D., & Gasson, C. (2012). A global survey of urban water tariffs: Are they sustainable, efficient and fair? *International Journal of Water Resources Development, 29*(1), 1–16, iFirst article.

Index